THE GO-BETWEENS

The

Go-Betweens

by David Nichols

Verse Chorus Press

© 1997, 2003 by David Nichols

All rights reserved. No part of this book may be reproduced, stored in or introduced into a retrieval system, or transmitted in any form or by any means (digital, electronic, mechanical, photocopying, recording, or otherwise) without the prior written permission of the publisher, except by a reviewer, who may quote brief passages in a review.

The original edition of this book was published in 1997 by Allen & Unwin (Australia). This expanded and completely revised edition was first published in 2003 by Verse Chorus Press.

Front cover photograph by Bleddyn Butcher
Back cover photograph by Peter Anderson
Design and layout by Steve Connell/Transgraphic Services

The author and the publishers wish to thank all those who supplied photographs and gave permission to reproduce copyright material in this book. Every effort has been made to contact all copyright holders, and the publishers welcome communication from any copyright owners from whom permission was inadvertently not obtained. In such cases, we will be pleased to obtain appropriate permission and provide suitable acknowledgment in future editions.

Country of manufacture as stated on the last page of this book

ISBN 978-1-891241-16-1
Library of Congress Control Number: 2003109772

Verse Chorus Press
PO Box 14806, Portland OR 97293
info@versechorus.com

For Stephen and for Mia

Contents

	PREFACE	9
	ACKNOWLEDGMENTS.	11
1	THE NEW VELVET UNDERGROUND	13
2	THE AUSTRALIAN GO-BETWEENS SHOW (1995)	16
3	BRISBANE.	27
4	"LET'S CAMP IT UP!"	32
5	"PASSENGER POP FOR TRAVELING MINDS".	43
6	"ROB LIKES THE WORD *GO!*".	50
7	FUNK! PUNK! SPUNK!	53
8	ZERO	74
9	THE SOUND OF YOUNG SCOTLAND	83
10	FROM BRISBANE TO MELBOURNE	95
11	*SEND ME A LULLABY*	104
12	*BEFORE HOLLYWOOD*	118
13	"HE'S THE LAST TO TAKE HIS COAT OFF"	130
14	"CAN YOU SHUT YOUR FUCKING MOUTH FOR A MINUTE?"	137
15	OUT OF STEP	147

16	*SPRING HILL FAIR*	154
17	*LIBERTY BELLE AND THE BLACK DIAMOND EXPRESS*	163
18	*VERY QUICK ON THE EYE*	170
19	*TALLULAH*	173
20	*16 LOVERS LANE*	190
21	PARTING COMPANY	205
22	DANGER IN THE PAST	215
23	UNFINISHED BUSINESS	241
24	*BRIGHT YELLOW BRIGHT ORANGE*	254
25	ELEMENTAL THINGS	261
	POSTSCRIPT (2011)	269
	NOTES	276

Preface

In 2001, I was interviewed by Fiona Dempster for her documentary on the Go-Betweens. Towards the end of the interview I found myself—weary, talked-out, a bit excited by my own unwarranted role in this whole epic adventure—lambasting Robert Forster and Grant McLennan for reuniting under the Go-Betweens banner to record a new album, *The Friends of Rachel Worth*, eleven years after they originally broke up the band. I said it was a callous financial decision, and claimed that a reunited Go-Betweens would inevitably let down the people who would go to their shows, buy the records, and participate in the process. I hope this outburst doesn't get used in the film, but I'll wear it if it does. After all, I participated in the process, too.

The Go-Betweens was first published in Australia in 1997 by Allen & Unwin; it was reasonably well-received and sold reasonably well. Revisiting it in the course of preparing this new version, I am appalled by its messiness. That said, when the original tome came out, even the subjects of the book were positive about it, though McLennan claims (and I believe him) never to have read it, and Forster, who fact-checked the final draft, felt that the ending—which, rather than eulogizing, discussed the importance of a brand name like the Go-Betweens to Forster and McLennan—was cold.

He's right, it was cold—but it was appropriate at the time. In 1996, Forster and McLennan, still more famous and popular for their work in the Go-Betweens than for anything they'd subsequently done as individuals, were showing every sign of returning to the old umbrella. Their manager was keen for them to do anything under the Go-Betweens name. Their record company in England, Beggars Banquet, had effectively dumped them as solo artists, while reissuing the Go-Betweens' albums in a uniform CD edition. And the willingness of Forster and McLennan to play shows together—and to work together on other projects—while refusing to make new Go-Betweens records was looking worse than perverse.

I wrote the original book because I wanted to write a book about an

Australian rock "scene," preferably one on the periphery, and preferably one with brilliant, funny, engaging characters. And of course I had always loved the Go-Betweens. Completely by accident, I picked the perfect time—two or three years after the breakup of the original band—to conduct my interviews: the ex-members were still fuming at each other, and their friends were still divided into camps, but there had been enough time for people to begin to augment their anger or distress with theories, ideas, and explanations. From a historian's point of view, it was a beautiful moment.

What you now hold is a rewritten (and even, due to the vagaries of computers, retyped) version of the 1997 book. Since Forster and McLennan have indeed recorded again together as the Go-Betweens—not once, but twice—and toured extensively, I have been able to pick up the Go-Betweens story and bring it into the present. The book still does not trace the "solo years"—the 1990s—in ardent detail, though, any more than it traces the early lives of the participants. It is a book about a band. And the band, as you will see, is greater than the sum of its parts.

Between the original book and this one I mapped out two other rock books which would cover the 1960s and 1970s in Australia the way this one covers the late 1970s and 1980s. One is about Sydney pop primitive Pip Proud, the other about New Zealand/Australian group Dragon. I haven't written them yet, but in the meantime I welcome the chance to return to my first book and improve it, or at least to replace the old typos with some new ones. This book was rewritten in an environment of domestic harmony, a Melbourne summer in West Brunswick, with a really good gelato shop up the road and a new Go-Betweens album—this time, a great one—spinning on the CD player. I hope the enthusiasm and the affection I have for this remarkable group shows through.

DAVID NICHOLS
Melbourne, 2003

Acknowledgments

I want to thank all the people who agreed to talk to me for this book. Not everyone listed here has been quoted directly in the final text, but their recollections, opinions, and ideas were invaluable. They are, alphabetically: Eric Auerbach, Colin Bloxsom, Leigh Bradshaw, Amanda Brown, Carrie Brownstein, Mark Callaghan, Wayne Connolly, Larry Crane, Robert Forster, Keith Glass, Robin Gold, Dave Graney, Roger Grierson, Phil Grizzly, Erhard Grundl, Mick Harvey, Alan Horne, Rowland Howard, Ed Kuepper, Peter Loveday, Irena Luckus, David McClymont, Clare McKenna, Grant McLennan, Ashleigh Merritt, Clive Miller, Steve Miller, Clare Moore, Lindy Morrison, Temucin Mustafa, Michael O'Connell, Alec Falao, Adele Pickvance, Matthias Strzoda, Peter Sutcliffe, Deborah Thomas, Glenn Thompson, Geoffrey Titley, Dave Tyrer, Victor Van Vugt, Robert Vickers, Clinton Walker, Dan Wallace-Crabbe, Peter Walsh, David Westlake, John Willsteed, and Andrew Wilson.

I was also aided enormously by: my mother, Jane Miller; Karin Bäumler, who gave me some invaluable advice; Mark Louttit, who was in on the GoBs' early days and gave me a copy of the early ZZZ tape which first inspired the wish to write this book; Bleddyn Butcher; Tony Moore; Karin Sprey; Michelle Cannane; Sophie Cunningham; Barry Divola; Wayne Davidson; Ian McFarlane; Graham Nichols; Bruce Milne; Gary Warner; Michael Conarty, who filled me in on the GPS business; Kristin Wallace-Crabbe; Bill Meyer; Fiona Graham and Bronwyn King, who read an early draft and asked sensible questions about who the fuck all the people were; Jen Matson, who gave me some interview tapes and was generally friendly; Ben Clancy; Dan Cross; Robert Hope; Jerry and Charlotte; Brigitte Salden; Mary Mihelakos; Shane Moritz; Richard Kingsmill; the staff of Fisher Library, University of Sydney; and the state libraries of New South Wales, Queensland, and Victoria, all of whom will no doubt be very excited to see themselves mentioned here (though frankly I can't remember why I thanked them in the original book—but I did, and I'm doing so again).

Ian Wadley was very helpful, too, as was Fiona Dempster.

Also, of course, Katherine Spielmann and Steve Connell of *Puncture* magazine and Verse Chorus Press, who have been supporting my writing for what must be about fifteen years and who gave me the other incentive (besides the ZZZ tape) to begin this work.

I was given valuable advice for this rewrite by my gobby friends Anthea Pitt, Elisabeth Vincentelli, Dan Waddell, and Nick Wilson.

And thank you to Mia Schoen for everything else.

A NOTE ON THE SOURCES

All quotes without footnotes are from interviews recorded personally by the author during research for this book from 1992 to 1995 and from 2002 to 2003, either in person or on the telephone: the list of interviewees appears in the acknowledgments. The interviews that were not conducted in person are those with the Supports (Leigh Bradshaw, Peter Loveday, Geoffrey Titley), Alan Horne, and David Westlake, all of whom sent me long letters from different parts of the world; and with Ashleigh Merritt and Larry Crane, both in the USA, who were interviewed via e-mail.

For the 2003 rewrite, Fiona Dempster very graciously gave me transcripts of all the interviews she conducted (in 2000 and 2001) for her documentary film on the Go-Betweens, and allowed me to make use of them here.

Other information was acquired by scouring a diverse assortment of magazines and newspapers, as well as material generously offered by members and friends of the band. Libraries tend to avoid archiving rock-music magazines (let alone fanzines), and sensible people tend to avoid accumulating them, so many of the articles on the Go-Betweens I have used in putting together this account were only available to me in the form of photocopies, clippings, or reproductions of old material on obscure web sites. This means that on rare occasions I have been unable to cite page numbers or other details regarding my source. I have provided whatever information was available to me.

1
The new Velvet Underground

> We might have been one of the most lauded bands in the country, but we sold bugger-all records. That's a shame. So let's not go on about it being one of the most lauded bands in the country, 'cause who cares? We didn't sell records, we weren't a popular band, and I'm sick of hearing about the fact that we were so fabulous—because if we were so fabulous, why didn't anyone buy our records?[1]

Lindy Morrison, speaking in 1992, three years after the demise of her most famous group, had a point. It is a point not at all diminished by the fact that she made it during promotional interviews for the pop group Cleopatra Wong, which she had subsequently formed with another ex–Go-Between, Amanda Brown.

It is well understood—even by those who have little connection to or affection for pop music—that for every group that "makes it," there are millions who don't even get their feet on the first rung of the ladder. Either they lack the commitment or the interest to emerge from the bedroom/garage, or they fail to score the all-important management/record deal. And should they pass these trials, their records may well simply fail to connect with a mainstream audience. There are even some pop groups who have no wish at all to cooperate with the whole system, thereby effectively bypassing the problem of "making it" or not "making it."

It is also generally understood by anyone who has thought about it for a minute that the recording industry is just that, an industry, where sales are the most important thing and, generally, quality takes a back seat. And that, presumably, is why "nobody" bought the Go-Betweens' records.

If there is any kind of success to be proud of having missed out on, commercial pop success might be it. In fact, Grant McLennan and Robert Forster, the Go-Betweens' founders and songwriters, claimed throughout the first incarnation of the group and throughout the 1990s to be extremely pleased with the fact that they did not come up with a hit record in their twelve-year career. As McLennan said in a 1996 interview to promote the rerelease of the original band's back catalog:

> Looking back, a lot of people would say that's unsuccessful ... It really doesn't matter. To me, the things I like and that a lot of my friends like have fallen under the floorboards a bit.
>
> I always thought to myself, what are we doing wrong? But by extension, what are we doing *right?*

Forster added: "It was quite freeing to realize, our group is so good, and we're getting nowhere. After a while, the lack of recognition was so absurd it was funny."[2]

"They never got anything like the attention they deserved," wrote *Melody Maker*'s Dave Jennings in 1990, on hearing of the group's demise and being presented with their *1978-1990* compilation to review. "Which means, sadly, that you may never have experienced the thrill that comes from hearing the Go-Betweens describe exactly how you felt the last time your emotions were pulled into unfamiliar shapes. The fact that the Go-Betweens never became massive is a disgusting injustice ... Take the Go-Betweens to your heart, where they belong."[3]

"The only problem with listening to the Go-Betweens now," wrote Andrew Male, reviewing their reissues in *Select* in 1996, "is they can't help but remind you how crap the eighties were. An example? The Go-Betweens produced records of quiet brilliance and got nowhere. Sting sang about a sodding turtle and became a millionaire."[4]

It wasn't just the time or place: the Go-Betweens remain just as much of an anomaly as they were fifteen years ago. The name shelters two singer-songwriters, whose individual styles clash with one another at least as much as they complement each other. Then there's the fact that the female musicians who have been full- or part-time Go-Betweens played instruments rather than singing, the group's Australian background, their literary and musical references, their contentious musicianship—so many rough edges that refuse to be streamlined. And, for all the journalists' gushing and fans' bluster about the hotline the Go-Betweens had to bedsitters' hearts, their songs are likely to be perverse, satirical, facetious, and hilarious as well as somber, reflective, and heartfelt—they are often all these things at once.

The classic quartet (Lindy Morrison, Robert Vickers, Grant McLennan, Robert Forster), 1983 *(Bleddyn Butcher)*

This is rarely a recipe for commercial success, even when a band looks and sounds as great as the Go-Betweens did.

Yet their songs continue to grow in stature and influence, and this has been affected little by Forster and McLennan's 1999 decision to reunite under the Go-Betweens name. The people who grew up with the Go-Betweens in the 1970s and 1980s spread the word in the 1990s, and new converts are made wherever their records are played. "We're going to become the new Velvet Underground, starting from now until the year 2010!" enthused Forster in 1996.[5] He is referring, of course, to the way that the New York band, despised and ignored when they were making records in the 1960s, went on to become one of the most influential rock groups of the last third of the twentieth century.

"The only people we appealed to," Morrison said in 1993, "were a fistful of wanky journalists and some university students."[6] Perhaps she is in the best position to know, having lived it. But even Lindy Morrison can't see into the future.

2
The Australian Go-Betweens Show (1995)

"Fucking heterosexuals, get a life!"

This admonition, yelled from a passing car outside Brisbane club the Zoo as we queue for a chance to see Grant McLennan and Robert Forster play a tribute show to their own days as the Go-Betweens, might give some of us pause to think. Not about why passing strangers would assume we were heterosexual,[1] but about why we're here and what we're hoping to experience. The sort of questions that we assume will not occur to people queuing for entry to other nostalgia events, like the traveling Manfred Mann show (which featured almost everyone from the original band—including both Paul Jones and Mike D'Abo—but *not* Mann himself), or for that matter the unbelievably successful Australian Abba tribute band Bjorn Again, or the post-reformation Buzzcocks. Are we trying to relive something from our (or someone's) 1960s/1970s/1980s youth? Are we privately hoping that it will be a night of special guests and reincarnations, a kind of *This Is Your Life* for McLennan, Forster, and the audience?

The Go-Betweens are the group the *Spin Alternative Record Guide* (1995) described as: "a band certain fans become obsessive for as they age, when the conceptual games of alternative start to matter less than music settling in upon a twentieth listen"[2]—high praise for the group's recordings, damnation for the passivity of their doughy middle-aged fans. And here we all are, "the fans," in Ann Street, Fortitude Valley, Brisbane, in 1995, almost two decades after the Go-Betweens' debut. Are we new Dark Ages ecclesiasts, only looking back to some divine act of inspired creation that we never expect to be bettered?

Strangely enough, on the whole, no. Inside the Zoo is a surprisingly youngish crowd. Too young to remember the full horror of the Bjelke-Petersen government of Queensland that ended in 1987, too young to recall the late 1970s days when Brisbane was so much of a non-place that residents would seriously ask themselves whether good creative work could be done there, decide it couldn't, and move south to Sydney or Melbourne. This audience is mostly made up of first-timers, people who would not have seen the Go-Betweens play live in the 1970s or 1980s, unless it was from the vantage point of their parents' arms. Now they sit cross-legged in the damp, dark, hot, big upstairs room eating the fruit salad their entry ticket entitles them to. The group onstage—Forster, McLennan, bass player Adele Pickvance, and drummer Glenn Thompson—has been jokingly dubbed by Thompson "the Australian Go-Betweens Show": as if they're a tribute band, like the still very popular "Australian Doors Show." It hasn't been advertised thus, but that's what "everyone" is calling it, anyway. So, even tonight's *band* is suspicious of where all this is leading.

Coming onstage to cheers, the first song they play is "To Reach Me," from the best Go-Betweens album, *Liberty Belle and the Black Diamond Express*. It's an interesting choice to lead off with—a middle-period rock outing with plaintive moments. "Head Full of Steam" follows, given a more up-tempo, straighter reading than the original. After these two Forster songs, McLennan chips in with the humorously maudlin "This Girl, Black Girl," a sea-shanty b-side from 1983. Then comes a rousing rendition of the co-written "Don't Let Him Come Back," a 1979 in-joke the two of them obviously still find funny sixteen years later. Then two ballads: McLennan's "Quiet Heart" and Forster's "Dive for Your Memory," both from what is still at this time the band's "last" album, *16 Lovers Lane*. McLennan's poppy 1986 non-hit, "Right Here," is given a faster, slightly country, outing, and is followed by a Forster b-side, "Rock 'n' Roll Friend."

Someone behind me turns to his friend and says, "What do you think? Do you recognize many songs?" I can't hear the answer. "In the Core of the Flame" is followed by the other side of "Don't Let Him Come Back," "People Say"; after they finish it, Forster comments that "the ending we played to that song is the only professional thing we've learnt in fifteen years." His 1984 ballad, "Draining the Pool for You," is followed by a stripped-back rendition of McLennan's first real stab at a pop hit, "Bachelor Kisses." 1988's "Love Goes On" and the first song the group ever recorded, "Lee Remick," close the set.

Of course there are encores. McLennan—with his usual provocative and infuriating sincerity—thanks the group and the Zoo "for making this gentle idea into something good—and we're glad we could do it in *Brisbane*." There is a huge patriotic cheer—the ironic not always separable from the naïve—in response. The two then embark on a rendition of McLennan's "Cattle and Cane," without the band; then a version of Forster's "Clouds," in the style of Simon and Garfunkel. For the second encore, the full band returns to deliver Forster's pre–Go-Betweens triumph "Karen." Someone, for some reason, calls out the word "rock!" from the audience, and Forster's response is typical: "Rock? We *define* rock." The show ends with McLennan's fluid "The Wrong Road."

Backstage afterwards, old and new friends congregate. Temucin Mustafa, the Go-Betweens' first full-time drummer, wanders in to speak to them for the first time since he quit the band in 1979. Outside, in the early Brisbane morning, it begins to rain lightly.

The next day, a prominent Australian promoter calls Forster and McLennan with a proposition. He's heard the Go-Betweens are more or less back together, and he wants to pay them more than they were ever paid in the 1980s to appear at his upcoming rock festival, provided they play under the recognized brand name. (Not long afterwards, with the same lineup, they will do exactly that—at a special show for French magazine *Les Inrockuptibles* in Paris, where the group receives rapturous applause and Forster enthralls the crowd by throwing one of his shoes and the sole of the other into the crowd.) The mainstream is starting to recognize that there's credibility to be gained—perhaps even, at long last, some money to be made—from the group and its name. Though they turn down the promoter's offer, this is the first link in a chain that leads to Forster and McLennan resurrecting the band name and trying once again for rock 'n' roll success.

But don't go saying that the Go-Betweens have now "arrived." Because the Go-Betweens "arrived" in January 1979, when they *arrived* at the studios of public-radio station 4ZZZ[3] in Brisbane to record an interview with their friends Allan Martin and Ashleigh Merritt.

Merritt was particularly fond of Forster and would drive the group to shows when they played at the Curry Shop or the Queen's Hotel. Martin was the station's "token cynic"; he'd also helped design the sleeve of the Go-Betweens' debut single, "Lee Remick."

The Go-Betweens were riding high on their notoriety at the time: on the strength of that one single, they had been offered a record deal with the British arm of hip US indie label Beserkley (home of Jonathan Richman). This was, of course, a highly unusual situation for an Australian group, let alone for one so far removed from Sydney and Melbourne, the two big population centers of Australia, where the music industry liked to think everything in Australian music happened.

The Beserkley offer had prompted Forster—at this time unquestionably the band's leader—to poach a second guitarist, Peter Walsh, who had been building a reputation with his own band, the Apartments. Walsh was to augment the basic three-piece of Forster on guitar and vocals, McLennan on bass, and Temucin (then known as Tim) Mustafa on drums. McLennan and Forster's delight and amazement at their good fortune brings out their humor, their way of bouncing off each other, and their good-natured arrogance throughout this interview.[4]

MARTIN: An interview with the Go-Betweens starting in five from now . . . one-two-three-four-five . . .
McLENNAN: Who counts down? I . . .
FORSTER: Dun-dun-a-dun-dun-a-dun-dun-dunn.
McLENNAN: [*In a high-pitched voice*] The Go-Betweens!
FORSTER: [*Sings the opening to "Lee Remick"*] Ba-ba-baba-ba.
MERRITT: That's them, that's the intro. So okay, fellas, start from the beginning. Who thought of starting the band, and why the name?
FORSTER: Ah, starting the band. I was playing in this other band, that

The first trio: McLennan, Forster, and Temucin (Tim) Mustafa, ca. 1978 *(Tony Forster)*

specialized in, sort of . . . funk and Status Quo.

McLENNAN: And Ry Cooder.

MERRITT: Interesting combination.

FORSTER: Yeah, it was, it was an interesting band. I could see they weren't going anywhere. They were called the Mosquitoes, then the Godots, and they've now changed their name to Curfew and they play in white satin. I just left that [band], because we were only practicing once a week and it was pretty off the track. I was writing these songs, [but] I didn't mix in musician circles so I had to teach someone, taught Grant the bass, because we got on personally and we liked the same music, and we just took it from there. The name of the band, the Go-Betweens, Grant will tell you how that came about.

McLENNAN: Oh, we were driving along in a car one time, going to the Exchange Hotel. We drove over the bridge there and we were just thinking of a few names and I think Rob came up with the Go-Betweens. Because, we since found out, we went between two types of music, maybe, or . . .

FORSTER: Basically there's night and there's day, and you try and go between that, and you find the twilight zone—and there lies the Go-Betweens.

McLENNAN: And Rob likes the word *go*.

FORSTER: Go-go dancer; if you gotta go, go *now*.

McLENNAN: And "between"?

FORSTER: And "between," yeah. Also, Grant and I saw ourselves as surrogate Alan Bates types. Um . . .

McLENNAN: More Ginsbergian, I thought.

FORSTER: Yeah.

MERRITT: The first time I saw you, I thought it was because of the film. But it's not to do with the film *The Go-Between*.

McLENNAN: At heart Rob's a little boy, I think, and I'm more like Julie Christie. I think that's the way it works.

FORSTER: Actually, it's not, it's more of a Rock Hudson/Susan St. James figure. And I call him Mac, but he won't call me Susan.

McLENNAN: Sally.

FORSTER: No, the trouble is he's not a great pretender—and my real name isn't Susan anyway—it's Glenda.

MERRITT: So you're right into films—is that it?

FORSTER: Um, well, Grant's into films. I'm not into films, I'm more into . . . astrology.

McLENNAN: I like fourteen-hour films.

FORSTER: Yeah, no, Grant's into films, um, and . . . so am I.

MERRITT: Do you get many ideas for songs from watching films? You have got a song called "Day for Night." And "Lee Remick."

FORSTER: Yeah, but "Day for Night" is just a title I liked. I was gonna write something on that but it drifted away from that. "Lee Remick" I wrote because I wanted...
MERRITT: To make money.
FORSTER: I wanted to write a song—no, not to make money... Well, I am going to make money. No, the reason I wrote "Lee Remick" was I just wanted to write a song about a movie star—and Lee Remick was my favorite so I wrote about her. It's as simple as that. There's only one other song that has basically a film ambience and that is "So Pretty." I saw a film called *The Collector*, made by William Wyler, starring the beautiful, gorgeous Samantha Eggar. I just put myself in Terence Stamp's shoes and came out with a song called "So Pretty." Actually, I also put myself in a Brisbane situation based on a girl I saw, that I know...
MERRITT: Okay, so you got the name of the band. Who was in the original Go-Betweens?
FORSTER: Grant and myself. It was just a two-piece and we used to turn up at gigs and borrow whoever was playing the drums.
McLENNAN: And *demand* to play!
FORSTER: Yeah, we played with Ronnie Ribbett's drummer.
MERRITT: When did you bring Peter Walsh into the band?
FORSTER: We brought Peter Walsh in about November. Combination of: the songs I was writing then were a little bit more spread out, a little bit more open, and we needed Walsh to flesh them out, we needed a fourth instrument. Also I could see we were going to be playing at places that were slightly bigger than the Curry Shop, i.e., the Queen's, the Exchange, and we needed a fourth instrument to add a few textures.
MARTIN: We've heard that Peter Walsh is difficult to work with, in fact...
FORSTER: That's true.
MARTIN: He's temperamental and he wants to be flattered.
McLENNAN: He's an artist.
FORSTER: Peter Walsh is a hell of a nice guy and he fits in quite well with the Go-Betweens.
MARTIN: But wasn't it extremely convenient that Peter Walsh did come into the band just as you were prepared to go to England for the Beserkley deal?
FORSTER: *Purely* coincidence...
MERRITT: I thought you had the contract, and then asked Peter Walsh.
FORSTER: No, no, that's true, yeah. We already had the contract. It's basically safety in numbers, there's four of us now. Basically we wanted Walsh on a musical level and he fits in socially, which is handy.
MERRITT: Are you happy with the drummer you've got?
FORSTER: Yeah, Tim's working out great, he's working out better all the

time. He fits in with the group well.

MERRITT: But I mean, he's not the same sort of person as you and Grant.

FORSTER: No, that's true. But it does balance well because Tim's a person we can rely on, and if anything he's a sort of a straight man for Grant and myself and it allows us to do more instead of having to compete with probably a third extrovert in the band.

MARTIN: He has been known to use the word "chicks" on occasion.

FORSTER: Ah . . . he has, but you know, he's also been known to wear Italian clothes and big, thick-heeled boots, but we don't try to change him, we're not trying to box him into any sort of image, he can do what he wants. As long as he doesn't use that word around Triple Z, we don't really mind.

MARTIN: Do you find it odd, I might even attack you on this point, that most of your reviews are not so much critical as "nothing" reviews, empty reviews, because they've really got no grounds to criticize the record upon, it's just so different.

FORSTER: Yeah, that's true, I mean Tony Parsons,[5] in *NME* . . . [6]

MARTIN: Did he review it?

FORSTER: Yeah.

MARTIN: Oh.

FORSTER: He didn't say anything substantial, he didn't put it down, but it was a typical Tony Parsons review where he didn't say anything but tried to show off part of his questionable intelligence. But the reviews . . . if you read the one in *Juke*,[7] that was a really good one, that person had it pretty well honed down to what we were doing.

MERRITT: What did they say about you in *ZigZag*?

FORSTER: Again it was the sort of review where they said they liked it—they said it had a power-pop quirkiness about it but had no staying power, which is probably true.

MARTIN: As far as the cliché goes.

FORSTER: Yeah, it's a single that isn't exceptionally deep.

McLENNAN: It's obvious, from most of the reviews anyway, that they haven't listened to the b-side.

FORSTER: No, none of them have listened to "Karen," which is a great disappointment. It's a pity.

MERRITT: We stop. We think. What can we ask?

MARTIN: We edit . . . afterwards.

FORSTER: You can ask about our backgrounds, what sort of schools we went to, stuff like that. How we met . . .

MARTIN: Not interested.

McLENNAN: Yeah, yeah, go on, Allan. I mean, this is the definitive tape.

MARTIN: Is it?
MERRITT: Yeah, this is going to be a one-hour special.
MARTIN: What deviant backgrounds do you fellows come from that caused you to put out singles like "Karen" and "Lee Remick"? You're pretty nonconformist considering your age group.
MERRITT: How old are you, Rob?
FORSTER: I'm twenty-one and Grant's twenty-one. Our background is mainly public . . . [*He corrects himself*] private schools.
McLENNAN: Greater Public Schools.[8]
FORSTER: And we came out of that environment. We didn't want to get a straight job, so we went to the University of Queensland where we both undertook arts degrees, with varying success. But the stuff we were doing there got us thinking. It's odd and creative. When you pick up a guitar you start doing things that come from that background.
MARTIN: It still doesn't explain why you don't play pinball or listen to AM radio.[9]
FORSTER: We both didn't really do that at school, either. It wasn't a conscious decision after we left school: "Oh look, we're not going to fall into that stereotype." It was just something we'd grown out of when we were ten or eleven years old.
MARTIN: Good wholesome clean fun.
FORSTER: Yes, basically that, yeah.
MERRITT: So what exactly was the Beserkley deal? How did you score the contract?
McLENNAN: Oh, yeah, right. We sent a few records overseas to various publications and record companies, and we didn't get any reply back for about a month. We got a few back from Australian record companies that said they weren't interested, that they just didn't think we were commercial enough, and Beserkley in England wrote back and said yes, they were prepared to sign us up and make a lot of money with us.
FORSTER: That was the first letter we got, and the first line was:
McLENNAN AND FORSTER: "We love the Go-Betweens."
FORSTER: And we go where we're loved.
MERRITT: And you fell for it.
McLENNAN: Oh, hook, line, and sinker.
MERRITT: How would you describe the music that you play?
FORSTER: It's like running water off thin, white strips of aluminium. It's just running off. It's open fields, it's sunlight . . . and *maybe*, in a moment of daring, it suggests a lost, primitive civilization. It's sunlight, it's horses, it's Indians on horses.
McLENNAN: And deer.
FORSTER: It's Indians on horses and deer, and it's running through open

fields. It's open.

McLENNAN: And flowers.

MERRITT: That's definitely a middle-American sound—Indians, horses, and deer . . .

FORSTER: Yeah, well if you can transpose that to Australia you get a sort of walkabout phenomenon, if you've ever seen the *Walkabout* film,[10] it's that sort of relationship. It's wandering through a desert, and it's trying to create some sort of music out of that sparse, open landscape.

MERRITT: Do you really believe that?

FORSTER: Yeah, it's true.

MARTIN: But does the band have that image? I mean, Peter Walsh certainly doesn't.

FORSTER: The band is variety . . . variety of personalities and image.

McLENNAN: Walsh is night.

FORSTER: We are day.

McLENNAN: We're day. We're sun, he's rain.

FORSTER: Tim Mustafa is um . . .

McLENNAN: Turkish.

FORSTER: Turkish and a full moon rising.

[*Muffled laughter, silence, break in recording*]

MERRITT: I can't believe it! Listen, you and Grant in particular are the cleanest-living two of the foursome. Why do you have such a clean image? Do you work on it?

FORSTER: No, we don't.

McLENNAN: We both love our parents.

FORSTER: We both love our parents. And also it's . . . There's people that do, and stay home and create, and there's people that go out and put on an outward superficial golden gleam of party-going and pub-crawling. We prefer to stay at home and write things and get things done.

MARTIN: Where do your influences come from?

FORSTER: Variety, um . . . it's that great mid-western Telecaster ring. It's also Bob Dylan in sunglasses talking to Françoise Hardy. I've listened to Françoise Hardy. And it's bicycles and boys, and it's also . . .

McLENNAN: Balloons.

FORSTER: Balloons, red balloons, and it's also . . . If you can imagine this, it's sort of sixties, but it's also trying to identify with the seventies, because I think we're very much a one-off thing, which pretty much [describes] the seventies. It's not a collective, communal music thing. It's very much me saying—this is the way I see things, if you agree with it, well, you'll listen to the Go-Betweens, if you don't, well, you know . . .

MERRITT: What would you say about the scene in Brisbane at the moment, the musical scene?

FORSTER: The music scene in Brisbane is full of bands that you see once and you never see again. They're just bands that play secondhand material, usually they don't progress. Elvis Costello named them all, they're last year's model.[11] Fuller Banks, you know. All this and no surprises from the Sharks,[12] you know, just forget it. Razar—Sex Pistols two years on. It's all boring.
MERRITT: Are there any bands in Brisbane that you like?
FORSTER: Mark Callaghan's a nice guy,[13] and um . . .
McLENNAN: So's Rob Vickers.
FORSTER: So's Rob Vickers, although Rob Vickers has left, sadly . . . Great sort of Keith Richard figure, looked permanently dead, without any drugs or alcohol. Rides a motor scooter.
McLENNAN: Listens to Dionne Warwick.
FORSTER: Yeah. Complete *fag*.
MARTIN [*Softly*] Cut.
FORSTER: The Supports are fun. They'll never be the future of rock 'n' roll.
MERRITT: Are you?
FORSTER: I look on them as sort of clattering rhythms. Pardon?
MERRITT: Will you be the future of rock 'n' roll?
FORSTER: No. I, I, I, *doubt* it. We could be.
MERRITT: But you want to be part of the present?
FORSTER: Yeah. I think we are very much a 1979 band, because we've got our ears open and we are progressing.
MERRITT: How do you think the tour'll go in London—well, in England . . .

Setting out to record "The Sound of Rain," with Peter Walsh *(Temucin Mustafa)*

FORSTER: There's no definite plans to go to England yet, we're still talking with Beserkley. We'd like to go, we're looking at March. And England, I think, has the greatest acceptance of new music, they're more open-minded. No closed minds there, you just walk in and you play, and they say they like you, if they do. Then they write it in the *NME* and people buy your records. Any country that can accept Jilted John, X-Ray Spex, and the Only Ones . . . there's a place for the Go-Betweens.
MERRITT: Well, if you don't make it to London, if the tour doesn't work out with Beserkley, do you look at staying in Brisbane or what?
McLENNAN: We'll probably stop over in Cairo, go all Egyptian or something.

FORSTER: Do you think so? I really don't think so. I'd like to go down south for a while and see how we go, but even if the Beserkley thing falls through, which I don't think it will . . . I can give you a scoop, actually. We are gonna sign the contract by Wednesday, which is the 31st of January. It shall be signed for sure.

MERRITT: Do you think about going down south before you go overseas?

FORSTER: I'd like to go down south, yeah. I'd like to go to Sydney where Double J[14] are playing us.

McLENNAN: I've never been to Sydney. I'd like to see Sydney, Rob.

FORSTER: Yeah, yeah. We'd like to play down there.

MARTIN: Doesn't Double J think the record's a joke?

FORSTER: Well, Double J's a . . . Uh, no. Um. No . . .

MARTIN: They laughed when they heard it.

FORSTER: Yeah, they may have laughed when they heard it, but they're playing it, which is the main thing.

MARTIN: They thought it was a *National Lampoon* comedy record.[15]

McLENNAN: Did they?

FORSTER: Well, they should have listened to "Karen," and they would have realized that assumption was false right from the word go. "Lee Remick" is very much a *fun* record. That's the period that we were going through and it was very much an up, good-time record.

MERRITT: Are you going to make any more good-time records?

FORSTER: Yes, but not, shall we say, as *simple* as "Lee Remick."

MERRITT: Do you regret making "Lee Remick"?

FORSTER: No, no. For the time we were going through, and considering that we'd only played two times before we recorded the single, I think it's a very good first-up effort after two months.

[*Silence*]

McLENNAN: It's an *excellent* first-up effort after two months.

FORSTER: I'd just like to thank Triple Z for putting us on air, especially Ash . . .

[*Tape ends*]

3
Brisbane

JOHN WILLSTEED: "What the fuck does that mean?" is my response to "Brisbane is the birth of punk."[1]

GRANT McLENNAN: "Brisbane is a place where you wait, and you wait, and you wait, and if a clipper ship comes in and they unload their tea, you just want to get on the ship and get out."[2]

Australian cities are bigger than most cities in Europe and North America. Not because of their populations—Sydney is the largest, with under five million—but because of the suburban ethos which prefers large blocks of land, and what critics call "sprawl," to denser settlement patterns. With a population of well over a million, Brisbane, 980 kilometers (610 miles) north of Sydney, has both beauty and drawbacks, like all Australian cities. It has hills, a river, stately nineteenth-century public buildings, and in some places a distinctive suburban architecture, notably the placing of houses on stilts so they stay cool in Brisbane's very hot summers.

As in other Australian cities, Brisbane's youth had taken rock 'n' roll by the scruff of the neck in the late 1950s and were still worrying at it twenty years later. The city in which the young Bee Gees cut their teeth also brought forth legendary sixties garage pop band the Wild Cherries and, just as importantly, hundreds of other, smaller rock groups with loyal local followings.

Unlike elsewhere in Australia, however, the Brisbane rock scene became inseparable from the local political scene from the late 1960s onwards. After a long political history in which the left had featured prominently, a coalition government of the two major Australian conservative groupings—the Liberal Party and the Country Party—took power in Queensland in 1957. The new state premier, Frank Nicklin, stayed in office for a decade, and on retiring was succeeded by longstanding second-in-command Jack Pizzey. Pizzey died in harness six months after coming to power, and was succeeded by a New Zealand–born farmer, Joh Bjelke-Petersen. Bjelke-Petersen did not look like promising leadership material at the outset, but he cemented his position over time with a commitment to what his government termed "law and order." A pivotal moment in this process was the forcible suppression of protests against the touring Springbok rugby team from racially segregated South Africa in 1971. Bjelke-Petersen was an extraordinary leader: though he often appeared doddering and foolish, his enemies soon discovered he was cunning, conniving, and heavy-handed. His government, while often described (not unfairly) as self-seeking and corrupt, appealed strongly to many Queenslanders, the majority of whom lived in rural areas. The Country Party's shameless pursuit of the best possible conditions for free-enterprise capitalism, at the expense of any other considerations, could seem almost benign in the golden glow of Bjelke-Petersen's shaky good humor and apparent inarticulateness. He was a standing joke to the rest of Australia, as indeed Queensland and its inhabitants have often been. But he shared with Ronald Reagan, for example, a "big picture" conception of politics, as well as a somewhat charismatic—if paternalistic—manner.

Brisbane in the 1960s—even in those early days of the Country Party's extraordinarily long rule, which lasted until a series of corruption scandals finally brought it down in 1987—was as keen to get into the strenuous celebration of teendom and the counterculture as the rest of Australia. Australian sixties rock was enthusiastic and vibrant: whether individual groups paid slavish attention to overseas trends or not, they always made sure they knew what those trends were, and were always somehow able to make them their own. There were few thoughts of exporting Australian rock to the world: people like Pip Proud made fascinating music that fell on deaf ears, and people like the Bee Gees got out as soon as they could. Other groups, like Adelaide's Master's Apprentices, Melbourne's Procession, and Sydney's Easybeats traveled to England and quickly discovered that pop success there, if it came at all, was short-lived and painful.

Brisbane's dance clubs in the 1960s—which were generally called discotheques, though in fact they featured live groups—must have been remarkable, especially the Sound Machine, which promoter and Brisbane patriot John Reid aka "the Brisbane Devotee," remembered ten years later as having "fluorescent posters, red and black decor, telephones on the tables so you could ring other tables."[3] The city was awash with evocatively named nightspots: the Red Orb, which regularly advertised in national "teens and twenties" magazine *Go-Set;* Adam and Eve's (later the Electric Circus); Snoopy's Hollow; the Ritz Ballroom; and Quentin's. Anyone sick of the crass commercialism of these venues—that is, of R&B covers bands delivering versions of contemporary top forty material—might turn to institutions of greater countercultural significance. There was Foco, for example, a Sunday night club in the Trades Hall, or, in the early 1970s, events organized by "How About Resisting Powerful Organisations," better known by its delightful faux-numbly-nostalgic acronym HARPO.[4]

Then there was radio. In the 1960s, 4BC, its call sign seeming to recall a lost primitive civilization, featured Beatles half-hours and sets of soul music. Late in that decade, the station celebrated and promoted its star DJ, Mike Ahearn, with concerts at which teenagers gleefully chanted "I will have no leader but my leader Mike Ahearn!" Radio would not inspire youth action to such an extent again until 4ZZZ was launched in late 1975, and even then it was hardly a matter of across-the-board devotion: 4ZZZ was apparently more a sounding board which the Marxists and the anarchists could use to attack the pot smokers, and then each other.

All sources seem to agree, however, that the early-to-mid-1970s saw an unprecedented slump in creativity. A few progressive rock acts meandered on, and heavy metal made a big impact—especially once a promoter named John Hein began putting together Black Sabbath covers groups to play the small circuit of suburban halls. One might explain this as the result of the kind of musical stagnation the whole world experienced at this time, especially with regard to vibrant, innovative live music. But Brisbane was doubly affected because of the decline of its live venues: as one observer put it, "the arse fell out."[5] Most clubs became bona fide discos in the 1970s sense: places where you went to hear records from elsewhere, not local bands, and certainly not local bands playing local songs. Police harassment of the young was certainly a major cause of this move away from live music: accounts differ as to why the police now found it necessary to raid live venues. One possibility is that in the Bjelke-Petersen government's "law and order" climate, police found it expedient to arrest young people for relatively trivial offences, such as underage drinking or swearing, because this boosted their charge sheets and their overtime without being particularly dangerous— physically or politically. It is also possible that rock 'n' roll venues—not in the same league financially as money-spinners like the brothels or strip clubs of Fortitude Valley—could not afford the kind of bribes "law and order" was beginning to expect in order to keep the police out of their business. The "Brisbane Devotee" told the *Cane Toad Times* that police interest was political, starting with the large-scale protests against the Springbok tour:

> The police became more the upholders of public morals, at least of the young ... Most of the dance activities were at the Uni, which has a measure of protection against the police, but anything held in the suburbs would have a few [police]. The police began harassing segments of the youth as part of their "moral duty" ...
>
> When every bank clerk started to wear long hair around '74, the commie radicals became that much harder for the Queensland police to recognize.[6]

Which is why, for the Devotee, punk came not a moment too soon:

> When the punks came along, the police found a new target. The Right to March demonstrators[7] had most of the southeast Queensland police force standing on the road in the sun looking at the assorted demonstrators.
>
> In this motley assembly they must have started to recognize the short-haired weirdos, some of whom had green hair, and wondered about them. You can imagine what effect a green-haired idiot has on the Queensland police. Loathing, distaste, hatred.
>
> These short-haired weirdos at the same time had a musical/cultural message going, which brought in new people. Every month of '78 saw new members of the "punk" community, and pretty soon you had a "movement," even if its message was ... "Rod Stewart Sucks."

The Saints were truly magnificent (Joe

So in Queensland you had this group growing that was political, with vague ideas of Anarchy, and now you have the Queensland Special Branch as the first cops through the door at punk dances.⁸

The Numbers, 1978. Robert Vickers on bass *(Tony Forster)*

This is not to say the advent of "punk" made a substantial difference to the number of venues in Brisbane in the mid-to-late 1970s, unless one counts venues like "Club 76," initiated by the Saints: this was what they called their house whenever they had a party. The decline of the venues and the politicization of rock are just two things that set Brisbane music of the late 1970s apart from the music of the rest of Australia and the world—with the notable exception, ironically, of parts of Eastern Europe.

Often the politics were blunt and strident: there was little room for humor when it came to resisting Joh. But then, you have to consider what anyone opposed to the Bjelke-Petersen government was up against. To follow the kind of lifestyle that people in other Australian cities took for granted—going out for the night, hearing a few rock bands who played music relevant to your world, drinking—was infused, in Brisbane, with a special kind of danger. The police could arrest you at any time, and effectively they could do what they wanted with you. Most residents of Brisbane—which had a more liberal climate than the rest of Queensland—seemed to consider themselves apolitical, and were comfortable with that. But to call oneself "punk" in Brisbane was to be part of a small, renegade movement. It was a choice fraught with greater risks than elsewhere in Australia—which is perhaps the main reason why Brisbane punk music always seemed to have that extra edge.

4
"Let's camp it up!"

DAMIEN NELSON: I remember playing a game of touch football with Robert at Uni once. Grant and I would play sport and get deadly earnest about it. It was quite a tight game and I remember to this day seeing Robert Forster running towards me with the ball yelling, "Let's camp it up! Let's camp it up!" I've never, never forgotten that. All these people were just standing there—"What on earth is going on here?"

He was very good at it too. To me, Robert and Grant always seemed to know what they were doing. I admired their gall. They had a lot of courage to get up in front of an audience and do what they did—especially in Brisbane.

Forster's way of turning sport—the reigning masculine cultural activity in Brisbane in the 1970s—into melodrama was typical of the sense of grandiose fantasy he brought to the everyday world. Andrew Wilson, a fellow student of Forster's at Brisbane Grammar School, remembers the way Forster played cricket:

ANDREW WILSON: I've reminded him of the way he was in the First Eleven cricket team at school. He used to practice at lunchtime, on the main oval, knowing full well he more or less had a captive audience, and under the guise of practicing his spin bowling he was in fact giving a private performance to the lower grades of the school.

Growing up in conservative middle-class Brisbane, Forster was soon using his "performance" personality to subvert another traditional male-dominated cultural system: the local rock scene.

He started his first band, the Mosquitoes, in 1975—the year he turned seventeen. "I'd just started playing guitar in the last year of school," he remembers. "Acoustic guitar, then I bought an electric guitar and an amplifier." His major collaborator at the time was a school friend, Stephen Hollingsworth.

> FORSTER: His parents had a house at Brookfield, a nice, leafy, huge house with a swimming pool, and we used to go there on weekends. He'd been listening to the Doors. I used to play guitar and this other friend used to do basic percussion, and Stephen used to ad-lib the lyrics and we used to record whole albums in a day. We'd start at twelve and finish at six. And we used to record it on a cassette player.
>
> I'd work out quite cyclical chord progressions, notes or something, and we'd start jamming, a vocal, someone on bongos and one or two guitars. We'd record eight or ten tracks, and then just listen to them. Then two or three months later, record another album. So we were doing these albums, they were pretty Doorsy-based—long, repetitive things, very dramatic. Stephen would sing or yell, some of the songs would be ten or fifteen minutes long.
>
> I wasn't much into the Doors at that stage. [Hollingsworth] would say to me "Go Robbie go," and a couple of years later I heard a Doors album and there's Jim Morrison saying to Robbie Krieger, "Go Robbie go." But I don't know, eighteen-year-old angst, I wasn't writing any lyrics, I was just coming to grips with playing guitar.
>
> Late 1975, 1976 [I formed] another band, called the Godots. This was a *real* band. Malcolm Kelly, who I knew from school, he was a real bass player. We got someone to play drums—we put up an ad, I think—a drummer who was still at school, and I was singing. Malcolm also sang. He was into the Doors, too. He had a good, vaguely conventional rock voice. That went for two years. It was a good band, it was mainly cover versions—it was *all* cover versions. We were doing early Beatles, Hollies, a little bit of Doors, and then old songs like "Shake Your Booty" by K C and the Sunshine Band,[1] "Heading in the Right Direction" by Renee Geyer,[2] "Knockin' on Heaven's Door," "Rockin' Robin," mainly sixties beat stuff, "You Sexy Thing" by Hot Chocolate, "To Sir with Love" by Lulu, "Rebel Rebel." It was a "Rebel Rebel"/K C and the Sunshine Band type of thing. And a lot of early Beatles—"I Saw Her Standing There," "I Feel Fine," "Eight Days a Week," really sharp early-sixties things . . .
>
> [We were] very, very pop, completely against everything else everyone was doing in town, because we did no heavy metal, which 99.9 percent of bands in Brisbane were doing. Rush, Deep Purple, Led Zeppelin just ruled, there was no diverging from that. They all looked dreadful, they sounded dreadful. We played some shows—three shows. There was no place to play except suburban dances. There was a big suburban high-

school dance thing and you had to have three hours of material. How were three teenage boys going to get three hours of presentable material? Also, there were all these bands who were technically so much better than us. There would've been two hundred bands in Brisbane who were better than us. None of them were taking the Hollies seriously. Or doing "You Sexy Thing."

These bands were rehearsing four nights a week, probably had day jobs, and were pouring all their money into buying equipment, which we weren't. I was at university, the other guy was at university, the other guy was at school. At this time the prevailing belief was that if you've got eight tons of equipment, you must be a better band than someone who's got four tons of equipment. I was immediately into the aesthetic of *as little equipment as possible*. Always look like you're completely undernourished in terms of equipment. Just to upset people . . . but also I liked the sound of it. This was a time when bands had two trucks' worth of equipment, and never played outside of Brisbane. They'd turn up at some suburban hall, and would take pride in the fact that it took three hours to get all their equipment out of the back of their vans . . . and then get up and start playing "Black Dog" or "Stairway to Heaven." This orthodoxy was so strong—the sixties didn't exist and the fifties didn't exist. The sixties existed merely as the creation of heavy metal. It was like—"early Beatles, early Stones, they didn't get it together, *man,* until 1969." And then music was invented. Jimmy Page invented music and Robert Plant invented singing. Nothing before. That's what it was like in Brisbane.

We realized after a while that [the band] wasn't going to work. But we kept going because we enjoyed it, we enjoyed playing. Not every Sunday but most Sundays. My father worked down at a factory at Eagle Farm. We used to play on the factory floor, amongst all these machines, unplug a lathe, or some huge big thing, and plug in and play, and it'd be like this huge big hall, it was like playing in a concert hall, with industrial equipment, with curls of steel everywhere. We'd sweep the concrete floor and set up drums, one guitar, bass amp, little vocal PA, two mikes, and start playing in this factory.

And the other thing—this was 1976, a band named after a Samuel Beckett play was, around Brisbane at that time . . . for one thing it had the word "the." It was "the" something or other. Every other band had a name taken from a Jethro Tull song title. One long word, or something with an X or Z at the end of it. And we were the Godots. I had this thing: "the band everyone's waiting for!"

We entered a Battle of the Bands competition, at the end of 1977. They called us "the Go Dots." Of course, it's only a short jump to "the Go-Betweens." I thought "the Go Dots" wasn't a bad misunderstanding.

We played one show, at the end of 1976, at the drummer's school. It didn't go all that well. Everyone had a light show ... and we didn't have a light show.

Any self-respecting Brisbanite who was young in the mid-1970s will be able—at least after a reflective pause and a sigh into their half-empty beer glass—to recall what happened in Brisbane in the mid-1970s to change the face of music. The Saints, of course. The Saints were formed by Ed Kuepper and Chris Bailey and in 1976 they recorded and released a single called "(I'm) Stranded" on their own record label. The reaction to this locally is probably hard to appreciate today, but would probably be best represented as: "no reaction at all." The Saints went on to become recognized as one of the best—if not *the* best—of the so-called Class of '77 (though in fact they predated even the Ramones by a couple of years). But in 1976 the Saints were too hard to understand, and what was hard to understand was hard to care about. There was little precedent for anything like punk rock at that stage, in Brisbane or anywhere, and what understanding there was of punk was of its sixties form—the "garage" groups. The main lesson later local groups learned from the Saints was that they quickly *got out* of Brisbane—leaving town was an ambition many felt was worth fighting for.

But although Forster had an abiding interest in the 1960s, and though "(I'm) Stranded" struck him solidly when he first heard it on the radio, his own breakthrough song about Brisbane and isolation was no rapid dirge. It was the plaintive, esoteric "Karen."

Robert being Lenny *(Tony Forster)*

The music to "Karen" was simple, and obviously influenced by Jonathan Richman, who had become something of an important figure in the 1970s with his trademark naiveté. Like "Lee Remick," the later song which it would be paired with on the first Go-Betweens single, the central figure of "Karen" is not the woman of its title, but Forster himself, lonely in Brisbane and pining for a connection to other worlds and exotic cultures. The exotic might be found in faraway cultural centers like New York or Paris, or in the female world, which was probably more alien still to the eighteen-year-old Forster.

There is a strong thread of asceticism in "Karen"; though its narrator returns to the theme of wanting affection, he also denies that his desire is sexual. It is the desire for knowledge: Karen, a composite character derived from a number of female librarians at the university library, helps him find the "right" authors: Hemingway, Genet, Joyce. Forster was asked to explain the song in 1979:

> FORSTER: Once I lost my wallet in the library, and the amount of anguish that they went through to try and find it . . . They were standing at the counter willing to help people and that struck me as some sort of social-worker, nun-type role that I could see coming out of being a librarian, so I wrote that song about them. I knew one of them personally and I was doing an assignment and I worked with another one that I knew.[3]

Quite apart from the fairly radical idea of idealizing women intellectually in rock, it was rare, before the mid-1970s, for serious rock songwriters in Australia to take on Australian subjects. The first big-league album to include local suburbs and place names is generally held to be Melbourne group Skyhooks' iconoclastic debut, *Livin' in the Seventies*, released in 1974. While it might be going too far to say that Australian songwriters had previously been terrified by anything that might mark them as living west of California, Australians did not seem to want to hear their own culture mentioned in pop music, and certainly it seemed ludicrous to expect overseas audiences to take an interest in such things.[4] Forster, however, hoped to push the Godots into new territory: that is, a lyrical exploration of the territory they actually lived in. He says he "started taking more control": the group entered the annual Battle of the Bands at the Brisbane Academy of Music in 1977.

> FORSTER: A lot of the big heavy metal bands used to enter because first prize was $5,000. They used to have heats Saturday mornings at the Academy of Music, downstairs, and so we entered. You had fifteen minutes and so you had to do about five songs. We all had quite short hair and I said, "Everyone wear a white shirt and black pants." And so we had this band "look." At that stage I'd just written "Karen," so we played "Karen," and maybe one or two other songs I'd written. We did "Sweet Jane."[5] We were a three-piece. My brother, who was a couple of years younger, got up from the audience and played bass without it being plugged in. So it looked like a four-piece—he put on the bass, pulled

out the cord and just stood there. And I sort of rolled around on the floor doing "Sweet Jane." People were just laughing. People were coming down from the music store upstairs; [we were] supposed to be doing *Led Zeppelin IV* or Styx, Journey, Wishbone Ash, all that sort of shit.

"Karen" went down very very well. They could tell it was not a *momentous* song, even though it was a *great* song, and they were laughing, which I thought was really good. I could see that if I could get away from this audience, people could appreciate the joke, or the insight, or whatever. And so that was the second show. We didn't pass, of course. Total disbelief.

I don't think the other members of the band enjoyed it. I think they wanted to compete with the other bands. And the fact that we were almost ridiculed . . . We did a gig about a week after, and the band broke up. They went into cabaret—I don't think they lasted too long. They just wanted to do "Black Magic Woman," "Honky Tonk Woman"—all songs that had "woman" in the title. Whereas I wanted to sing about *girls*.

In 1976, 1977 I was trying to change the direction of the band because all these records were coming out. The Ramones' first album, which I had really early and I worked out three or four of their songs. These guys couldn't see it; it wasn't complicated enough. And they'd become better musicians, we all were, and so they wanted something to show off, and I wanted to do a song off *Station to Station* by David Bowie. When punk came, that was the flow-on from the early sixties stuff. They weren't interested.

The next step for Forster, if he wanted to continue playing music, was to find people with personalities strong enough to challenge his own. Naturally—and this probably would have been the case even if the year had not been 1977, "Year One" of the do-it-yourself ethic—musical skill took a back seat to such aims. Eleven years later, Forster described this time to *Sounds*:

> FORSTER: I remember spending twenty-one Saturday nights at home in a row—that was my record. My parents were going out more than me and they were trying to push me alcohol, trying to get me to get involved, and I just started to realize that I had to get out and that's when I started writing songs. I knew [that] to break the chain of Saturday nights I had to get up onstage.[6]

The Brisbane of his youth, Forster went on, was "a town where you have to look for people, where you have to put out certain sounds, almost wear certain kinds of clothes—and just hope that someone will walk by that you can grab." His someone was, of course, fellow University of Queensland arts student Grant McLennan. Forster recalled that McLennan "was carrying a film mag and a Ry Cooder record" when they first met. "The film mag I approved of, the Ry Cooder record I was cool on."[7]

This kind of cultural flag-waving was a legitimate way to make friends in Brisbane in the late 1970s, according to Robert Vickers, who moved in the same circles as Forster and McLennan.

Grant McLennan *(Clinton Walker)*

ROBERT VICKERS: If you walked down the street with a Nico album, and somebody who was interested in Nico saw you, they would probably stop. Oh, definitely, without a doubt. You really did judge people quite quickly by their tastes and that was very important. And you needed other people to be involved. Just someone to share it with. And if you did see someone walking down the street with a Nico album or *Big Star 3*, that was enough. If you saw someone on a train even *dressed* in a certain way, you might talk to them.

McLennan came from a boarding-school background. His father, a doctor, had died when he was four, and he had been sent to Brisbane's Church of England Grammar School a few years later.

McLENNAN: I'm the eldest child. We moved around a little bit, and after my father's death we moved to where my mother grew up, which was in Cairns.[8] I spent a few years there and then I was sent away to boarding school at quite a young age. Then I went on to university. I turned seventeen in my first year, and around that time my mother remarried and we moved to a cattle station about three hundred miles west of Cairns.

The McLennan family were rural conservatives, and boarding at "Churchy" was a family tradition:

McLENNAN: My father went there; I've since found out Robert's father went there. Everyone in my family went to boarding schools. Mother went to one. Aunt went to one. Uncle went to one, brother, sister, first cousins went . . . Most of those people from school were kind of country boys. A lot of them didn't go on to university or tertiary education; they went back to the farm or cattle station.

A creative child, but one who needed to escape into fantasy, McLennan wrote "ballads in the Australian tradition—like Banjo Paterson, and as I discovered other poets I just mimicked their style." In 1983, he recalled a formative school experience common among precocious children whose elders underestimate their ability:

> McLENNAN: I had written a poem and the housemaster accused me of stealing it from someone else, and said that I'd copied it out. I said I hadn't. I insisted on this and I was punished—corporal punishment.[9]

He had also been extremely interested in cinema from an early age:

> McLENNAN: As a kid I used to cut out reviews from lots of magazines— I wouldn't have seen any of the films—and stick them in a scrapbook. I always liked film, it was always an improvement on life, to quote Truffaut, and I just liked the stars of the screen. I applied at film and television school at the end of my senior year at boarding school, but they said I was too young, and to get back to them when I was twenty-one. Twenty-one seemed like years and years away, so I went to university. It was just a thing to do. I didn't question it.

Forster's account of their first meeting almost gives the sense of the blissfully unaware younger McLennan being spied on, then seduced, by the older figure—although a Ry Cooder record might not have been the most appealing tail feather for McLennan to waggle. McLennan's first memory of Forster, however, is of quite a different courtship display:

> McLENNAN: I'd never seen a six-foot-two person with a nappy on.
> There were two groups in our drama class: we were doing Hamlet and I was playing Polonius. Robert's group were doing *The Rocky Horror Show,* and I thought, "appalling taste." Robert played the monster. He struck me as an impressive specimen. And very unusual, with the eyebrows together and stuff. I thought that was good makeup. Then we kind of mingled, then we ended up in the same class. He was reading the same kind of books I was interested in. I was reading *NME* and he was reading that [too]. We both liked Nick Kent and the same kind of records, like Mott the Hoople. When Patti Smith's *Horses* came out, that was a

great record for the two of us. And then we were just complete and utter lags, you know, in class.

McLennan has often characterized his relationship with Forster as a non-sexual homosexuality:

> McLENNAN: We were in Queensland, which is a very macho state, and Brisbane symbolizes everything which is disgusting about Queensland. We were pushed together at university in our foppish attitudes towards theater as well.[10]

He was also able to indulge his taste for cinema. He wrote film criticism for the university magazine, *Semper*,[11] in which he was able to preview films he was programming at the university's Schonell Cinema. One of his reviews—of Robert Altman's *Images*—pinpoints McLennan's own dilemma, as a member of a very exclusive elite. He writes that "a good film is one the viewer reacts favorably to, rather like the statement 'I like oysters because they taste nice.' The critic might like a film that 1,000 people detest. That doesn't mean the film is good; after all, not everyone likes oysters."[12]

McLennan and Forster's shared tastes in cinema, theater, and music set them apart from most of the people they had ever known, but university also outlined for them the kind of ideas and creative avenues that existed in the wider world. McLennan embraced the opportunities to the extent that he was quite successful academically. Forster was not.

> FORSTER: University was for me to bide my time. I was buying time . . .
>
> [In] London or Paris or New York or San Francisco, if you don't want to exist on a nine-to-five level, [the university area] is sort of the bohemian area. That's where the coffee shops are, that's where the art cinema is. There's houses to rent, there's people to meet, you go and do it. This is what people do all around the world. But not in Brisbane in the mid-seventies. I left school and it was like . . . nothing. And that was the hard thing. There were no older people here.
>
> You read about the groups in London and you read biographies of the Sex Pistols or Television, whoever, and there's always older people from the 1960s still on the scene. And they were either controlling things, or at least telling people, "Oh yeah, back in the sixties I saw the Stones, I saw this, I saw that"—and the younger people go, "That's a helpful link!" In Brisbane—no one. Everyone over the age of twenty-two was working in an insurance office. And so I had no one I could sit around and listen to who'd go, "I didn't get a job until I was twenty-four and I knew these people and we sat around and smoked dope—everything's worked out

fine. Groovy." I had no one like that. It was scary. And the only thing I could think of in my semi-coherent seventeen-year-old brain was university.

It was a great disappointment to my parents because I'd been accepted into law, and just before the first semester started I changed, to the eternal disappointment of my grandmother and parts of my family. But I chose arts right at the last minute, and I immediately started falling down a ladder.

I'd been extremely successful at school; at school, I found a lot more freedom than later at university. I could do anything I wanted at school. It was a lot more creative, a lot more satisfying, a lot weirder, if you like. Which I thrived on. And as soon as I got into university and started handing in assignments, I was called aside and told, "If you want to do creative writing, we have little courses . . . but we don't want creative writing." And of course this is the way I'd written through school. And got good grades. I used to hand in schoolwork with photos. I'd take photos a lot. At university you were supposed to hand in a paper. I handed it in in a box—a cardboard box. It was rejected. And so there was a bad spiral. From being the schoolboy genius, I go to university and become the town dunce.

My parents were very unhappy with me—it almost led to breakdowns of relationships with certain members of my family, because I was failing. The problem was, I was the first person in three or four generations of my family to go to university. And with no academic background, *they* couldn't understand.

Fortunately, at university I did meet some people. I met a woman by the name of Virginia Clarke who was a very inspirational, pivotal person. She walked into my first class in 1975. She came from Inala, and she was a big fan of the New York Dolls. She was someone I could relate to, and she became a friend.

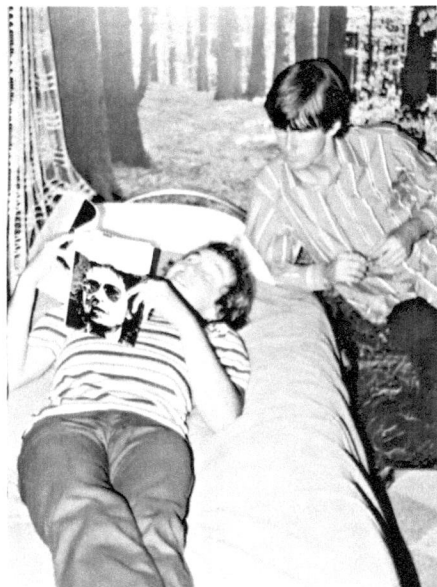

Cinemaphiles *(Tony Forster)*

I used to spend all my time in the library. I'd start to read and I'd jump—I'd have an assignment on the Enlightenment in seventeenth-century France, and I'd end up reading about Timothy Leary in San Francisco in 1967, and I could link them. I'd spend a whole day in the library and I wouldn't have anything to show for it. I used to read lots of books about the sixties and fifties, because I was interested in how I got to where I was, eighteen years old and confused. I'd read a lot about the Beat Generation, and Paris in the twenties. It was a holding time.

By the end of 1977, Forster had dropped out of university and McLennan had completed his degree. Forster would occasionally suggest to McLennan throughout 1977 that they form a rock group, but McLennan—perhaps daunted by witnessing the Godots' Academy of Music show—resisted such challenges until his studies were over. By then he was still only nineteen—presumably still too young to apply himself effectively in the film world. Which did not mean, however, that he was hungering to play music.

> McLENNAN: I said, "I can't play." I guess I wanted to be a scriptwriter. He didn't try and persuade me too much . . . He was scratching around on guitar and it just seemed like that was what he wanted to do. I was interested in something else. Music was the *last* thing . . .
>
> He didn't twist my arm and he didn't seem disappointed, because Robert was obsessed with what he wanted to do. He was always walking around in his own world.
>
> At the end of 1977 he rang up and said, "You're finishing [university], have you changed your mind, do you want to start a band?" And I said yes.
>
> You know, it was: "Why not?" It wasn't like: "Oh, yeah, let's get a band together!" It was just: "Why not?"

5
"Passenger pop for traveling minds"

McLennan and Forster began rehearsing together in late 1977. In early 1978, they attended a "punk dance" at Baroona Hall, walking distance from the center of Brisbane, where the Numbers and Robbie Ribbett and the Toadettes were playing. They asked the Numbers singer, Mark Callaghan, whether he'd let them perform a couple of songs. Of course he consented—this was a common way for bands to get their first shows. They then asked Gerard Lee, a Toadette they vaguely knew, if he would drum for them. The songs they did were "Lee Remick" and "Eight Pictures."

Lee was a good choice to support the Go-Betweens' debut; he was probably the most literate drummer in Brisbane. He'd published a small, limited-edition book of poems and a short-story collection, *Pieces for a Glass Piano*, which included a tale about a confrontation between an exotic friend called Lindy and an Ann Street greengrocer. Lee's 1982 book, *True Love and How to Find It*, is as eloquent a summary as you could find of the dichotomies and ironies of personal politics in Brisbane in the late 1970s. Ronnie Ribbett and the Toadettes—the name had been inspired by the band's first show, at a benefit for the *Cane Toad Times*—were a 1960s-style group who considered themselves "too well adjusted" for punk rock.[1] The Numbers, on the other hand, were entirely punk rock, and probably better adjusted than the Toadettes. From their covers—"(I'm) Stranded" and other Saints songs—to their originals, with titles like "Yellow Cake" and "Teenage Depression,"[2] their attitude was entirely anti-conservative and pro-reality; they were also unapologetically professional.

This was the first of a number of unannounced, and more or less unplanned, shows by the Go-Betweens. Clinton Walker, a budding rock writer in Brisbane who would soon move to Melbourne and start a fanzine, *Pulp*, and a radio show on 3RRR with his punky Melbourne friend Bruce

Milne, reminisced about one of these late 1970s Go-Betweens shows in the Adelaide-based music magazine *Roadrunner* at the end of 1979. The bands that night were what we would now call "traditionally" punky—the Survivors and the Leftovers, but Walker saw "two fairly nondescript fellows" take the stage: they "fumbled their way—drummerless—through two songs that were obviously the product of their own inexperienced hands."

> WALKER (1979): There was nothing particularly "good" about their "performance," but something about it impressed me. Probably its unique "style." I left Brisbane soon afterwards, and promptly forgot the whole incident.³

An early show, 1978 *(Tony Forster)*

Whether Walker was trying to indicate heavy irony or light ambivalence through the rampant quote marks is now difficult to divine. What the *Roadrunner* piece did herald was the beginning of a long and not always healthy friendship, and an even longer and usually healthy critical to-ing and fro-ing. Walker was lauding Forster and McLennan's achievements from the outset, but that didn't mean he'd let them get away with anything he didn't approve of. In 1984 Walker conducted a lengthy interview with McLennan in which Grant recollected those early shows:

> McLENNAN: I bought an old bass, an Ibanez, and Robert knew nothing about bass but he knew [that] if it was a 4/4 song you'd play four beats to the bar, so we used to practice every now and then in my bedroom with an amplifier. Robert was writing a lot of songs at that stage, a lot of songs.

A couple of weeks after the Baroona Hall debut, the Go-Betweens did "about five songs" at a university show. Bruce Anthon, a legendary drummer in Brisbane punk circles and a member of the Survivors, offered his services, "so we used him a few times," McLennan told Walker. "Then we placed an ad in Brisbane newspapers for a female drummer, and a couple answered, but they were worse than we were on our instruments."⁴

Exotic dreams of female drummers aside, Bruce Anthon was a valuable asset, and his early support of the fledgling group boosted their profile and their credibility. The Survivors were a dynamic three-piece, who had risen meteorically in the Brisbane scene with covers of Kinks and Small Faces hits. Though they denied any "punk" or "new wave" tags—"only two of the numbers in our sixty-song repertoire are new wave," they told the Brisbane *Courier-Mail*[5]—they signed a five-album deal with Melbourne's "punk" label Suicide.[6] For the Go-Betweens, the offer of support from Anthon was invaluable.

Forster was the sole songwriter in the Go-Betweens for the first two years of the band. McLennan had actually written one song, he now says—when he was seventeen, he and his sister had performed this composition, "The Lady of the Lake," on guitars for their grandmother. This had not, however, led him into a flurry of songwriting, and was his only composition to date. Forster was writing songs quickly, but the group still filled their set with covers. Forster remembers these including the Monkees' "You Told Me" and "You Just May Be the One," the Byrds' "It Won't Be Long," the Easybeats' "She's So Fine," and the Velvets' "We're Going to Have a Real Good Time Together." Andrew Wilson, who had been at school with Forster and was soon to form his own band, the Four Gods, recalls the first night he saw the Go-Betweens, at a hall in Woolloongabba, where the group added "Hang On Sloopy" and Jonathan Richman's "Roadrunner" to these gems.

Bruce Anthon *(Tony Forster)*

> ANDREW WILSON: It was actually the night Clinton Walker's sister and another girl who I think had studied with Robert at university had agreed to be go-go dancers. I walked in to this scene of two girls go-go dancing, obviously very drunk. Lisa Walker, I remember, was swigging from a bottle of vodka and she dropped the bottle and was dancing in the glass—and sort of upstaged the band a little bit. I remember seeing blood on the stage. It was a pretty memorable performance.

The group also played many shows at the Curry Shop. This venue, in central Brisbane, advertised itself with a bizarre cartoon of a naked, elderly man who looked as if his visit to the basement eatery had given him chronic diarrhea. More than two decades later, Peter Walsh and Robert Vickers recall the Curry Shop with wonder:

> VICKERS: A dive, very small. It was, in fact, a curry shop. It was a place where you could buy curry and eat it, if you chose. A small basement—there was an alley in the back which opened into the store. It had a

definite feel of squalor.

WALSH: It was dangerous to eat there. I don't think I ever ate there. I *played* there.

VICKERS: It was certainly perfect for the time. It had columns, wooden columns, all through it; you were always up against a post. It looked like there were walls everywhere that had been taken down except for the uprights. A little tiny stage, and you couldn't see anyone playing onstage because everyone could stand up front. You couldn't hear anything—but you were *there*.

WALSH: You could hear the amps, and you could hear the guitars. The dressing room doubled as a urinal. I thought the people who ran it were hippies, and they meditated on a Sunday night, they had people to put you to sleep. And then someone must have said, "You should have some rock 'n' roll!"

VICKERS: That's one of the interesting things about punk in Brisbane, the connection between punks and hippies. This crossover. Shared houses, with hippies and extreme punks living together.[7]

Vickers recalls Blondie showing up at the Curry Shop, on the seminal New York new-wave group's ill-fated (and reputedly heroin-flushed) first trip to Australia. The Grudge, the band Vickers would shortly join and who would then become the Numbers, were playing that night.[8] Walsh has fond memories of Debbie Harry vomiting in the Curry Shop toilets. Vickers remembers, "We all got to talk to them and that was pretty amazing. It was a really happening place, and everyone from out of town obviously knew about it."

This was the Go-Betweens' live habitat: perhaps they figured the sooner they got to vinyl, the sooner they could escape it—physically and spiritually.

When, in May 1978, Forster and McLennan decided they would record a single, it was not Bruce Anthon who accompanied them into the studio but Denis Cantwell, the Numbers' drummer. Mark Callaghan was also present, though no one—least of all Callaghan—remembers why. They recorded at Window Studios, which was usually used for recording advertising jingles as well as what little rock and country music was being produced in Brisbane at the time. "We got it out of the phone book," recalls Forster. It turned out to be a fortunate choice: "It was twenty-four-track, it had good microphones. We did it in three hours. It would have been only about the twentieth time we'd played those songs ever. Started at nine o'clock in the morning."

Forster with Mark Callaghan of the Numbers *(Tony Forster)*

Like "Karen," "Lee Remick" is much more a song about a lonely boy in Brisbane idolizing and failing to connect with women ("My life is desperation/But it's only infatuation") than it is about Lee Remick, the movie star. Forster does, however, manage to toss in several hilarious lines, which serve to make it even more unique: it's a comedy record, but it's a sincere comedy record.

"It was one of the first songs I wrote," Forster said, eighteen months after recording "Lee Remick." "I wanted to write a love song. But I wasn't in love with anyone, so I just projected it towards that screen image. I didn't know anyone I felt strongly enough about to write a love song for."[9]

A week after recording "Lee Remick," the Go-Betweens acquired another drummer. Her name was Lissa Ross, and she lasted long enough in the band to be included in their first major press appearance: the "Rory Gibson's Scene" column of the Brisbane *Telegraph*. Gibson—who railed against punk rock generally and the Suicide label on the same page—raved about the Go-Betweens' courage, if not their music:

> A Brisbane band has launched themselves into the music business in a way most groups would not have the guts or conviction to do.
>
> They are the Go-Betweens, consisting of Robert Forster, guitar; Lissa Ross, drums, and Grant McLennon [*sic*], bass.
>
> Together for only three months, the band decided to record a single first without building a following or "paying their dues" by gigging for years before recording . . .
>
> Describing the Go-Betweens' music, Rob, tongue in cheek, said: "You

could call it passenger pop for traveling minds."

You could also say the style is rock 'n' roll along the lines of Talking Heads, a New York group acclaimed as the new Beatles, but the group say their music is a lot warmer and less jerky.

Forster was obviously overdoing the positive angles when he spoke to Gibson. He explained his plan to put out more singles after "Lee Remick"—whose release date was given as three weeks away—then release material by other bands, and "then spend money on expensive gear and do all the pub and club circuits." "We should be successful," he told Gibson. "All that is needed is to think positive, have enough faith to go ahead, and do everything well."[10] In the caption to the picture that ran with Gibson's article, McLennan was called "Brad," which apparently led to no end of ribbing from his friends for years afterward. Forster claims the article produced an immediate turnaround in the attitude of his parents, who had previously been antipathetic to his music.

Lissa Ross did not last in the group much longer than the photo session; she was soon succeeded by the first full-time Go-Betweens drummer, Temucin Mustafa (who at the time called himself Tim). By the time the "Lee Remick" single was released in September 1978, Mustafa was listed on the sleeve as a member of the band, although he hadn't played on the record, where Denis Cantwell was thanked for "the beat."

Born in Cyprus, Mustafa had come to Brisbane with his family in 1963, and was instantly more of an outsider than any punk rocker could ever have made himself. "We were the only Cypriot Turks in Queensland," he says. "In those days they'd say, 'Ah, ya bloody wog'—all that sort of stuff—even the Greeks themselves!" Mustafa had found Forster and McLennan via an ad, probably placed in a record-shop window, and probably accompanied by a list of nonmusical "influences" along the lines of the sixties TV show *Mod Squad* and comedian Bob Newhart. Mustafa auditioned with trepidation:

> MUSTAFA: I wasn't experienced, I think it was my first band. I just went in, said hi to the guys, sat down, talked a bit. I think they started playing a few tunes, I followed them, that was it. They had no experience themselves, actually, they were just plucking away on strings and so forth. I'm thinking, "Well, I'm pretty bad, so okay, that's great!" We started playing and went off from there.
>
> I was just the drummer, basically, attached to the band. I didn't get any artistic input. I didn't blame them for that, they were mates. I was there for the experience, anyway. The guys, they would wear jeans,

pointed shoes, whereas I would be the outcast—I was a dressy type of guy. I was so shy—I lacked confidence, for a start, I just played. Nowadays I'm completely opposite, completely extroverted.

I put some lyrics to the guys once. They laughed. I thought, "Well [*clears throat*]. Take it away. Next!" It was just completely different to what their music was, anyway. I had a go, it wasn't anything you'd scream over.

McLennan, Mustafa, and Forster *(Tony Forster)*

Although Mustafa was exotic and talented—the Go-Betweens would hardly have settled for less—it was obviously an odd alliance, and while Forster and McLennan have always been full of praise for his playing, there was nevertheless a distinct divide. Mustafa was being pulled in a number of different directions.

> MUSTAFA: My dad, being of Turkish background, he'd say to me, "Oh, you're working with a band? What time you coming home?" But when we got $75 an hour playing a certain venue, he'd go, "Oh great, yes, good stuff! Carry on!" That sort of thing. Then I'd have friends in other bands going, "Oh, they're not very good. They're shithouse, don't play with them." They were either jealous or—I don't know what, but I ignored it.
>
> I had a sort of girlfriend at the time who was saying, "You've got no time for me! Why don't you give up the band?" Do this, do that . . .

Mustafa, however, whose life until he got a car and joined the Go-Betweens had been insular and almost entirely family-oriented, was now having new experiences with the group:

> MUSTAFA: Once I was going along to the University. On Schonell Drive, I think it was, there were a lot of speed bumps. I didn't know that. Had all my drums in the car and all the guys in the car with me—I'm driving along—all the drums went bang! I went, "What was that?" They said, "Don't you know, it's a speed bump!"
>
> "What's a speed bump? Shit!"
>
> "Slow down, there's another one coming up!" I'd never heard of them!

6
"Rob likes the word *go!*"

The Go-Betweens' name must have been chosen partly as a cinematic joke reference to director Joseph Losey and screenwriter Harold Pinter's 1970 adaptation of L. P. Hartley's novel, *The Go-Between*. A song named after the film star Lee Remick by a group named after a film provided yet another aspect of their campaign for more cinema references in rock. Forster is still immensely proud of "Lee Remick" and claims that, had this been his sole record release, he would not mind being remembered only for what was essentially a novelty record.

There must also be a certain self-deprecating aspect to the name, the same sort of self-effacement present on "Karen" and "Lee Remick": "I come from Brisbane"—itself a sore indictment—"and I'm quite plain." The importance of the go-between depends on the message he or she is bringing. Translated into the terms of the songwriter relaying a "message" to an audience, there's great value in a messenger, though Forster and McLennan's contemporaries in late-1970s Brisbane would have sneered at anyone who claimed to bear a message. Another Go-Betweens associate from the 1980s, David Westlake, called his band the Servants, presumably after another Losey/Pinter film, *The Servant,* a 1963 British drama starring Dirk Bogarde. Ciphers, messengers, carriers were all around.

Yet the position of go-between, while it might be lively and exciting, is rarely a positive one, as Leo Colston, the eponymous hero of *The Go-Between,* discovered. Colston is in transition between childhood and adulthood, between the nineteenth and twentieth centuries, and between social classes—even before he becomes the "messenger of the gods." This messenger, incidentally, is condemned for the message he carries, though he barely understands it. Film buffs Forster and McLennan would also have

(Tony Forster)

been well aware of the sentiment expressed by Art Garfunkel's character, Alex Linden, in Nicolas Roeg's film *Bad Timing:* "To be in between is to be no place at all." Being on the periphery, outside the picture, is essentially what "Lee Remick" is about. But "Lee Remick" is a joyful and funny song, and there's nothing bleak or mournful about its narrator. Disembodiment, lack of connection: it's only a stupid pop record. An avenue to something or someone else. Such is the role of a go-between's record.

To be a go-between was far from a negative role in McLennan and Forster's eyes. They were in between so many places, swamped by a cultural flood. While they faced the reality of Brisbane, the heat, parental pressure, and the influence of punk rock, they also yearned for New York in the 1960s and 1970s, Paris in the 1920s and 1950s, and were fascinated by Timothy Leary, Bob Dylan, Tom Verlaine, Françoise Hardy, Samantha Eggar, Richard Hell, Blondie, and the Erasers. All of this was siphoned through a strange, anomalous Brisbane rock group called the Go-Betweens.

Were they also the kind of go-betweens who deal in contraband, and profit from the experience? In 1977, the year the Go-Betweens began, Christopher Isherwood published *Christopher and His Kind,* the second volume of his memoirs, which includes a description of a go-between called Gerald. Gerald would sell a stolen painting to "a collector who didn't mind enjoying it in private," he smuggled arms, intruded on commercial deals and so on, without compunction: "a great deal of money would pass from hand to hand. The hands in the middle were Gerald's, and they were sticky."[1]

(photographer unknown)

Isherwood later became a favorite of Forster's, but it is unlikely that he had read *Christopher and His Kind* at this time. Nevertheless, the idea of a go-between with sticky fingers is an intriguing one, and McLennan and Forster would not have hated the idea of themselves as urbane diamond thieves—like Cary Grant in *To Catch a Thief,* perhaps—though Isherwood's Gerald is far shadier than the suave Grant of Hitchcock's film. Nevertheless, this go-between matches our men: the contraband in question is underground American and European style, Warholiana, *nouvelle vague* cinema, and Monkees-like verve.

Forster and McLennan have occasionally referred to the Go-Betweens name in terms which suggest they were the recipients of the message, but they needed other members in the band to "go between" them. This is perhaps best explained as the kind of stance you take when you have abandoned your original modesty and are looking for a way to be arrogant with its remains. But if they were trying to turn the former self-effacement into an edifice of distinction, it didn't work. Late in the Go-Betweens' career, journalists would attempt to rein in the meaning of the name. Ralph Traitor of *Sounds* magazine reasoned rather pallidly that "the Go-Betweens, as their name suggests, liaise for us between what pop is and what it can be, showing the human side without artifice."

And perhaps that is the best explanation of "the Go-Betweens" as a name: it can take anything you wish and deliver it with any meaning you would like firmly pinned to it. Note, however, that most friends of the band—though not anyone in the band itself—like to use the friendly-derogatory term "the Gobs" when speaking of the group: a gob being, of course, a British/Australian noun and verb for a big phlegmy spit. The group were soon to discover that if you lean towards self-effacement there will always be people around willing to help you get the job done properly.

7

Funk! Punk! Spunk!

The Toowong Music Centre was a small record shop—"just a square box, one side fronted onto the arcade, the other side on the street"—run by Damien Nelson between 1976 and 1982, and owned by his parents. It was handy for the University of Queensland, and advertised in publications like the *Cane Toad Times* and *Semper*. Nelson trod the fine line that record-shop proprietors often had to tread in the late 1970s, as "new wave" battled with the old established bands in the racks and in the hearts of his customers.

> DAMIEN NELSON: Grant McLennan used to sit across the arcade in a little coffee shop or take-away food place every afternoon. Some afternoons he'd come in and ask about records and advise me on what I should be stocking. One day he came in and my brother, who had been working in the shop, had just left. Strangely, it was Grant who suggested he should work there . . .
>
> There were some artists we had in there that I never thought much of. Kris Kristofferson, Jerry Jeff Walker . . . [but] Grant would go, "Genius! Great talent!" Oh, really? And because Grant was reading the *NME* he'd suggest, "this person's quite interesting, really big overseas"—and I'd look out for them.

Nelson gave McLennan a part-time job. Eventually, the line between actually working there and just hanging out listening to what McLennan now calls "god-awful" records became blurred. "Damien would say, 'When people come into the shop and they want to hear a record, you have to take that one off.' And we kind of . . . *didn't*."

> NELSON: One night Grant came into the shop—I was working late, had a flagon of wine, getting drunk—and he suggested, "Why don't we make

a single?" Because he'd started a group with this boy Robert. And when I said yes, that's how I got to know Robert.

People had been making independent records in Australia for decades before 1978, just as they had all over the world. If there was a difference in the late 1970s, it was that better distribution mechanisms were developing—for instance, import-record shops would also stock obscure, self-produced local records. More importantly, at least some consumers were starting to regard low-budget independent product as at least as valid as mainstream, big-budget material, if not superior. Forster, McLennan, and Nelson's Able Label wasn't entirely about being taken seriously as a "real" record label—like its first release, it hedged its bets with humor as well as presumption by displaying as its motto the words, *If it's Ready, it's Able*. Nelson recalls the financial details:

> NELSON: As I remember, I put in, oh, it would have been anywhere between $800 and $1,000,[1] and I'm sure they put in that amount of money too. It was looked on as very much a venture between us.

All the young dudes: Gerry Teekman, Forster, Graham Alsthorpe, Damien Nelson, McLennan *(Tony Forster)*

The Able label was intended to provide a forum for a "sound" or "scene" sympathetic to Forster and McLennan's vision: guitar-pop groups with what was then considered to be a sixties sound, as opposed to more modern, progressive, electronic, or heavy rock. Eventually, the Numbers (who had been the Grudge and were soon to become the Riptides), the Apartments, and the Four Gods would also release singles on Able. Nelson recalls, though, that all except the Go-Betweens' singles were funded by the individual groups: "It was like, 'Here's the label, if you want to use it, go ahead.' I really only had the money, I think, for the Go-Betweens."

And there were limits on what could be released on Able. When the English-style punk band Razar demanded of Able that they release their debut single, the anti–police-state song "Task Force," they were turned down. The band then released it themselves, but defiantly used the catalog number AB002. The Numbers single, released almost simultaneously with "Lee Remick," was therefore numbered 003. Small skirmishes like this made Nelson feel he was not cut out to run a record label, as he freely admits.

NELSON: I found dealing with the musicians quite a stressful activity. In lots of ways they just speak a different language—not so much Grant and Robert. Grant and Robert you could talk to about films, sport, politics, books. [But] a lot of the others were so *egocentric*, so *wrapped up in themselves*. I remember meeting a lot of musicians at that time, and there was this feeling of, "What can we get out of you?" I found a lot of it quite tiresome. Not the Go-Betweens, I must say. Robert and Grant I looked on as my friends. And I still do.

In case the grooves of the record itself did not adequately declare its influences, the Go-Betweens managed to slip more onto the sleeve of "Lee Remick": "This is dedicated to John Fogerty, Phil Ochs, Michael Cole, Natalie Wood and that Striped Sunlight Sound." The back cover featured "an interview with the band":

> Q. What are your influences? A. Different coloured socks. Q. Do you speak French? A. Non. Q. What do you think of the New Wave? A. Godard's a good director. Q. What are your ambitions? A. To be the fourth member of the Mod Squad.

Though the band had a test pressing of the "Lee Remick" single soon after the recording session—Mark Callaghan, whose record player wasn't working, broke into Forster and McLennan's house to play it to his housemate, Robin Gold—the single was not released until September, five months after it was recorded. Part of the delay was due to the fact that Forster, McLennan, and Nelson, ignorant of the vinyl-pressing process that allows the labels to be stamped into the vinyl as each record is made, had ordered a thousand circular gummed labels, which then had to be moistened and stuck to each record by hand.² By the following January, the group claimed to have sold five hundred copies of the first pressing of seven hundred, no mean feat for a Brisbane band, even at a time when vinyl singles had much greater currency than they do today. The record had been distributed in Sydney and Melbourne by Robert Vickers, who lugged it—along with the "Sunset Strip" single his own band the Numbers had released on Able—to various record stores in the south. It was reviewed in the overseas press, where perceptive critics pointed out that the band was Australian and the music sounded sixties-ish. Rock entrepreneur Kim Fowley, who was visiting Australia at the time and had signed up a Beatlesque outfit called Beathoven, called the Go-Betweens at the Toowong Music Center to tell them he was bored by the time he got to the second verse of "Lee Remick."

Fowley had promoted the hard-rock all-female group the Runaways a few years before and produced some Jonathan Richman demos, but his supposed high-beam insights into the music industry often proved to be no more than bluster. During his visit to Australia, he improvised a song about Australian music for the benefit of a *RAM* journalist:³

> Don't you Aussies know that you're no longer a colony?/Why don't you perfect your own rhythm and harmony? . . . /You don't have any scope at all/You really think so small . . . /If you tried to be a world citizen you might just get off the skids . . . /Your days are numbered because you can't think international/You've got to be more daring/You've got to be the kings and queens of push and pull/You've got to think real big/You've got to do it if you want to keep your gig.⁴

It's testament to the times that this was reported without comment by *RAM;* a few years later the sentiments expressed by Fowley would have been followed by some resounding cheerleading on behalf of Australian music.

Though Fowley would not have known or cared, he was provoking something that Melbourne critic A. A. Phillips, writing in the 1950s, called the "cultural cringe." The cringe was, in essence, a continued concern about—in a sense, the inability to judge—the value of Australian creative work in comparison to that from overseas. (Phillips was thinking particularly of Britain, and so were most of the Go-Betweens' contemporaries.)

However, just as the shock humor of Barry Humphries in his fifties satires of Melbourne suburbia showed Australians a way in which they could begin to evaluate their own culture in literature, so the shock humor of punk/new wave began to give young Australians the freedom to thumb their nose at overseas domination. There was Dave Warner's song "Just a

Suburban Boy," the work of the Reels, the Saints, the Sports, and Mental As Anything. All these groups and more tried to pinpoint—usually for the purposes of satire—the Australian cultural condition. Phillips wrote in 1958 that the opposite of the cultural cringe was "not the Strut"—that is, not breast-beating, arrogant patriotism—but "a relaxed erectness of carriage."[5] The groups that sang about Australia with humor and understanding contributed to this new perception of the nation in the way that a hundred Little River Bands or Olivia Newton-Johns—Australians who were successful internationally just by dint of their professionalism and homogeneity—never would.

In this climate of change, "Lee Remick" opened up new doors for the Go-Betweens. Forster, recalling their live performances from this time, claims that audiences "liked us, they couldn't help it."

(Courtesy Temucin Mustafa)

> FORSTER: We had "Lee Remick" and "Karen" and it was quite obvious these were the two best songs in town. I'm not wishing to brag here, but no one ever put anything better to vinyl at that time, 1978. We started playing these songs ... You can't imagine, in 1978, playing "Lee Remick." People were completely for it, and so were we. It just leapt through. And it was so different. A lot of people were trying to write pop songs and were trying to do formulas from overseas. Trying to rip off this or that—I'd *taken* the leap and seemed to have done something which was my own. And this made it more exciting.

"Lee Remick" served an important purpose for the Go-Betweens. They were able to use it as a promotional tool for their music and their particular wit. Soon copies of the single were being posted to magazines and record labels around the world. The winning response ("We love the Go-Betweens!") came from the English arm of US label Beserkley Records, the self-styled "Home of the Hits."

Beserkley UK had been set up in late 1977 when Matthew Kaufman, who had founded the label in Berkeley, California, in the mid-1970s, tried to leverage the European success of his US bands into a fully fledged UK label, with former Island Records GM Fred Cantrell as its head. Beserkley's star performer was Jonathan Richman: his "Egyptian Reggae" was a top-ten hit in the UK in 1977. And Richman was presumably the reason the Go-Betweens had sent them a copy of "Lee Remick," although Forster had little interest in the work he was turning out in the late 1970s. The label's other American acts—Earth Quake, Greg Kihn, and the Rubinoos—tended to plough a rather lean furrow of forced-fun rock, although they had some success in mainland Europe. And the other bands signed directly to Beserkley UK—the Tyla Gang, Smirks, and Engineers—were hardly distinguished. Certainly, the Go-Betweens would brighten the Beserkley roster.

Beserkley's plan was to rerelease "Lee Remick" and "Karen" as the a-sides of two separate singles. The contract called for two further singles, and then—if the label was happy with the band's commercial prospects—an eight-album deal. Mustafa had a lawyer look over the contract; he pronounced it unsound, but the group signed it anyway.

Beserkley, it was clear, also expected the band to make their way to the UK to play shows to promote their records. Panicking, Forster visited Peter Walsh at home—where he was dining on hamburgers and claret—to ask him if he would join as second guitarist.[6]

> WALSH: I had just split up with my girlfriend at the time and I thought this would be a splendid revenge: "I'll just leave Brisbane and everything behind." They were going to go to England. I think the reason they were interested in me was I had a Fender guitar. My huge talent had nothing to do with it, but my Fender guitar . . .
>
> I didn't know them very well, I never socialized with them. The people I hung out with were a bit more worldly than them. I was incredibly shocked to see the boy-scout bunk room they lived in, with posters of French movie stars on the walls. I do remember signing a contract, an 8-album contract. Damien had a photographer there!

McLennan, Walsh, and Forster in the Mustafa family's living room *(Temucin Mustafa)*

Walsh had first met the Go-Betweens in the Toowong Music Center. Even if he hadn't socialized with them, he was already part of the same crowd. He knew their friend Robert Vickers, who was his neighbor in Indooroopilly—they had met when Vickers heard Walsh playing and singing a Graham Parker song over his back fence. Walsh had been making a name for himself in the

Apartments, a band in which he had teamed up—in a similar manner to Forster and McLennan—with Michael O'Connell. The Apartments made great guitar pop, though their set was still mainly covers. "He'd just virtually burst onto the Brisbane scene," Forster recalled in 1985, "and everyone was really impressed with him." Vickers believes Walsh "thought the Go-Betweens were a bit of a joke," which was not a completely unfair assessment of the group at this time. McLennan and Forster, for their part, regarded Walsh with the same kind of awe they had for Vickers:

> McLENNAN: He had lots of great stories. He seemed a very exotic character, and of course played it to the hilt—very funny. He used to live in this hut behind a house and listen to *Highway 61* twenty-four hours a day.

Peter Walsh with the Apartments *(Graham Aisthorpe)*

Another point of connection with Walsh clearly appealed to Forster: "He didn't finish his degree either." For Walsh, though, the differences were greater than the similarities:

> WALSH: My rehearsals with the Apartments were—not Fellini's *Satyricon*, but *berserk*. We'd all be speeding or drinking, there'd be this fierceness, and it'd be overwhelmingly loud. That was my belief, ever since I had started playing electrically, [that] you had to be out of it—that was how you made great music. But to arrive at Robert's place at two o'clock in the afternoon—"Would you like a cup of tea? We've got some scones." These tiny little amps, having to turn down: it was just an eye-opener.
>
> I liked various things about the music but I couldn't relate to it emotionally. I thought it was kind of clever—much more clever than anything I could do. Some very quaint propositions there were, too. A song called "Strawberry Rock," Robert doing twelve-bar. Robert was writing about ten songs a day. He'd try to write an Easybeats song, for instance. Which is something he's lost, but I think it's a *good* loss. They'd never say it, but you could tell which part of the record collection he'd listened to in the two minutes it took for him to write that song.

The four-piece Go-Betweens took their campaign to the backblocks when their friends, the Supports, suggested they join them on a double-decker bus tour of north Queensland.

The Supports were Leigh Bradshaw (vocals), brothers Peter and Ralph

Loveday (guitars), Geoffrey Titley (drums), and Robert Wheeler (bass). Bradshaw had met Alan Reilly of the Grudge through her late-night radio show on 4ZZZ. He had introduced her to Titley, who had in turn met the Loveday brothers and Wheeler through a mutual friend, Dave Tyrer. Titley had designed a Warholesque silk-screen poster to advertise "Lee Remick."

Leigh Bradshaw and Peter Loveday of the Supports (Tony Forster)

Like the Apartments, the Supports hadn't written many songs of their own. They ran on that old standby, "fun," in the form of "punked up" versions of pop songs like "It's My Party," alongside obscure new wave/punk covers such as Lene Lovich's "Cuckoo Clock." The Lovedays had family connections in north Queensland, and the tour was a Supports project into which the Go-Betweens were drafted as headliners at the last minute. Tim Mustafa had work commitments, and couldn't go. It was the month Joh Bjelke-Petersen became the longest-serving premier of Queensland.

PETER LOVEDAY: I think [the tour] was Geoffrey's idea. We drove up north, scouting around, trying to get some bookings. Most people said, "Yeah, yeah, fine. When you're up this way let us know. You can play a few nights in the lounge bar if you like."

Everything was more or less arranged. We'd invited the Go-Betweens along but up until the day we were to leave they hadn't given us a definite yes or no. That morning Robert dropped in while his washing was in the laundromat. He said that he was coming and that Grant and Peter Walsh would catch up with us along the way. We set off for Toowoomba at thirty-five miles an hour. Robert smoked Gitanes and sat on the platform reading a thick novel. I think he wondered what the hell he'd got himself into. There were quite a few people who'd come along for the ride. Andrew Wilson was there, an important instrument in animating the crowds.[7] Someone brought a sack of carrots and a sack of potatoes, although I don't remember ever eating carrots or potatoes. Everything was groovy. The bus behaved and we headed north. The top floor was carpeted and there were a couple of deckchairs up there and a sunroof.

The first few dates we did with just us and Robert. We turned up at the venues and played one or two nights, just like they said. In the afternoon we'd drive the bus through town with Robert hanging off the platform shouting "Rock 'n' roll, rock 'n' roll!" and singing snatches of "El Rancho Rock" (a kind of Mexican number, with lyrics that changed from day to day) with his guitar. We'd have dinner and then the gig. I can't remember exactly, but I think we played two sets on these occasions. First Robert played—things like "Karen," which often lasted quite a long time, "I Am an Architect," "Roadrunner," and the crowd pleaser, "El Rancho Rock." Then the Supports would play the second set. The audience was bemused but usually friendly, or at least only verbally abusive. We'd stop off at the bottleshop, then drive the bus out of town or up the beach a bit to pass the night. Of course there was some drinking, partying, and sitting round the campfire.[8] From the top deck we spied on the local scene, which got a little rowdy on the beach at night. It took a long time to get *up north*. We stopped in all the towns, usually at the park, or sometimes at the public swimming pool, if there was one. Whenever we stopped, Robert would run off to the public toilets with his only piece of luggage, a small school case. We often wondered what was inside that case—dirty magazines? haircare products? clean underwear? If we stopped at a park, a game of cricket inevitably ensued.

At about this time, Robert started talking about the "Inner Circle": who was in it, or wasn't in it. It was all very much like *The Partridge Family* crossed with *The Untouchables*.

At one stop-off, Forster and Bradshaw set off from Rainbow Beach to visit the wreck of the *Cherry Venture*, which they believed lay a few miles down the beach. The walk actually took them eight hours altogether in the tropical sun, and they were badly sunburned by the time they returned. "They didn't arrive back until after the soundcheck," remembers Loveday. Bradshaw recalls that she and Forster "hopped around the stage with more than characteristic vigor that night, our pain dulled only by large quantities of tequila."

The bus tour met up with McLennan and Walsh in Gympie, 127 miles north of Brisbane. McLennan's strongest memory of the trip is of his interactions with Leigh Bradshaw: "I've never been slapped so many times in my life—'It's the way you said it, Grant, not what you said.'" Bradshaw, however, claims that the only time she hit McLennan was at a Zero show, during an argument over the merits of drum machines (she for, he against). Maybe it was in anticipation of being punished for his smart-arse one-liners that McLennan joined the tour late:

> McLENNAN: Walsh and I didn't want to go in the bus. We hitched, and we said we'd meet them in Gympie at eight in the morning. We were doing a kind of Woody Guthrie thing—we were walking around Gympie and found this bakery and slid open this door and there were all these flour sacks and we stayed the night. We had a couple of bottles

of Star Wine and drank that and played guitar until this security guy came around and kicked us out and we checked into a motel. And so the bohemian kind of thing disappeared really quickly. In the morning I *found* twenty dollars, which paid for the room. Walsh was just playing cards, smoking dope. He couldn't stand hanging around in that sort of scene so he flew back. Yeah, he *flew* back—he always had style.

Judging from Peter Loveday's similarly Star Wine–soused memories, Walsh was the wild card of the touring party.

LOVEDAY: Walsh didn't take too well to the tropical heat. He drank a lot of Star Wine to keep cool and had to be saved more than once. He got out through the sunroof and traveled on top of the bus, which didn't always clear overhead power lines.

Titley remembers a show at Rainbow Beach as yielding the best crowd response. To Loveday, their one show at the Rockhampton YMCA was "the pinnacle of our northern success." The local *Morning Bulletin* even ran a small piece on the Go-Betweens:

The story goes that the Go-Betweens go between Bob Newhart and T-Rex, and that if the world ended tomorrow morning, the Go-Betweens would sleep in.
  Their music is said to have "a distinct flavor of sunshine and deep blue water and perhaps in a moment of daring, there is even a suggestion of a lost primitive jungle."

The story ended on a particularly cryptic note—presumably due to an uncomprehending sub-editor—with the stark sentence, "When they started on the city circuit, their sound was purified."[9]

Geoffrey Titley recalls the Rockhampton show as the scene of a cultural clash typical of the late 1970s:

TITLEY: We played a gig organized by the resident DJ at the pub. He was heavily into disco music. We turn up and see a billboard outside saying *Funk Punk Spunk! Come and see the Supports and the Go-Betweens!*[10] He carried this line on. After he'd done his set on the turntables he announced, "You're about to see the punkiest, spunkiest, funkiest band in the town—the Supports!"
  Leigh, who didn't particularly like hecklers at the best of times, let alone disco DJs, let forth with a torrent of abuse over the PA to this guy at the beginning of the set. That set the tone of the evening.

The relative success of this small tour whetted both bands' appetites for travel. Shortly after returning to Brisbane, the Supports split and Titley and Wheeler relocated to London. The Go-Betweens expected to join them there shortly, as they still had their Beserkley contract and the world was about to become their collective oyster. On returning to Brisbane, the group placed a small item in the *Courier-Mail*:

> Two Brisbane bands this week returned to town in the double-decker bus they used as transport for a fourteen-day working holiday. "We wanted a short holiday and to play to some new audiences," the Go-Betweens' lead vocalist, Robert Forster, said yesterday. "We're thinking of doing more trips west, south, and north of Brisbane."[1]

It was now that Forster and McLennan were interviewed by Ashleigh Merritt and Allan Martin for 4ZZZ, and the interview (reprinted in chapter two) clearly reveals their exuberance at this point. The new songs the Go-Betweens recorded for their Beserkley b-sides are so slick in comparison to "Lee Remick" and "Karen" that they sound like the work of a different band. They also show what an excellent addition Walsh was to the lineup—his guitar on "The Sound of Rain" and "I Want To Be Today" gives the tracks exactly the kind of radiant feel a small Australian group would have wanted for braving the shores of the United Kingdom. "I Want To Be Today" is a deliberately trite, Monkees-like reworking of the Easybeats' classic "Friday on My Mind"—not an inappropriate source of inspiration for a Beserkley single, considering that a crass cover of this classic Australian song had been a b-side for the first Beserkley band, Earth Quake. "I Want To Be Today" has never been released and probably never will be.[12] On the other hand, Forster and McLennan are still gleefully proud of the flippant, pseudo-misogynist "The Sound of Rain."

The master tapes were duly sent off to Beserkley. By the time the package arrived in London, Walsh was already out of the band. He had played only his second[13] show with the Go-Betweens, supporting the Sydney group Flowers (who later became internationally successful under the name Icehouse).[14] At the time, Flowers were primarily a slick covers band with new-wave overtones, producing note-perfect renditions of Sex Pistols and Graham Parker songs.

A short while later, Forster and McLennan returned to 4ZZZ to record another interview with Merritt and Martin, and explain their decision to dump Walsh:

FORSTER: It just came to both Grant and myself that although both bands are vastly different, Flowers, for their four-piece sound, were putting out a much more proficient and professional sound. When we got up there as a four-piece, our sound was getting a lot closer to Flowers', but we had nowhere near the professionalism or the tightness. We sounded like a very, very poor version of Flowers, trying to do the same thing. But if we're a three-piece, people can immediately see, and hear, that we are trying something different.

MARTIN: Why didn't you stay a four-piece and bring yourself to the musical prowess of Flowers?

FORSTER: I'd never want to be as tight as Flowers. And with Peter the volume certainly was there. That comparison could be [made] not just with Flowers, but with any other four-piece, five-piece Sydney-Melbourne-Brisbane band.

Peter Walsh re-formed the Apartments, who stayed together as a band until October 1979. Since then, apart from a brief period in the early 1980s with Out of Nowhere, "the Apartments" has simply been the name Walsh uses for recording and performing his own songs. He has not played with the Go-Betweens again, but he will nevertheless return to our story shortly.

Meanwhile, Forster, McLennan, and Mustafa still intended to travel to Britain to be a Beserkley band—until the encouraging letters and phone calls stopped coming, and word began leaking back to Australia that the label had gone bankrupt. Some Beserkley staffers, including Cantrell, made further overtures to the group, suggesting they might want to record for Cantrell's new label, Zilch, but the name itself was hardly encouraging. The signed Beserkley contracts were never sent back to the UK. In hindsight, this was very fortunate: some artists found their contracts with Beserkley UK were still binding despite the label's liquidation. The main loss to the Go-Betweens—apart from a certain amount of dignity—was the loss of the original masters of "Lee Remick," "Karen," "I Want To Be Today," and "The Sound of Rain," which have never been recovered. In 1985, Forster claimed that Fred Cantrell—a "thorough scoundrel" in his eyes—had the tapes. "He's a roof tiler now, so where those tapes are I don't know."

Luckily, the Go-Betweens learned to swallow their disappointment, or simply keep a range of options in mind, early in their musical career. Instead of going to England straight away—but not discounting a trip later in the year, with or without a record company—they recorded a second single at the same studio[15] they had used for their previous forays. It was May 1979, and the songs were "People Say" and "Don't Let Him Come Back." "People

Say" was a slightly surreal mid-sixties–style pop number featuring Malcolm Kelly, who had played guitar in the Godots, on organ. Mark Callaghan recalls being given the important duty of flicking a switch on the organ during the recording to change its sound between the verses and choruses. "Don't Let Him Come Back" was a Forster/McLennan collaboration on a generic vendetta song, which they decided would be about Walsh, "dressed in black . . . in his apartment." Forster and McLennan insist they did not then, and do not now, feel any hostility whatsoever to Walsh. Walsh entered into the spirit of things, however, with a riposte: his "Help" on the Apartments' EP *Return of the Hypnotist* featured the possibly smutty image of McLennan and Forster as "choirboys dancing cheek to cheek."

"People Say" was released in May on the Able label in a yellow, red, and white silk-screened sleeve; fictional girlfriends "Jacqueline" and "Candice" were thanked on the back for contributing "tambourine and harmonica."[16] That May also saw the first of the so-called "Teeki tapes" recordings, in which the Go-Betweens' set was captured by their friend Gerry Teekman, who owned a stereo cassette recorder.[17] Teekman's recordings are the only time that many of the "one hundred songs" Forster and McLennan boast of on the sleeve of the 1986 reissue, *The Able Label Singles* EP, actually made it onto tape. Some of the songs are symptomatic of the problem described by Walsh—listening to too many records by other people.[18] Others are just downright weird—like "Day for Night," which Vickers still finds astonishing:

> VICKERS: [Forster] was just obsessed by sixties songs and mixing that [type of] melody with an odd slant on the lyrics, an original lyrical stance. "Young Australia, don't do drugs, not unless you've done them

before." Some of these songs were great: "My mouth feels like a jetty where young ladies walk." You would just be standing there [thinking], "what the fuck is that?" Unbelievable lyrics. You just wanted to *talk* to him. There was a whole bunch of other songs that were not so well arranged, bits and pieces thrown together with funny couplets.

The group also covered Bob Dylan on the Teeki tapes, delivering "Most Likely You'll Go Your Way and I'll Go Mine," in a faux-Dylan accent. Dylan—specifically the mid-1960s version—was certainly a particular obsession for the group. They posed for photographs in front of the poster of Dylan that had appeared as one of the pictures on the sleeve of "Lee Remick," McLennan in a t-shirt imprinted "Get Outta the Car Ochs," an enticingly obscure reference to an argument Dylan and Phil Ochs once had during which Dylan insisted Ochs get out of the car they were traveling in.[19] When McLennan and Forster drove to Sydney together to master "People Say," McLennan read Dylan's *Tarantula* out loud on the way.[20]

The Lemons: Mark Callaghan, Forster, McLennan
(Tony Forster)

Forster and McLennan were not devoting themselves exclusively to the Go-Betweens at this time. They had many other irons in the fire in Brisbane. The first of these was their covers group, the Lemons, which played two shows. Forster remembers that this group came about when Mark Callaghan dropped in one day at the Toowong home he shared with McLennan. Callaghan mentioned that a function to be held that night needed an additional group due to a last-minute cancellation. There and then, they decided to form the Lemons.

FORSTER: [It was] Grant, myself, Mark Callaghan playing guitar, Dennis Cantwell on drums, and Alan Reilly the guitarist from the Numbers. I know we did "Who Are the Mystery Girls?" by the New York Dolls, "Love Comes in Spurts" by Richard Hell and the Voidoids, maybe some sixties stuff, "A Kind of Hush" by Herman's Hermits. It went really well. The first show was just a muck-up [for] architecture students at a QUT[21] end-of-term party. I was singing and jumping around, and Mark Callaghan was playing guitar—at that time he was only singing in the Numbers. We were sort of falling apart, laughing, forty people were there. Then we played a second show at the Exchange, which was a serious show. Everyone was standing around with folded arms.

The Lemons died under scrutiny, though a similar project, the Hawks, soon followed. And there were other Forster-McLennan projects to fill the time—for example, their fanzine *Torn Curtain* (they took the name from a song on Television's *Marquee Moon* album, though they would have been aware that it was also the title of a Hitchcock film). *Torn Curtain* was to express in print the various Go-Between obsessions. McLennan, who had already proven his skill as a critic, probably took to this with more gusto. While Forster had a way with words in conversation, and of course in lyrics, the McLennan touch was more suited to print. The two drew up their plans on Pablo Cruise notepaper they got from the Toowong Music Centre: McLennan was to write about gay "punks" the Tom Robinson Band, the Clint Eastwood film *The Gauntlet*, New Wave cinema (to extend the connection made on the "Lee Remick" sleeve), and novelist Tom Robbins, as well as reviewing the film *Jubilee* and the Rolling Stones single "Miss You." Robert's articles were to be music-centered, but were still an eccentric mix: the Numbers, the Beatles' pre-Ringo *Star Club* double live album, Television's album *Adventure*, Bruce Anthon, Patti Smith's "Because the Night," and the "Lyrics of Byrne."[22] But although the first issue of *Torn Curtain* seemed as if it might be fascinating, it was never finished. There were too many things to do. Damien Nelson often shared in the pair's imaginative schemes:

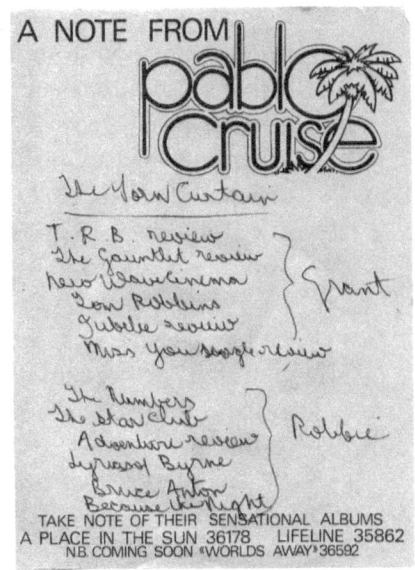

(Courtesy Robert Forster)

> NELSON: There was often talk of us starting a club somewhere. Robert suggested the name "The Vanilla Ego." There was talk of all sorts of things going on in there. And the thing is, in Brisbane at the time, it would have worked. There was this really bold thing among people—anything went.

Nelson was able to point the group in one direction: that of film and video. He invited the Go-Betweens to create a TV commercial for Nelson's record shop, the Toowong Music Centre. Nelson, an ardent Dylan fan—he even wrote to *RAM* in 1978, defending Dylan from a hostile critic—came up with the idea of remaking the "Subterranean Homesick Blues" sequence from D. A. Pennebaker's 1965 Dylan documentary, *Don't Look Back*. The image of Dylan, in an alley, holding up signs displaying key words from the song, has been influential ever since the film was released. Brisbane cineaste and director Robin Gold, who was present at the shooting of the commercial, believes that no one involved had actually seen *Don't Look Back*, and that they had only heard of the scene. Damien Nelson's father funded the commercial, which was made in black and white (in the face of heavy opposition from technicians and television stations in what were the early days of Australian color television).

The group recorded the backing music at a studio in Indooroopilly. When they arrived for the session, Forster and McLennan assured Nelson they had the song ready. Then, he remembers, "they disappeared for about five minutes. And I know now what they were doing—they were writing it. And they recorded it!"

Forster sang the song, which opened with the alarming nonsense of "Some glass camels don't even run/Some poor witch and her revolving gun/Shifts down, runs down, in her fur gown." But he only appeared briefly in the commercial, which starred McLennan holding up handwritten signs featuring the words: WHO?/GETS/ONE/DOLLAR/OFF/ALL RECORDS/AT/TOOWONG MUSIC/NOW/EVERYBODY/EVERY/BODY. The visuals and music were not synchronized, so—unlike the original "Subterranean Homesick Blues" clip—the music was merely a surreal backdrop to the visual quote.

> NELSON: We got a film guy, Jan Murray, and he did it in an alleyway one morning. It looked fantastic. It's a real lost classic.[23]
>
> You see Robert Forster at the beginning. First shot, Robert pokes his head round the alleyway. The final shot is of Grant walking—high shot from above—over "Toowong Music," the letters put on the ground.

McLennan's memory of the commercial is not dissimilar, though it contains more vomiting:

> McLENNAN: I was sick as a dog that day. I'd been up all night. We shot in this alleyway next to the Black Cat, which was a little café then.[24] I think McDonald's is there now. But there was this great laneway, very much like the start of *Don't Look Back*, and I had this houndstooth double-breasted kind of Dylan suit that a friend of mine used to wear in the 1960s—she

Toowong Music Centre TV ad; McLennan as Dylan

got it out of mothballs. I thought I was Bob Dylan. I felt as sick as Bob Dylan on that '66 tour. We shot it early in the morning before people went to work, and Damien's sister Theresa was there, Damien was there, Robert was there, I was there, Robin [Gold] was there. All I remember was getting sick and getting in the car and vomiting all the way to Bardon.

The advertisement was shown at least once, possibly twice, on late-night television in Brisbane. "My parents never saw it, thank God," says Nelson. "I'm sure if Dad had seen it he'd have hit the roof!"

Advertising was a field which greatly appealed to Forster and McLennan:

FORSTER: Grant and I used to look at products. As a game, I'd go round the kitchen and pick up [something like] Vegemite. And we'd rattle off five or ten advertising slogans. Products around the kitchen. We were flying! We thought we were geniuses. The band was always the flagship: "If the band becomes famous, everyone's going to be interested in these ideas. We've got to get famous." The group was the get-famous thing—once that happened, we could go, "Surprise, surprise, everybody, yeah, we're pop stars but we've got all these other ideas and we're goddamn fuckin' geniuses. You thought you were only getting two moptop pop stars, what you're getting is Truffaut and Godard! We're the Orson Welles of rock." It didn't happen.

Though the Beserkley deal had come to nothing—it was to be the first of many failed recording contracts—Forster and McLennan were still determined to go overseas, and would ultimately do so for the first time later that year. They would not be deterred even by the departure of their first full-time drummer.

> MUSTAFA: Two things: I felt that maybe I wasn't getting much input into the band, and secondly, girl problems. I was really naïve then. When I did leave, the guys were saying, "Everything was just going great—it was picking up, we were getting there." [But] they were hinting before that they wanted a female drummer, from Zero, to come in, and I said, "Here you go, guys." I didn't leave on a bad note. We sat in the car for a long time talking about it. When you look back, you think, I'd love to have hung around. But I'm not regretting.

Earlier drummer Bruce Anthon was drafted back into the group for their last few Brisbane shows. They planned a farewell performance at which—with the addition of Anthon and the Apartments' Michael O'Connell—they supported themselves, under the name the Hawks.[25]

They also found time to add to their filmmaking experience in the time remaining before their overseas trip. The most important project was the McLennan-scripted *Heather's Gloves*, a romantic film with overtones of Polanski's *The Tenant*. Robin Gold—who had been part of the crew for the Toowong Music Centre advertisement—said of this film that it "was an attempt to take a risk. It has intelligent dialogue and a story that demands something of the audience . . . It's a great picture."[26] He spoke too soon, for the film was never completed.

McLennan, who—with considerable justification—did not regard the Go-Betweens as a full-time pursuit until they relocated to Melbourne in 1981, was not content to just play bass to Forster's songs. Two local film productions allowed him to flex his cinematic muscles: the first, *Escape to Beaver Mountain*, was a farce from the outset, however. Damien Nelson rolls his eyes when it's mentioned.

> NELSON: Oh God. See, that was interesting. When we filmed that, all these people were involved. There was one party scene every man and his dog was in. It was this really vibrant sort of feeling, everyone getting involved and seeing what they could do.
>
> At the time—I have a suspicion—because I'd helped fund a single, people thought I was some Peggy Guggenheim type, liberally doling out money for the arts. I remember we'd be driving around with a bloody

generator in the boot of my car, ferrying people from place to place so they could film.

Robin Gold is the only one involved in *Escape to Beaver Mountain* to own up to having memories of its content.

> ROBIN GOLD: A lost classic. Some people would say, "deserved to be lost." An ambitious project, it was actually color, sixteen mill. It probably would have run about twenty-five minutes. We let this chap in—he wanted to make a film, he had a camera, equipment, and a lot of money. He and I just *hated* each other on sight, but we managed to convince him to put up a few thousand dollars. He wanted to shoot it—it was his camera. A script was hastily put together. A lot of it was shot in an abandoned woolshed. It involved kidnapping schoolgirls. There was one scene we stole from the Monkees where we had a bomb with a lighted fuse on it and everyone was tossing it around and someone threw it out the window.
>
> Robert refused to learn his lines and improvised shamelessly, so no one had their cue to say *their* lines. It was mainly Robert with a quiffed hairdo and young teenage girls in school uniforms, because Damien's younger sister and all her friends wanted to be in it.

What McLennan claims to remember of the film seems even more unlikely.

> McLENNAN: It was more a kind of Famous Five, you know, Enid Blyton kind of thing but mixed with very hardcore pornography. And being eighteen, seventeen, nineteen, or whatever, it was very infantile. I haven't thought about it for many years. It was a very good title for a Walt Disney film.

Shortly after this, McLennan wrote the screenplay for *Heather's Gloves*:

> McLENNAN: I first met Robin, I think, at the Queens Hotel. The Stranglers were playing. Robin was going on about making a vampire film and it was going to be very kind of sexual and psychotic. And that struck me as interesting, because I've always been fascinated with vampires. Robin was making films and he asked me [to] write a script, 'cause I'd reviewed films and written about them. And watched a lot of films and read a lot of books about them. I said, "Yeah, okay, as long as you shoot it in black and white." I don't know why, I had probably seen *Manhattan* or something like that, and so I went away and wrote a script. It was full of Godard touches, and Truffaut, Preston Sturges—lots of stuff. It was a first effort. Not bad.

Filming of *Heather's Gloves* was completed,[27] in black and white, for which Gold took responsibility—he said later that he "didn't want a film associated with the muddy, murky, fuzzy color of other Australian films."[28] It starred Jane Oliver, Michelle Andrings, Ross Ramsay, and Robert Vickers as William (William was the character McLennan had based on himself and given his own middle name).[29]

> ROBIN GOLD: In my mind I had it as a collaboration. I thought it would be a Michael Powell/Emeric Pressburger kind of collaboration, and I remember saying, "Grant, do you want to play the lead role?" and he turned me down flat. He said, "No, it's finished. It's in your hands." I read the script a few times, it was very personal, quite esoteric. It had some lovely imagery and some lovely moments but what the hell it was about, I didn't know. I tried to broach the subject with Grant and say, "Let's talk about this," and he'd maintain that his job was done. I had a strong sense from Grant that he didn't want the artistic integrity of his film compromised in any way . . . Fair enough from his point of view, but a bit rattling for me, not knowing what it was about. I got Robert Vickers mainly because he looked good in a suit and sunglasses.

From Gold's point of view, *Heather's Gloves* was a chance to capture a Brisbane which was fading fast:

> GOLD: Spring Hill tumble-down, three-story New Orleans–style boarding houses, diseased old palm trees, bats hanging off power lines, flapping there for weeks, rotting away, and always the smell of rotting pawpaws in somebody's garden. Overgrown grass, old weatherboard houses that had never been painted, looked about a thousand years old—that's what we liked, that was our special Brisbane, and that was the Brisbane everyone else was embarrassed about; [they] wanted to get rid of [it] and put up a shiny new Brisbane we could show the world. That's what *Heather's Gloves* came out of. We knew it was going to disappear and we wanted to capture that funny gothic Brisbane. Moreton Bay Figs . . . that kind of moody atmosphere.
>
> There's a few moments in the film that hold up quite nicely and I wouldn't be embarrassed about. Robert Vickers smoking a cigarette under an old lamppost—it was about midnight when we shot it—opposite the old Central Station, which I don't think is there any more—just a great old Brisbane image. There was another sequence where Robert and Michelle, I think, realize they are in love with each other, and they run down the street, and it was a really nice tracking shot, a street in New Farm that was completely overrun with Moreton Bay Figs—the only light

that got through was little pinpricks of dappled light. And they were just running. It made no sense but it was a beautiful, quite surreal image.

The Australian Film Commission decided not to provide the funding that would be required to complete *Heather's Gloves*. Firstly, according to Gold, they felt "black and white was totally inappropriate"; they also objected to Vickers because "he looks like George Harrison in 1965." This was, of course, a comparison everyone involved in the making of the film would have adored.

In addition to McLennan's sixteen-page *Heather's Gloves* script, he and Forster were also writing a screenplay they planned to send to James Garner. McLennan now laughs at their presumption. "Shit, we've got two records out—we can write for James Garner! Of course he'll do it, Robert, of course he'll do it. Just get him the script!"

> McLENNAN: It was about a detective and it had a very surreal end. Kind of a genre thing set at the Gold Coast and involving jewels and diamonds. At the end he goes swimming, scuba diving, because these diamonds are supposed to be in a wreck or something and he finds this hole like a manhole in the bottom of the ocean and he opens it up and there's a ladder and he goes down the ladder, shuts the hatch, and he sort of walks up and through and down and up more ladders and keeps on walking— in a frogman suit—and he sees another ladder and he opens the top of the manhole, pushes it open and he's in Pitt Street[30] and there's a jewelry store. That's the end of the film. We both thought that was hilarious.

Leaving Brisbane for their planned trip to London would put an end to these flights of fancy. McLennan and Forster had to decide whether they would be making films, running a club, editing a fanzine, coming up with hypothetical advertising campaigns, or just following Forster's nose-to-the-grindstone musical vision. Before settling this, Forster indulged himself one more time with another band, and in the process made a connection that would cement the Go-Betweens' success and notoriety.

8
Zero

Of all the Brisbane groups of the late 1970s and early 1980s, only Zero rivaled the Go-Betweens for creative twists and turns. John Willsteed, who much later became a Go-Between for a year or so, was a long-term member of Zero, and Forster had been playing with Zero throughout 1979. But the strongest connection between the two groups was Lindy Morrison.

Like Forster and McLennan, Lindy (born Belinda) Morrison came from a middle-class background, but she had reacted more sharply against it. She had graduated with a degree in social work, and subsequently worked with Aboriginal people[1] in Brisbane. She discussed her early working days with Marie Ryan of *RAM* in a 1987 interview:

> MORRISON: I completely changed from being a protected middle-class girl to just discovering what an incredibly racist country Australia was. Remember when the Labor government set up all those services run by Blacks for Blacks, like the Aboriginal Legal Service? I was the first white social worker in Brisbane involved in those kind of groupings.
>
> People didn't want to come to offices, so I did most of my social work over pool tables in pubs. I passed on an incredible amount of knowledge about how to pick up benefits or how to get their kids out of homes or how to get a house, but I learned more from them than they learned from me. It was fantastic, but really, it was a mistake to be a white person working in those black set-ups.[2]

To complicate this, she was in a relationship with Aboriginal activist Dennis Walker, son of well-known Aboriginal poet Kath Walker (who later took the name Oodgeroo Noonuccal). Morrison recalls Dennis Walker's peers wondering, "What was a black man doing with a white woman at that stage, when blacks were solely fighting for themselves, and had every reason to be?"[3]

Leaving social work, she traveled to Europe in the mid-1970s, and on her return became an actor in Queensland's Popular Theatre Troupe. It was acting that brought her to drumming. In a modern-style production of *Macbeth* (she was Lady Macbeth), she performed a song while playing drums. By the time she was accepted into the radical Australian Performing Group in Melbourne—which within Australia's left-of-center experimental-theater scene was certainly a recognition of considerable talent—she had decided that she would abandon acting for drumming.

Her first band was Shrew, which played between 1976 and 1978. In a 1984 interview she described this band to journalist Frank Brunetti:

> MORRISON: We were an acoustic girls' band with saxophone, clarinet, double bass, drums, piano and a singer. We did covers of songs like "In the Mood," "Chattanooga Choo Choo," forties pop songs. We were a political women's band.

Leigh Bradshaw also got involved after meeting Lindy Morrison at 4ZZZ while Morrison was working with a women's radio program called *Through the Looking Glass*; soon Bradshaw was singing swing tunes with Shrew as well as delivering punky covers with the Supports.[4]

> MORRISON: Shrew went up to 1978. I was living in a house with these boys and they said, "What the fuck are you doing playing acoustic instruments?" I could hear the Sex Pistols and the Slits and the Gang of Four, and I could hear those drummers doing what I could do, but the boys were still years ahead of me in playing skills. So I started asking around town who would play with me.
>
> I'd thought that rock 'n' roll would never have any relevance for me because of what I'd heard in the early 1970s. Then I heard this stuff and I couldn't believe it. It was everything I would have hoped to have done. Songs like the Slits' "Typical Girls" . . . it was everything that I was thinking then. "Anarchy in the UK," "Blank Generation"—I was just so fucking lost as to what my direction would be until I heard this stuff.[5]

The Gang of Four were a highly influential British post-punk group who dealt in angular, polemical rock/pop that was both witty and direct: they were all men until 1982, when they gained a female bass player. The Slits were an all-female punk group moving in a tribal, primal direction; in 1978, they acquired a male drummer. In both groups the rhythms were sharp, immediate, usually simple, and much more stripped back than in ordinary "rock" drumming.

MORRISON: Towards the end of 1978, I met these two girls called Deborah and Nikki. They were sixteen, seventeen, lesbians, and they didn't give a fuck about anyone. They stood up to everyone. Men used to say rude things to me and I just used to say "Fuck off" and run away, but these girls would fight. They'd hit men! I met them at a party and said, "Look, I'm a drummer and I want to play with someone. I want to play with women."[6]

Zero, in its initial stages, were Deborah Thomas aka Debbie Zero, Irena Luckus aka Irena Zero, Vicki Allen aka Nikki Nought, and a psychiatric nurse whose name is now forgotten, and who would soon be replaced by John Willsteed. Deborah Thomas' recollection of meeting Morrison is that she was a "great blonde goddess, [a] tall Aphrodite." Morrison was invited for a jam:

MORRISON: I turned up in my little car with my drum kit and as soon as I arrived they gave me about four Seconals—I'd never used barbiturates before. And I set up the drum kit and just played for five or six hours, just the two girls on guitars and me. Irena turned up during the afternoon with her kids and stayed for about ten minutes and listened and went away. From then on it was every day.[7]

Despite its reputation as that fearful curiosity/novelty, an all-woman rock band, Zero was in fact never that strict. Besides the above-mentioned five, the group briefly featured another hetero couple: John Hunt on bass and Barbara Hart on saxophone, who steered the group in a "folky political" direction. Hunt and Hart were pushed out at the time John Willsteed came in. He would come to share the creative heart of the band with Irena through its seven-year history—later as Xero (they recorded one EP, *Lust in the Dust*, under this name), and also as Xiro. Willsteed—like the members of the Numbers/Riptides—had been an architecture student, and had also been a member of Fuller Banks and the Debentures, a band inspired by the Tubes (and one of the groups Forster had so cavalierly dismissed in January '79 as "last year's model"). But in this new world where the long hair/short hair gap was widening daily and a bit of a trim was a stepping stone to a whole new lifestyle and outlook, Willsteed had recently lost his mane and begun casting around for a punk group to play with.

WILLSTEED: I'm not sure how [joining Zero] happened. All my recollections are a bit hazy. Alcohol-related brain damage! I remember meeting Lindy—I remember the moment even—and very soon after that

Lindy Morrison, ca. 1979 (photographer unknown; courtesy Robert Forster)

I joined the band. They had someone in the band that they wanted to move, so they got me, probably as part of moving that person out rather than because they wanted me around.

I was walking in Kelvin Grove, in Brisbane, on the other side of Victoria Park from the Royal Brisbane Hospital, and Lindy was driving a red moke. I think it belonged to a man called David Giddings, who she had a relationship with but I don't think he was around. He was in that British a cappella band, the Flying Pickets. Morrison was older than me,[8] and very loud and flamboyant, attractive. I'd never met anyone like her . . . I have yet to meet anyone like her!

I was walking with this boy, Gary Warner, and she knew him, and she stopped and gave us a lift somewhere.

Morrison has fond, almost maternal, memories of Willsteed and Warner in the late 1970s:

MORRISON: They were both your devo artists, they used to wear computer bits all the time and jewelry made out of electronic parts and they were really wild and scatty and did magazines and were very punk/

new wave. They were most dedicated to leading that kind of anarchist art life [in Brisbane]. Which I didn't understand. It was very Dadaist, which I did understand, I thought Dada had happened, so to me it couldn't happen again. I'd been to Zurich. I'd seen all of that stuff. To them it was all really new and exciting. They were all into Dada and surrealism and futurism.

They used to come over, I lived at Wellington Street, Petrie Terrace, they used to come over and sleep in my bed. We'd never, ever have sex—they were like my pet little brothers, and I adored both of them.

Zero had been together a short time when Morrison joined. She now claims that Willsteed's entry into the group was "a big mistake; it ruined Zero."

MORRISON: See, Zero was essentially a dyke band. Irena was a pretty straight woman, she was influenced by punk—she changed overnight, cut off her hair and dyed it—and soon she was fucking John, and that changed the whole dynamic of the band and Deborah and Nikki, who had previously been lovers, left. And then of course it became a heterosexual band and that was a shame, because as a dyke band it was fabulous.

Willsteed, unlikely of course to see his entry into Zero as the ruination of it, takes refuge in the technical details.

WILLSTEED: Zero were a political rock 'n' roll covers band but then doing punky, new-wavey songs of the period—B-52s, girly things, not *girly* things but inspired by the Slits and Raincoats and stuff like that. British pop/punk stuff. That went off for a while, we started playing around a bit, and it sort of all went quite well. A very volatile band, though, two of the women were in a relationship and they were just constantly brawling, so it was very . . . It was hot, probably, Brisbane summer, people are always volatile.[9]

When Nikki and Deborah left Zero they were replaced by Michael O'Connell, formerly of the Apartments.

MICHAEL O'CONNELL: Looking back on the whole thing, Zero was probably Irena's band more than anyone else's. Writing songs with Zero was very interesting; rehearsal-room stuff was so good with John. I could come to Zero with the real beginnings of a song and it would turn into a song. John Willsteed virtually showed Lindy Morrison how to play the drums. In the performing process the spotlight was mainly on Irena and myself.

Willsteed is adamant that Morrison, too, was involved in songwriting for Zero, although she denies it:

> WILLSTEED: Lindy did write, musically, a couple of songs. She probably wrote lyrics, then had some idea of the melody, so it would have been worked out by Michael. She probably would have sat down with Michael and gone through some ideas. A major part of the pleasure of the process of being in a band was sitting around working things out.
>
> We were living in Queensland in the early 1980s when it was really restrictive and it wasn't an easy place to live if you were young. A lot of places we'd play were continually being closed down by police; there was nothing subtle about it.

Everyone knew everyone in Brisbane, one way or another. Zero and the Go-Betweens came to share a practice room. In 1979, Forster began playing a set of songs that were unsuitable for the Go-Betweens with Zero as his backing band.[10] Morrison and Forster were soon spending an enormous amount of time together, working together on Robert's songs in the rehearsal room shared by both the Go-Betweens and Zero. Forster's addition to Zero was a pragmatic arrangement:

> WILLSTEED: Robert must have been new to me even though I'd seen them play probably. He had this three-piece backing band—Lindy and Irena and I—and we had Zero, so we could sell it as two bands. It was cheap. Zero and this other band, which was sort of like the Robert Forster Band only it didn't have a name.
>
> Robert came along and had all these songs, so we didn't have to make up a whole new bunch of songs. We went over to Stradbroke Island which Zero [alone] probably wouldn't have been able to do, but with Robert we all went together. It was, "throw Robert in the truck and that's an extra two brackets [sets]." But I'm not sure of the machinations of how that came to be . . . This tall guy just got up and sang some songs. The Go-Betweens must have had some sort of popularity, not with me, but certainly some sort of following. I don't really remember what the response was like.

On the other hand, everyone remembers the response to the developing relationship between Morrison and Forster:

> DAMIEN NELSON: Robert and I went to see Talking Heads at Festival Hall[11] and Lindy was there. Seeing the way Robert and Lindy spoke to each other, I thought, "Oh, yeah, something's happening here." Which

was quite amazing, because to me Robert and Grant just seemed like these completely androgynous types who would never be interested in the opposite sex. Robert in particular.

Androgynous, or homosexual; for many at this time it was an academic distinction. Certainly, the lionization of Hollywood stars was recognized as a "camp" pursuit. Robert denied all in the ZZZ interview, where he equated homosexuality with a kind of detached heartlessness: "We aren't the Melbourne camp crowd in sort of strange campy forties gear . . . It's straight, it's not—we aren't sort of campy people saying 'Oh, let's do something interesting in rock.'"[12]

The evolution of Forster's description of women in his songs is, however, worth tracing. The females he portrayed in "Lee Remick" and "Karen" were idols and ideals. Another early song, "So Pretty," was based on the film of John Fowles' novel *The Collector*. The women of "Eight Pictures" and "The Sound of Rain" were subjects of violence—although the former was only "shot . . . with my Kodak,"[13] the latter was definitely shot "right between the eyes." In the early 1979 ZZZ interview, Forster was taken to task for such objectification by Ashleigh Merritt:

> MERRITT: So generally what sort of role do you assign women in the songs that you write?
> FORSTER: The women in my songs are usually either objects of desire, or . . . yeah, basically they're objects of desire that I'd like to communicate with. But unfortunately I can't.
> [*Break in recording*]
> MERRITT: Well, why can't a person like you, Rob, who writes such brilliant songs, communicate with other people?
> FORSTER: I can communicate with other people. But the women I want to talk to, there's basically this horrendous sex thing that comes up. Immediately you start talking to women they put up some sort of defense guard, where I can't really communicate with them.
> MERRITT: Would you consider that a particularly sexist attitude?
> FORSTER: No, it's not sexist, I don't degrade women, I don't put them on any sort of pedestal . . . I . . .
> MERRITT: But you cannot relate to them.
> FORSTER: I can, but they seem to have this sort of great sexual thing where it seems to be . . . where they *rightfully* feel, I know, a lot of men will press themselves upon them, and they think, "Oh, here comes another one." I just wish I could sit down and talk to them. But . . . there seems to be this barrier there. I suppose it could be my fault, I don't know.[14]

Merritt was one of the more politically aware 4ZZZ staff, and certainly saw nothing wrong—and why should she?—with quizzing a pop-song writer about sexual politics. She also had romantic designs on him at the time, she later admitted, and this clearly affected her opinion of Lindy Morrison, who by now was spending more and more time with Forster.

> MERRITT: It was clear to all that Lindy was going to snaffle up our Robert, and nothing and nobody (including Grant, who tried very hard) could stop her. She had her sights set on getting into a successful band, or some boys with talent.
>
> You'd have to say that our Robert was a naive young thing, and no match for the older, been-there-several-times-before, Lindy. The struggle for Rob's soul (between Grant and Lindy) was something to watch.

While Merritt and all their other friends watched, the Forster-McLennan relationship was rejigged—and the Forster-Morrison one began.

(Tony Forster)

> MORRISON: Robert and Grant ... were both virgins when I met them. They were twenty years of age and really scared of what they perceived as *bad* women. They had very well established ideas about what women were.
>
> I will never, ever forget that for the first six months Grant would never come into Wellington Street. It was 1979. Wellington Street was a wild house, that's where I lived with this woman called Bronwyn who ran the Curry Shop. We had a huge sunken bath that was like a swimming pool, and we used to have parties there all the time. We were bad girls, we smoked pot and had naked baths with anyone who came to the house at any time. We weren't having rampant sexual orgies, we were just *completely liberated*. Rob and Grant entered that world and Rob—it took me six months to get Rob into bed. It took me six months to realize he was a virgin. I mean, I just thought he wasn't interested in me. Once I sorted that out it took me a *day* to bed him. But I knew I wanted to for six months, and he was visiting all the time.
>
> I think that I got Robert onto pot, because we were smoking pot

continually, Bronwyn and I. Grant would never come in. He would sit outside in the car for an hour, and wait. We had a party and he wouldn't come. We were the bad women.

Morrison and Forster's relationship was consummated on an excursion Zero took to Stradbroke Island to play a show at a pub there. As Debbie Thomas recalls:

> THOMAS: Irena was terribly drunk the next day and she was throwing the Stradbroke Island pub's champagne glasses off the cliff in the name of art. We came down onto the beach because we knew that Lindy and Robert had done it the night before—we'd had our ears against the door, we were laughing our heads off, we could hear them squealing away in there. I don't know how they figured it was a nudist beach but they both came down onto the beach completely naked. It was like one of those teen commercials—they held hands and ran off down the beach together. It was his "she took my hand and made me a man" kind of day—his big day. "How could you, Lindy?! what have you done to this boy?!"

> MORRISON: We went to Stradbroke Island for a Zero gig and we had our first fuck, and he was so overcome by losing his virginity and the joy of sex, that he went for a walk down to the beach and he didn't return in time to get the bus back. I went back to Brisbane on the bus and he had to stay overnight, didn't have any money, had to sleep on the beach. We all went back on the bloody bus which he missed because he wandered off to contemplate nature and the mysteries of the universe—because he'd had his first fuck. I didn't hear from him for three days. Here I am, I'd finally got his pants off, and—the bloody guy—as soon as he does it he disappears down the beach and when he finally gets back to Brisbane doesn't even ring me for three days!
>
> I fell in love with Robert. You fall in love with someone and there's no more thinking—you have to be with them. And why did I fall in love with a twenty-one-year-old? That *is* incredible. I never thought he was like twenty-one. But he was such a beautiful person.

9

The Sound of Young Scotland

In an interview with *Sounds* in 1984, by which time the Go-Betweens were firmly based in London, Robert Forster recalled how he felt in 1979:

> FORSTER: At the time I had this idea of the Go-Betweens as a very maverick group, traveling around the world doing one-off singles with lots of independent labels. Sort of musical missionaries, if you like.[1]

As every Australian—and for that matter every Londoner—knows, London is full of Australians. Whether they are seeking the heart of a crumbled empire, undergoing a rite of passage, or just taking the opportunity to bong and booze with one another in exotic circumstances is hard to tell. Luckily Forster and McLennan—whose 1979 trip was part holiday, part fact-finding mission, and part work—knew a good many Brisbanites who had already settled there. Geoffrey Titley of the Supports, for instance, had not only moved to London, he had joined the Desperate Bicycles, a group known for having released some of the first D.I.Y. singles in the UK.

> TITLEY: Robert and Grant came over to England at the end of 1979. Robert was staying with friends of his parents. I don't think he was that comfortable there. I remember one night he got home and he'd forgotten to take a key and it was quite late at night so he just kicked the door in ... Soon after that he came to stay with me.
>
> I was staying at a flat in Highgate with Robert Wheeler[2] ... I think Grant at that point was off to Egypt for a holiday.[3] I'd joined the Desperate Bicycles, [who] were heavily into recording. The only other time I'd been in a studio was at 4ZZZ, so I had the bug, and one day I suggested to Robert [Forster] that we make a recording, 'cause he was always playing guitar.

He and Robert Wheeler and myself went into the studio and did two songs that Robert had written . . . The engineer said, "What's the band called?" As far as I knew the band didn't have a name, but Robert said, "The Reason Why."[4] So that was it! [The band] started a few days before that and finished in the studio.

The Forster of the 1990s considers the two songs by the Reason Why to be among the few genuinely regrettable things in his career. Certainly they explore his art-rock leanings much more than anything he ever did with McLennan, who apparently still teases him about them periodically. Nobody seems to remember whether they were entirely new compositions, or songs he had been playing with Zero a few months earlier. The eclectic drumming Geoffrey Titley employs certainly has the clipped, mathematical feel of Lindy Morrison's style at the time. One song, influenced musically by the Gang of Four, explores a very different side to the expatriate experience from "I Need Two Heads," which he wrote at the same time; its refrain runs, "There's no place like Hell/There's no place you know so well."

Another former member of the Supports, Peter Loveday, was also ensconced in London by the time Forster and McLennan arrived.

PETER LOVEDAY: I think when Robert went over to London he was staying a while with Geoffrey. He had a job in the X-ray department of a hospital, hoping that Paul Weller would come in for an X-ray so that he could "look inside his head and see all the songs he was going to write."

The hospital, according to McLennan, was St. Mary's, Paddington. He also says that while working there, Forster stole an X-ray of Nicolas Roeg.

The Go-Betweens were, as far as Forster is concerned, as much of an anomaly in London as they had been in Brisbane:

FORSTER: We arrived in London with acoustic guitars. We were the first people walking around London with them . . . this is late '79. You could virtually be booked and put in jail for having an acoustic guitar. I don't know who the last people were in London who had acoustic guitars or played acoustic songs to A&R people. They just thought we were completely nuts. They'd say "Oh, yeah. Send us a demo tape." We'd go, "We don't have a demo tape, we've got our acoustic guitars, we'll come and play you some songs."[5]

I thought it was fantastic. Completely immediate. You can see that they play, they're sitting on two chairs and they're playing you the songs. If I was an A&R person I'd think: "I wish every band would come and do this." But we were just laughed at. No one was interested. We went to Virgin. We went to Rough Trade and played "People Say" for Geoff Travis and he said "It's too commercial." I was just: *"What does that mean?"* Too commercial? You just kept running up against these orthodoxies. "No, you have to sound like the Gang of Four. You have to sound like the Fall. You have to sound sort of scrapey and scrappy, [with] the lyric way down in the mix."

They thought it wouldn't fit into what was going on. We arrived at a good moment and a bad moment. We only had half a dozen good songs in 1978. So if we'd gone over then, we would've—whatever time we'd gone over, it would've been the wrong time, we wouldn't have been able to fit in. You know the week that "Lee Remick" came out? If we'd been there that week, it would have done really well. We would have been famous. Then. In England.

Forster, as usual, places himself at the margins and finds it a good place from which to take a critical view:

FORSTER: We weren't dropping the right things, we weren't saying the right things. The fact that we were young, talented and knew a huge amount about music—we knew everything that was going on, we listened to everything—but the music we liked was New York–based. We knew we couldn't go to New York, there was no system there. We had our favorite bands—I really liked the Only Ones, I really liked the Pretenders—and I saw these bands and they were just loud and heavy. I liked their records—"Kid" by the Pretenders and the first Only Ones album—and then I go to London and see them and they're sort of . . . guitarists rubbing their groins—this was the sort of thing I thought I'd left behind in Brisbane! Sure, Chrissie Hynde was great, but why's she got this shitty band with her? Peter Perrett's great but he'd got these old cock-rockers with him. I saw the Gang of Four and the Fall and Scritti Politti and all these bands, and no one really knocked me out. Still, it was good to go to London in 1980. Of course, a few years later everyone was walking around with acoustic guitars—they still are.

Almost before punk began, people were discussing its demise. Still more were attempting to divert it in some way that would best serve their own purposes. And it didn't take long before the diversions became more interesting than punk itself, which had already started to look weary by the end of 1979. The English bands of 1980 were drawing their influences from a diverse range of possibilities. Forster was particularly taken with the Pop Group and the Raincoats, and both he and McLennan were excited by the Gang of Four. Of course, they'd already heard songs by these bands on record, and in live cover versions played by Brisbane groups like Zero. But as Forster said, "In Brisbane, musically, we're [enrolled] in a school, but we're just doing it by correspondence, and then suddenly you go over to London and you're actually at the college."[6]

At the start of the new decade, it was the turn of Alan Horne and Edwyn Collins to try to hijack that elusive "spirit" of punk. Independent record labels had sprung up in their hundreds in the UK since the beginning of punk. They ranged from larger labels like Rough Trade—which also comprised a shop and a fledgling distribution network—to small but highly influential ones like Zoo, New Hormones, Step Forward, and Fast Product. These labels rarely managed to place singles in the mainstream charts, but they had the attention of weekly music papers like the *NME*, and many of the bands whose careers they launched went on to lasting popularity.

Collins' and Horne's bizarre vision, hatched in their hometown of Glasgow, blended their favorite 1960s music—Motown, Creedence Clearwater Revival, the Lovin' Spoonful, and, most importantly, the Velvet Underground—with that of one most undeservedly unsung 1970s British punk, Vic Godard of Subway Sect. Their label, Postcard, operated with the catchphrases "The Sound of Young Scotland" and "Funky Glasgow Now!" Horne was its proprietor (though "perpetrator" may not be too strong a word), as well as the manager of Collins' band, Orange Juice. Orange Juice were boyish and apparently happy: they produced colorful, off-kilter singles with bright guitar sounds and good-humored, intelligent lyrics delivered in Edwyn's delightfully syrupy voice. The first singles—"Falling and Laughing," "Blueboy," and "Simply Thrilled Honey"—appeared in oddball uniform Postcard sleeves with cowboys and cacti. The Postcard Records of Scotland logo was a cat playing a drum. The overall effect was a kind of deep feyness, if such a thing is possible. The attitude was, perhaps: "Pop music has no meaning, it's forgettable trash; but since we all know that's *not true*, that pop music means a lot to a lot of people, then here's the forgettable trash to treasure." In 1980, Postcard brought forth three sensational Scottish bands: Orange Juice; Josef K, from Edinburgh, with frilly shirts and blurry photos but, it must be said, a brilliant songwriter in Paul Haig; and Aztec Camera, a glorious pop group starring the teenage Roddy Frame. It was, of course, the perfect scenario for McLennan and Forster to wander into, but what was the likelihood of such a thing happening?

In 1981, when the Go-Betweens' association with the label was almost over, Postcard records produced a slender manifesto known as its *Brochure*, with the four bands' biographies executed in beautiful copperplate. The Go-Betweens section tells the magical story of how Edwyn and Alan happened across a copy of "Lee Remick" in the Rough Trade record store:

> "Lee Remick" and especially "Karen" was classic rubbish, sounding like Lou Reed when he was working for Pickwick Records.[7] We scribbled a note explaining we had no money, wanted to put out their single, blah, blah, blah, and slipped it under their door with a copy of "Falling and Laughing" and left for Glasgow never expecting to hear anything more from the Go-Betweens. Two days later a letter arrived: "Thanks for your interest, we had to break into someone's house to hear the record. We found it an interesting and courageous effort, considering the musical climate. It reminded us of us!" More letters were exchanged and we started to get some idea of what they were like. The groups they liked were the same as us—the Velvets, Byrds, Creedence Clearwater, Lovin' Spoonful. They'd never heard Subway Sect.[8] "Brisbane is anything but funky, merely persistent dry winds, the threat of a storm, and a form of music that hardly ever rises above these circumstances, hence that striped sunlight sound: guitar, bass, and drums producing a thin, vulnerable sound based on emotion and melody. Our answer to the tropics."[9]

The account Alan Horne gave much later of the events surrounding his and Collins' first encounter with the Go-Betweens is less enthusiastic, less sparkling with pop magic than in 1980, when he and Postcard had something to sell. Now, he'll happily burst his own balloon:

> ALAN HORNE: We made the first Orange Juice single end of '79 and then in February we were down in London—probably distributing the record which was a case of [having] a whole lot of records in the back of a car and going round to various shops in London. One of our ports of call was Rough Trade, which was in Kensington Park Road at the time. The shop had a wall full of records, and one of the singles was "Lee Remick." Every record under the sun was there, actually. But Edwyn and I had actually heard this record on the Peel show a year or so back, and we were going through a period of thinking we had to have a couple of groups on the label, primarily to get attention, to make it look like a label rather than just an outlet for Orange Juice.
>
> I guess it was sort of calculated in a way with the other groups, Edinburgh's Josef K—"let's find a group who's sort of current in that post–Joy Division sound,[10] wear all black and look the part for the time." [But] with Orange Juice we were very worried it was too far ahead of its time, fell between two camps, wasn't mainstream enough to be played

on the radio and wasn't so obviously left-field in that silly way that was going on at the time in Britain, that kind of daft, non-musical, don't even remember . . . "gothic" . . . don't even know what terms they used to use, *nonsense* music like Joy Division, Bauhaus. We weren't too sure it would be very easy to get Orange Juice noticed, so a lot of this padding round the label was kind of calculated and the idea of an Australian group seemed like a great novelty. If a small provincial label from Glasgow, Scotland, had an Australian group it'd be more serious—that was the appeal of the band, I suppose.

The other thing obviously was the record. ["Lee Remick"] was all right, it was kind of a Jonathan Richman–influenced thing and that appealed to us a bit. And we found out from the girl behind the counter[11] that they were not only staying in London at the time but were in fact in a sleazy down-market hotel in the same street we were staying in, in Sussex Gardens. We went to visit them. They weren't in, so we wrote a letter and stuck it under their door with a copy of "Falling and Laughing." And then headed up the road back to Glasgow. I don't know if we were actually sure we'd hear from them again. And a couple of weeks later we got a letter back from them. [It] said they'd broken into someone's house to hear the record on a record player because they didn't have one, this kind of nonsense. And that they thought it was great, they were really excited and they wanted to come up to Glasgow, blah blah blah, so that obviously was quite interesting.

McLennan and Forster took a train to Glasgow in March 1980. Orange Juice bass player David McClymont recalls driving Horne to the railway station to pick them up. Horne was apparently so fearful that the two Australians would turn out to be long-haired hippies that he was fully prepared *not* to pick them up if, on driving past, he didn't like the look of them. Luckily, they passed the audition.

Forster stayed with McClymont, and McLennan with Postcard pals Robbie Kelly and Anne Hogarth. Their first meeting with Edwyn Collins has assumed legendary status for Forster and McLennan, though Collins' most enduring memory of it is that "they went to the food cupboard and ate everything."[12] Forster remembers walking into a room in Collins' flat to be introduced to him:

> FORSTER: Edwyn was down on his hands and knees listening to the first John Fogerty solo album. He turned to me and said, "Do you think that second guitar is a Stratocaster or a Rickenbacker?" I just looked at him and I went, "We've found 'em!" This was where . . . It wasn't in London.

It was right here. They liked the Velvets, they liked Creedence, they liked Dylan. It was guitars, and it was songs, no bogus avant-gardism.

McLennan was similarly taken with the Postcard crowd:

> McLENNAN: It was just a great time. They were our age, they didn't take music too seriously, music wasn't the only thing they were interested in, they were just great. They drank. Alan wanted to be Andy Warhol, dyed his hair and wore glasses. They were ambitious, they were snotty-nosed—*hated* the rest of the Glasgow scene. They were completely opposed and opposite to everything that was going on. A groovy little gang.

McClymont says Brisbane and Glasgow are extremely similar: "They've both got massive inferiority complexes, Glasgow about London, Brisbane about Sydney."

The Go-Betweens were added to the Postcard stable. Forster had a new song, "I Need Two Heads," which was paired with an older, pre-Europe "song about irritation,"[13] "Stop Before You Say It." Postcard had engaged Alex Ferguson, of the seminal and brilliant experimental punk group Alternative TV, as producer for a number of its releases. With their usual pragmatism when it came to drummers, Forster and McLennan asked Orange Juice's Steven Daly to record with them, and the group cut their third single, a much jerkier and less poppy proposition than the previous records.

Of "I Need Two Heads," Forster said at the time: "I was being confronted with so much information over there, my head was just spinning, and I remember walking down the street thinking: 'I need another head to take all this in.'"[14] It appears, however, that this cultural confusion worked both

ways, because—as Horne's recollections reveal now—the Go-Betweens gave as good as they got. Horne's memories of McLennan and Forster during the two months they were in Glasgow seem to say more about his own strangled asceticism than about the Australians:

> HORNE: We certainly thought they were hippies. The thinking we had at the time was based on a lot of punk and Jonathan Richman ideas, we had an antidrug stance—we were horrified by the fact that they just rolled up. They seemed a lot older than us and a lot more laid-back. We were incredibly neurotic and wound-up—we'd scream about town being neurotic and mental, and they were just sitting around smoking their dope. Yeah, we did think they were hippies and that was quite a bad thing in our book at the time but I think we took to them to a certain extent.
>
> They sat around all day doing nothing but smoking dope, watching TV, and talking about crap TV from the sixties. We got the impression that Australians got all this secondhand American TV—stuff we don't get over here. They talked about these dreadful—obviously dreadful—sitcoms and comedy shows from the sixties. Musically, I guess they knew a few things we were into, Velvets and all that stuff. They were a lot more conventional in that they were into the New York punk scene onwards and I think they were interested in a lot of things happening in Britain at the time, although they would probably play that down now. The Cure, I think, and Joy Division—I think they were into that. Of course, to us those groups were lower than dogshit. We were interested in the fifties, the sixties, disco, Chic, Motown, Stax, and we wanted to get a black thing into music. And the Go-Betweens were the whitest of white groups.

It is difficult to imagine much of a connection between black music and promotional photographs from this time showing a pale Edwyn Collins in schoolboy shorts lying on a manicured lawn. But this is Horne's fantasy and it must be said that it was, and is, utterly enjoyable. Fortunately, every record released on Postcard was magic.

As for Horne's feeling that McLennan and Forster were older than the other Postcard stalwarts, there would have been at most a two-year age difference. The impression they made was presumably conveyed by their more worldly perspective—although Brisbane was a parochial city, McLennan and Forster were among its least parochial offspring. Horne, who seemed to prefer things to be *felt* rather than *known*, was obviously also rather irritated by McLennan and Forster's insistence on being *interested* in things—old TV shows, and groups he loathed, like the Cure—as though they were tourists.

HORNE: To a certain extent I wasn't terribly keen on the Go-Betweens' music, I liked *them,* liked having them about. They weren't nearly as bad as Josef K, whose music I just really detested, to be honest. To me it was just *Orange Juice* at the time, Orange Juice were really way ahead of the pack, everything else was just so-so. But it was fun having them about and I liked Robert quite a lot, he seemed to be quite a wacky character. Grant I don't remember so much, he seemed a bit more booky, a bit more boring, also a little bit snide. But I remember he used to go around calling me a middle-class faggot, so I feel quite justified in [saying] this stuff!

During their time in Scotland, the Go-Betweens played three shows. According to the *Brochure:*

> April was the month for Funky Glasgow Now. In an effort to get noticed by the less astute members of the Great Rock Public, we fixed up two concerts, in Glasgow and Edinburgh, with Orange Juice, (rarely to be seen on stage before), Josef K, and all the way from Australia the UK debut of legendary unknown cult group the Go-Betweens. Videos and recordings were made, members of the audience got onstage and performed between the groups, members of the groups got offstage into the audience. A Glasgow audience for once managed to dance to a group. Warhol on a Clydeside level. The start and finish of any Glasgow "scene." The Go-Betweens fell in love with Glasgow, they recorded a ridiculous interview with Radio Clyde explaining how they toured with a rodeo in Australia playing country and western versions of "Anarchy."[15] They played in a cafe one dinnertime, went to Malcolm Fisher's for scones, and watched TV.[16]

One of these shows was captured on very lo-fi cassette: Forster and McLennan, probably mindful of temporary drummer Steven Daly, kept their set short and simple. All the songs previously released on record and a few new ones, like "Hope," were delivered in a competent, if slightly stilted, fashion.[17] One audience member, David Westlake, remembers the group striking him as "fragile and quirky" with "lots of space." "They seemed to have this irony going on. Sort of intentional anticlimaxes. Which manipulated the listener's expectations." Forster, who had expected that the audience "wouldn't clap and [that] someone would shout, 'Well, nice one, but you come from Brisbane'"[18] wrote elatedly to Andrew Wilson:

> We played last night at the Glasgow Technical College and won. Groups play a lot less here and when they do it's sort of an event. We know so many people, and have friends. People come up and talk to us and we

know as many people here as we do in Brisbane.

The other group on Postcard Records are Orange Juice who are excellent, not because we know them, but behind the Gang of Four, Raincoats, and the Cure their [sic] the next, sort of fantastic.

We live close to the city, and Glasgow looks sort of grim, but it's such a short walk only five minutes and the city center for the entire population is very small. Went to the country last week, and lay down in green grass, beside a small river and I thought of so many things including how I was going to get home, but Alan arrived in his car.

Edwyn Collins recalls Forster asking him at this time, "Do you think you can be a punk rocker and still love the leaves?"[19]

Understandably, Forster was wondering how he fit in:

Groups here in Glasgow seem split between punk and new music (spelt with a K) and too much is catalogued [i.e., pigeonholed]. London is far too much at the center of things for its own good.[20]

Once again, Forster was coming to feel that the best place to be was outside the mainstream, observing from a distance. The Glasgow experience was, however, necessarily temporary. As Forster remarked a few months after leaving Funky Glasgow:

The next choice would have been having to spend four months there . . . buy gear and find a drummer and a practice room. We used to break into old council tenements, set up our gear and practice, then leave quickly—no one has practice rooms there and money's very hard to save in the UK, so I thought I'd come back. I had to sell my guitar to come back, as it was.[21]

McLennan seems to have been relatively financially secure on this trip—secure enough, at least, to go on to New York after Britain to visit Robert Vickers and Peter Walsh—but Forster obviously was not. Much of this first British experience seems, in fact, to have been associated in his mind with breaking and entering. Staying in Glasgow and awaiting the release of the new single was therefore not a tenable proposition. In any case, it probably would not have been the best decision, quite aside from the fact that he had a lover in Brisbane whom he missed. But the duo's achievement on this trip—a UK single release as one of a batch of exciting, trendy new groups—was, once again, something close to miraculous for Brisbanites.

It was assumed for some time back in Australia, where the obsession with pigeonholing was at least as rampant as in the UK, that the Go-Betweens were now "a Postcard band." But there was no Scottish follow-up, and the label itself soon lost its indie identity when Postcard—and Orange Juice, for whom it had been constructed—got hitched to major label Polydor.[22] However, snatches of letters from McLennan and Forster are reproduced in the *Brochure* as though there was an ongoing relationship between the band and the label:

> "Two Brisbane bands doing cover versions of our songs. Can't get 'Lovesick' out of our minds.[23] Grant and I doing Edwyn and Alan impersonations, no one knew what we were talking about. Has Malcolm [Fisher] been arrested yet? We miss Glasgow but have that glorious Orange Juice tape so when I'm traveling round the rodeos with my brother I will have something to listen to."
>
> September: "Was talking to the drummer in the Cure, he asked me if I'd heard Josef K. Robert Smith wants to produce our next fifteen LPs. Heard the Bunnymen LP—it stinks. Have been invited to play with the Laughing Clowns—best band in Australia. Today the temperature reached 37°.[24] This is serious, Alan, my Burns Nu Sonic will not stay in tune due to the heat. Please line up dates in Paris immediately."
>
> October: "Our rehearsals are coming on, our sound is hypnotic. Television circa 1974, lots of ballads and snare rolls. Imagine George Harrison fronting the Velvets 1965."
>
> December: "We've just returned from Sydney, played three dates. Can the Go-Betweens be the Art band on Postcard? Robert is listening to Broadway musicals and I'm listening to fifties jazz."

Returning to Australia was something of a triumph—an especially sweet resurrection in the wake of the Beserkley fiasco. Certainly, the Go-Betweens fared better than Orange Juice, who split from Alan Horne and signed to Polydor, then split in two leaving only Collins and McClymont from the original band. Soon afterwards they had a hit record with "Rip It Up," but artistically they were a mere shadow of their former glory.

The Go-Betweens' successes were a long way removed from the mainstream record charts, but they were successes nonetheless. Back in Australia, Keith Glass, owner of Melbourne's Missing Link label, which had put its ugly purple-and-blue label on releases by the Birthday Party, Whirlywirld, and (for one release only) the Laughing Clowns, had contacted

Postcard and acquired the right to release "I Need Two Heads" in Australia.

> KEITH GLASS: I paid an advance on the record, the Postcard record. I made the contract up. I have a piece of paper somewhere saying "I will pay you x amount of dollars . . . we'll license this." That record might even be licensed to me or my descendants right now, I don't know, I haven't checked up. I've never heard from anyone, ever, involved with Postcard.

This action was to shape the next steps in the group's recording career. The single was released in the UK in June 1980, after Forster and McLennan had left, and it reached number six in the *NME* independent charts among a top ten of (mainly) wonderful singles, including Delta 5's superb "Try," the Au Pairs' "It's Obvious," and Orange Juice's "Simply Thrilled Honey."

> HORNE: They went back to Australia, and we put the single out, and I think it got Single of the Week in one of the papers; it sold some, but it didn't sell very well. Everything else on the label started selling, we started picking up press and the label became the hip thing. So the record eventually did okay—but it was always the lame duck of the label, I'm afraid! Just because they were in Australia. There was no group, no photos, it was like running a race and tying your feet together. We really didn't see it as practical and sensible to continue. I rarely came across them after that.[25] How did they fit into the Sound of Young Scotland? Well, they didn't. They weren't young and they weren't Scottish!

10
From Brisbane to Melbourne

> McLENNAN: This is going to sound completely romantic—we always envisaged the band with a female drummer. I suspect it has something to do with the Velvets. At that stage in Brisbane, there were only one or two women playing [drums], all the rest were men. Maybe it was just to be different. Maybe we thought, somewhat sexistly perhaps, that a woman would soften the band.[1]

In the Go-Betweens' scene of the late 1970s, the inspiration was of course to some extent Mo Tucker of the Velvet Underground, pure and simple, although Tina Weymouth of Talking Heads represented a seventies version of the same kind of thing, perhaps—a woman in a band primarily as an instrumentalist, not the focus of the group and not the singer. There was perhaps also an underlying sexual aspect, too, as in both cases the woman in the band was playing a rhythmic role. Forster was also looking, as usual, to powerful nonmusical influences: he was hoping to fill the "Go-betweensmobile":

> FORSTER: When we started we had Lissa Ross playing drums. Grant and I, one of the things we based the group on was *Mod Squad*. I just loved that combination—two guys and a girl, a fantastic lifestyle. We also needed solidarity—we were in Paris for about a month, we looked for a drummer there too. There was one new-wave record store—we put up a note for a female drummer, we wrote the note out in French—but no one applied. That would've been cool, a French girl drummer.
> We loved *groups*! I can't think what the stereotype would've been then of a two-person group. Now you've got the Pet Shop Boys, all that kind of stuff. [But] we were called the Go-Betweens, so you needed more than two. We had to have *people* in the group. Like Creedence—[we]

loved going from album sleeve to album sleeve, "Look, his hair's reached his collar now," "Thank god he's changed his shirt by the third album."

It is probably unfair to accuse Forster and McLennan in retrospect of inverted sexism or tokenism in actively pursuing a female drummer. We should also grant someone like Lindy Morrison the sense to know if she was being patronized.

Certainly, Morrison was not the kind of "woman drummer" the two Go-Betweens had in mind when they would try to pick up women at dances with the winning line: "Uh . . . you don't play *drums,* do you?" In fact, she was very much at odds with the founding Go-Betweens' image of themselves. She was not likely to fall in with their flights of fancy involving Warhol-style clubs with girls in fishnet stockings on trapezes, nor to have the respect they did for a more traditional sexist like Bob Dylan. But she was, of course, a perfect strong and intelligent third personality for the group, as well as being something of a local celebrity: she was loud, vivacious, and political.

Forster realized this even as—soon after his return from London, but while McLennan was still in New York—he invited another woman, Clare McKenna, to play drums for the Go-Betweens. He did this despite an explicit request from McLennan, who recalls, "I told Robert, 'do not do *anything* until I get back.'" Interviewed at the time for the short-lived Brisbane rock magazine *Backstage,* Forster told Graham Aisthorpe about the new-look group, with McKenna on drums and David Tyrer on guitar. Tyrer had previously played with the Poles, one of Forster's favorite groups, and was also a regular cartoonist for the *Cane Toad Times.* Tyrer, Forster explained, "has a Roland guitar synthesizer." And, he continued, "Grant will be joining us, playing bass, when he gets back from New York."[2] Dave Tyrer also brought a song of his own, "Born to Rebel," which—if the title is anything to go by—would hardly have been a comfortable fit with the typically wry and apolitical Go-Betweens fare.

> FORSTER: I came back from Scotland before Grant—Grant went back via New York. I got back and I had a cassette of "I Need Two Heads." Going away for six months, coming back, "I Need Two Heads." Sonically fantastic. I was excited—I should have waited—I don't know, I was just keen. Got Clare in, she played drums, she was also a part of the Zero crowd. And David Tyrer—who had played with the Poles for a while. He was playing in that Magazine-type style.[3] There was a show offered at Caxton Street, with Zero. So [when] Grant came back I'd sort of formed

the band.

But behind all of this—and why it's confusing for Clare, and unfair—was [the fact that] before I left I'd started a relationship with Lindy Morrison, and that sort of continued while I was away, by mail, but when I came back—I was at my parents' house—we didn't resume the relationship straight away. So there was a little bit of confusion.

MORRISON: I was seeing someone else at the time but it wasn't a serious . . . I was seeing Colin Bloxsom.[4] And I only saw him seven times, to be exact. Colin and I always laugh about it now. I was filling in time, I was lonely. I was a twenty-eight-year-old sexually active woman, I wasn't going to wait around for Robert—a twenty-one-year-old who didn't know if he was Arthur or Martha.

FORSTER: I'd been away for six months. Coming back, *everything* had changed. This is going to sound like a hideous cliché, but . . . the 1970s were over. That golden '78, '79 time was over. Music had changed, everything had changed.

I came back and was staying in my parents' house, and David Tyrer got me a job at Queensland University, and it was all wrong. And then Lindy and I started up again, and then Grant and I had a meeting with her, "Do you want to join the band?" She said yeah. She left Zero. That was a big break. They were a big scene, they were the most social band in town . . . crowds of people around Zero. For her to leave that and come over to us, that was a big step. So there was a sort of power shift . . .

I mucked it up. It was two people, Lindy and I, coming together—and Clare in a way was treated unfairly and badly by me to an extent.

These events revealed a change in the dynamic between Forster and McLennan. Before their overseas trip, in 1979, Forster could play as "the Go-Betweens" with the Supports backing him. By mid-1980, McLennan, returning from New York to find a new band assembled without his consent, could veto the arrangement. "I was pissed off at him, actually," he remembers. "Well-nigh furious. By that stage I felt [the band was] very much fifty-fifty. The new incarnation wasn't pop enough for me. Too English-sounding."

As it happened, neither of the newly recruited Go-Betweens minded very much being given their marching orders:

TYRER: I was sort of aware that things weren't too good and I didn't see much of a future in it. I ran into Robert—I remember it well because Robert was lying on the footpath, he had a nosebleed . . . He must have been drinking and bumped his nose or something. He was actually lying on the footpath with somebody—I don't think it was Grant—and he just said something like, "it's not working out, it'd be best if you left." And I just nodded and said, "I know, it's not really the right thing."

Forster had obviously had little conversation with Tyrer before enlisting him; there were bound to be problems in the Forster-McLennan songwriting guild given Tyrer's desire to bring his own songs to the group. In any case, Tyrer was hardly in sync with what he saw as the sixties style of the Go-Betweens, and returned with relief to his own group, the punky Bex Crystals.

Clare McKenna already knew Lindy Morrison from "early days feminism stuff." Of the Go-Betweens, she recalls practicing in "that lovely old building behind the *Sunday Sun* in the Valley." This was the rehearsal room started up by the group Swell Guys, which both Zero and the Go-Betweens came to use as well. "Zero used to practice on the ground floor, the Go-Betweens used to practice upstairs. I remember we found a lot of old glass photographic plates there."

> McKENNA: They were probably more conservative than I wanted to be at that stage. I was discovering other stuff. And I really disliked Bob Dylan intensely! They were absolutely besotted with Bob Dylan. I thought he was a whingeing miserable bastard and they thought he was some poet from on high. So I guess I never really related to them.
>
> To me, they were pretty formal. I just wanted to get in and do stuff and I remember going to the practice room and getting into it and they were very unwilling to get their hands dirty! They were very much still private-school boys. I wasn't interested in that stuff. I wanted to lash out, really. I think to me that was reflected in the music. I was just discovering drums by the seat of my pants.

Forster feels remorse for edging McKenna out of the group, but she feels she left of her own accord and that her next drumming gig—she replaced Morrison in Zero—was much more enjoyable. The Go-Betweens' music was, she says, "too controlled for me":

> McKENNA: I wrote them a postcard from a ferry in Sydney. I remember I was a bit shy about saying I didn't want to play in the band any more and I didn't quite know how to say it. I think I sent a postcard—"I won't be at practice on Monday—or thereafter!" Who knows, they may have been very peeved. They were all so *serious* about it.

Despite Zero's casual ways, it seemed to shock all its members when Morrison resigned. Michael O'Connell, who quit at the same time, explains:

O'CONNELL: [Robert and Grant] came back and they would come and see Zero, and Lindy started playing with them—and Lindy just announced one day she was going to quit and play with the Go-Betweens.

The band was divided: Lindy and me, and John and Irena. John and Irena were living together, or dating or something. Lindy and I had songs I was particularly pleased with—there were two axes in the band. When Lindy said she was going to leave, that was the end of my power base.

IRENA LUCKUS: It was terrible. Lindy and I had worked really well together. We'd get into the practice room without the boys, we'd play whatever we wanted to. We went so far from the beginnings to a certain stage, we were getting somewhere in Brisbane. We always had guests come in, we'd have friends. That was the nature of Brisbane. Everybody would play with everyone else. It was sad to see Lindy go, but it was inevitable, because she had this relationship with Robert.

Debbie Thomas, who had left Zero by this stage, sums up the Zero experience as entirely dependent on "who you were sleeping with." To the remaining members of Zero, this ultimately made Morrison's defection understandable.

Lindy Morrison was instantly accepted as the third Go-Between—in a way that Tim Mustafa, for instance, never really was—but relations were never smooth between her and McLennan. Apart from differences in temperament, each considered themselves Forster's best friend. For five years—their

Forster, McLennan, and Morrison outside the house Forster and Morrison shared in Hughes Street, North Carlton, Melbourn

relationship was to fall into chaos around 1984—Morrison was winning the battle for Forster's affections. She feels that McLennan made no secret of his displeasure at the way Forster had been taken from him.

> MORRISON: He actually said in front of me one day—we were traveling somewhere—"It was all so easy when it was just the two of us, Robert, and now it's so hard that there's three." He actually said that in front of me. I was of so little value to him that he would say things like that in front of me. And it's true, I'm sure it was a lot easier when there were two.
>
> God, I mean, I'm sure it was awful for him—he and Robert used to do everything together and then Robert and I [did] everything together. We were inseparable.

Morrison was the eighth person to play drums with the Go-Betweens, but it soon became very hard to imagine the Go-Betweens without her, especially since she played an integral part in their rise to the next level of fame—making albums and videos, touring nationally and internationally. Nor was it merely that her unique playing style welded itself successfully to the band, even if that was the most important thing. She also made an invaluable contribution in terms of organization and publicity. To many new Go-Betweens fans, she was the member of the band that made it different.

The new group traveled to Sydney in April 1981 to record a single for

Missing Link. Label owner Keith Glass came up from Melbourne to supervise, and the Go-Betweens recorded three songs with Birthday Party engineer Tony Cohen. "It Could Be Anyone" was not released, and would later be rerecorded for the first album. Forster's "World Weary"—for which Tony Cohen "flicked a switch" and, Forster says, "suddenly I was transformed into John Lennon"[5]—emerged as the b-side to "Your Turn, My Turn," which was largely a McLennan composition, although sung by Forster. This was McLennan's first great foray into the epic ballad, and it remains one of his most successful—and most poignant—works. The recording also featured Laughing Clowns pianist Dan Wallace-Crabbe (who claims he is still waiting to be paid for the session).

This was not the first trip the new lineup had made to Sydney, however. At the end of 1980 the Go-Betweens had gone south to play their first major shows in Sydney and Melbourne, opening for the Laughing Clowns and the Birthday Party (arguably the two hottest independent Australian bands at the time—and now their labelmates on Missing Link).

Clinton Walker has argued that the Paris Theatre show in Sydney was a consolidating and defining moment in the Australian music of the period.[6] Forster's description of it shows how momentous it seemed to him:

> FORSTER: We flew down—it was like, the little Go-Betweens—and we sat at the back of the Paris, this huge big theater. We didn't introduce ourselves, just walked in, off the plane, sat down—and there were the Birthday Party, up on stage, the most beautiful band, fantastic clothes, everything had this sort of *angle*, smoking cigarettes in the best way. They looked incredible. Then they started playing these songs and we were just overwhelmed. They were all very theatrical, it was like some sort of Shakespearean production watching them play at soundcheck! We were sinking in our seats.
>
> Then they get off—this noise, this beautiful noise, very funny—and we recover from that, still up the back of the theater—then the Laughing

Clowns get on. And they're just phenomenal again in a whole different region. A brass section, these ten-minute songs, Ed's just fantastic . . . Jeffrey Wegener drumming. We're like—fuckin' hell, what are we going to do here? It was one of the most nervous shows I'd ever done in my life—merely because I'd sat through the soundcheck!

The Laughing Clowns' music was highly crafted and intricate. The core of Ed Kuepper and Jeffrey Wegener, always accompanied by a magnificent brass section, and usually by Louise Elliott on saxophone, were impossible to beat—difficult even to imitate.

The Birthday Party were something else; blending the Stooges, Pere Ubu rock, and Australian gothic, they were loud, ratty, and spectacular. They were also, understandably, extremely influential, especially in Melbourne in the early 1980s. Indeed, by the time they made their first trip to Britain in early 1980, there was already a nascent scene of Birthday Party copyists. Forster is correct when he says, "It was a great bill—Birthday Party, Go-Betweens—because obviously we weren't imitators like everyone else that played with them."

The Birthday Party, the Laughing Clowns, and now the Go-Betweens were beginning to be perceived as the spearhead of a new campaign of confident, forthright Australian rock bands who would go abroad and show London—the old capital of the Empire, yet also the city that Australians felt had the cutting-edge music scene—a thing or two.

Lindy Morrison was well on the way to realizing her ambition of leaving Brisbane and Australia. Overseas travel had been the reason she'd wanted to hitch her wagon to Forster and McLennan's, despite their perverse immaturity: "I felt they were fantastic artists. They were just unique. There was nothing like them in Brisbane, nothing." At twenty-eight, she had made a third career change, and this time it would be something that took her beyond the narrow confines of Brisbane political scenes and the Bjelke-Petersen government's overbearing manipulations. Forster and McLennan were a decent gamble.

> MORRISON: Not only were they unique—the most important thing [was that] they were very ambitious. And I was always ambitious artistically. I wasn't gonna hang around Brisbane, I wanted to get out, I wanted to do something that was artistically unique, I wanted to make a name for myself as a creative person, I wanted to be known as someone who had produced something. I looked around everywhere. I couldn't

have got Zero to move. There was no one else whose prime ambition was to get out of town and make a name for themselves through art.

In fact, the Go-Betweens were not the only strong unit to leave Brisbane and take something out into the world—the Saints had done it before them, leaving for Sydney (briefly) and then London in the first half of 1977. But by the end of 1978 they'd fallen apart; Ed Kuepper had returned to Australia and subsequently put together the Laughing Clowns. The Riptides, too, had managed to get out of Brisbane—but for a pop career, not for art, and their attempts to make the right music-industry moves did them in.

In the end, the Go-Betweens didn't go directly from Brisbane to London. As they had learned more about Melbourne—where the Birthday Party had established themselves, and where their record label, Missing Link, was based—it became clear that they didn't have to wait for an overseas opportunity in order to escape the limitations of Brisbane. By the second half of 1981, McLennan, Forster, and Morrison had left for Melbourne. For Forster, the effects of the move were particularly welcome:

> FORSTER: I'd lost it. Grant started to write really well, and Grant's songs were by far the better [ones]. I mean, he wrote "Your Turn, My Turn." His songs were a lot more melodic than mine. I knew I didn't want to keep writing "Lee Remick," because it would just get to be an embarrassment as I got older. I didn't want to be twenty-nine, thirty, and still writing the sixteenth revision of "Karen." It was an adolescent song. I was twenty-three, twenty-four, and I had to somehow write something that meant something to me as a twenty-three or twenty-four-year-old.
>
> Melbourne saved us. As soon as we arrived in Melbourne, I exploded again.

11
Send Me a Lullaby

> FORSTER: We went down to Melbourne and people really liked us. We were getting good crowds, we met all these people through the Birthday Party. They were all very sharp and artistic. We had a great time. We were writing songs!
>
> Lindy and I lived in a house in Carlton, a little house, then we lived around Richmond . . . November 1981 till May 1982. The band exploded there.[1]

Whereas Brisbane was a place you left as soon as you could, a city that retained little sense of its musical history, Melbourne was well aware of its history and sure of its own importance. This appealed to the group:

> FORSTER: We met a lot of people [who] told us about Melbourne 1978, 1979, 1980. I used to sit and listen to people, and became an authority on the Melbourne punk scene from 1978 through 1980 just because people were telling me about it. So I'd go, "Right, so that person left JAB and is that the same person who played bass in Teenage Radio Stars for two weeks? And this person was in Whirlywirld . . ."

Melbourne had a burgeoning and productive new-wave scene in 1981 (although the term "new wave" was already sounding hokey by then). Where Brisbane bands tended to rail against the state and institutionalized corruption (with good reason), the underground Melbourne groups weren't forced into such a polemical stance. What they had, along with a vaguely skewed and angular feel, was something sophisticated and interesting, in the ways that the Go-Betweens were themselves. The members of the Birthday Party were private-school boys like McLennan and Forster; like McLennan, Nick Cave had spent time as a boarder at an exclusive private school. The member of the group McLennan got on best with, though, was Tracy Pew, probably because they had a similar world view: Rowland Howard has said of Pew, "everything was a private joke to him, and only he knew the punchline."²

> FORSTER: Grant always got on well with Tracy. He was a real man's man and I couldn't do that macho thing. Grant can. Tracy was an absolute gentleman in doing it—knives, and all that . . . a real adventure man.

For his part, Forster was closest to Cave and Howard at the time; he would not get to know the reticent Mick Harvey, who later collaborated on the first Robert Forster solo album, until later. He is unstinting in his praise for the Birthday Party as people and as musicians: "They were charming, friendly, creative, intelligent, and they were a great band."

There were other exciting Melbourne groups, too. Equal Local was an instrumental synthesizer group with jazz and pop influences who, against all odds, shone. Bryce Perrin, the group's double bass player, would visit Robert and Lindy in their Carlton house. Lindy hated his group, but marveled at his range of neatly-ironed cotton pajama tops, which he wore as shirts. There was the Fabulous Marquises, with one Mr. Pierre (who had played in JAB and the Teenage Radio Stars) on vocals, Edward Clayton-Jones on keyboards, and Chris Walsh on bass—they were very poppy and fairly unsuccessful. There was also International Exiles, and Hunters and Collectors (who at this early stage in their career would dress as New Romantics rather than in the bricklayers' outfits they adopted later). Plays with Marionettes were one of the hot groups on the circuit, one of many bands featuring Nick Seymour on bass before he struck gold with Crowded House.³

The most influential and interesting groups—at least that's how it seemed—had their records released by either Missing Link or Au Go Go records, which were effectively the same label at the time, run respectively by Keith Glass, owner of the Missing Link record shop, and Bruce Milne, who worked in it. The shop, in Flinders Lane, dealt in import records of all sorts: Ted Nugent rubbed shoulders with Desperate Bicycles, and the Go-Betweens' "I Need Two Heads"—released on Missing Link under license from Postcard—sat on the counter with the Buzzcocks and Marillion import singles.

According to Glass, "Bruce [Milne] decided what went on Au Go Go and I decided what went on Missing Link, but we both worked on all the records past that stage, in terms of wandering around looking for distribution." Glass had recently maneuvered a chart hit by licensing a reworking by London

Address: 239 FLINDERS LANE, MELBOURNE, 3000, AUSTRALIA   Correspondence: BOX 5159AA, MELBOURNE, 3001, AUSTRALIA

Phone 63 5507   Telex Extdis AA57059

AGREEMENT BETWEEN "THE GO-BETWEENS" (THE ARTISTS) AND MISSING LINK RECORDS (THE COMPANY)

1/6/81.

1. The parties shall enter into an agreement to record sufficient material for an album of not less than 30 minutes duration, within six months of the signing of this document.

2. Such signing will bind the artists to record exclusively for the company within the period and for a further period of 3 months during which time the company shall have the option of calling for a further term of nine months and a second albums worth of material.

3. Any material recorded for the company and released commercially shall not be re-recorded for any other party within a two year period from the lapse of the agreement.

4. For the above the company agrees to pay the artists a royalty of 7% of 100% of records sold (less sales tax only) within Australia and 5% of 100% (less relevant taxes) in all other places.

5. Such royalties will be paid 60 days from the end of each quarter year.

6. All decisions relating to marketing, exploitation of likeness, name, choice of tracks in all instances shall be a matter of mutual decisions between the parties and must have their full agreement.

7. In respect of original compositions, not otherwise subject to publishing agreements, the artist grants to the Company the right to administer said compositions for a deduction of 25% of the amount due each composition, the Company agrees that such control ceases at any time the artist should decide to place his compositions with a publisher.
Such royalties will be paid at time of performing royalties.

SIGNED for THE GO-BETWEENS   SIGNED for MISSING LINK RECORDS

_____   _____
_____   _____
_____
_____

art-rockers the Flying Lizards of the old chestnut "Money."[4] Such novelty records had been his stock-in-trade before: he had recorded and released "Salute to Abba" by Australian comedy character Norman Gunston, and licensed English satirist John Bird's "Idi Amin"—a big hit in Canberra—for his earlier label, Electric.

Missing Link had a pressing and distribution deal with RCA, which certainly provided better access to the mainstream than the Go-Betweens had ever had with Able or Postcard. Nevertheless, at a time before there was network radio there was still little chance that people outside the major cities in Australia would have the opportunity to hear the Go-Betweens, let alone be induced to buy their records (although the video they made for "Your Turn, My Turn" was shown on the commercial music show *Nightmoves*).

From Keith Glass's point of view, however, the money that might be made from the Go-Betweens was less likely to come from local sales than from overseas licensing. He had heard that at least two British record labels—Statik and Rough Trade—would be interested in licensing a Go-Betweens album. Before it was even recorded, he agreed to a deal with Rough Trade, which allowed him to count on sales for a Go-Betweens album in Europe as well as Australia, and to budget for an album accordingly. He recalls spending $12,000 on the recording of what became *Send Me a Lullaby*; Lindy Morrison remembers it as $8,000.[5]

The Go-Betweens wanted Rowland Howard and Mick Harvey to produce their first album, but the Birthday Party were about to head back to England. And they were just as happy to work again with Tony Cohen, who had produced their recent single. In a later interview, Cohen remembered very little of the sessions for *Send Me a Lullaby*, or even the name of the album. But he did recall that the group were "really fun people," who would "just sit there and play their guitars for three hours nonstop, just playing and playing. I've never seen anyone do that and not get tired of it. And what they came out with was really brilliant in a simple way."[6]

Perhaps uncertain of the quality of their songs, and also still reeling from their experience with British groups, the band gave Cohen license to experiment with recording techniques and sound. He spent a whole night miking Morrison's drums in an upstairs room at Richmond Recorders:

> COHEN: It was in the middle of winter and they were huddled around radiators, and they had the guitar amplifiers downstairs. By the time we'd set up all night, with mike leads going up the stairs, the sun was coming up. So we've got the trains going through East Richmond station, and the

phones ringing at nine in the morning, and the typewriters and all that on the record.[7]

Although only Tony Cohen seems able to hear them.

The Go-Betweens had a considerable backlog of songs to select from for their first LP. But they shunned almost all their earlier material, as well as half the songs they had demo'd for Missing Link in Brisbane earlier in the year. They chose instead to record their latest material, even though they weren't always sure of its quality; the record, they decided, should be more like a newspaper than an archive.

One factor in this decision might have been Forster deferring to McLennan, who had recently written excellent songs like "Hold Your Horses" and "It Could Be Anyone." Morrison recalls that Forster had been anguished, for a time, about McLennan's desire to write songs himself; by this time, though, the issue had clearly been resolved. Of the songs demo'd some months previously, "One Thing Can Hold Us," "Ride," "Arrow in a Bow," "It Took You a Week" (retitled "The Girls Have Moved"), and "Careless" remained. "Eight Pictures" (which, along with "Karen" and "Lee Remick," was one of their first songs) was recorded at this point to showcase aspects of the Go-Betweens in their earliest form—their off-the-cuff humor mixed with paranoia—combined with the band's newest attributes, in the form of Lindy Morrison and her remarkable drum solo. More new songs were written during the sessions.[8] The end result reveals a group struggling with new dynamics. Forster and Morrison were now working constantly on the technical and rhythmic angles of rock music, while Forster and McLennan continued to explore their old cultural obsessions.

During the recording of the album, Forster and Morrison were interviewed for *Waves*, the magazine of local public-radio station 3PBS. Morrison tantalized readers with cryptic news of a special guest on the newly recorded LP, telling them "his name is Numan Freudski and he plays saxophone. He plays on three songs and they sound really good! He wears a hat when he plays saxophone!"[9] "Numan Freudski" was, in fact, James Freud, who had only the previous year had a top forty chart hit with the song "Modern Girl." Having become disillusioned with pop music (although still interested in a large intake of drugs), he had shaved his head and was hanging out with Tony Cohen, who also led a very drug-oriented life at this time. He probably seemed a bit of a faded star at the time (though his biggest commercial success—as a member of the Models—was yet to come), yet involvement with someone like Freud must have appealed to Forster and McLennan, with their bizarre, campy dreams.

> FORSTER: We had mutual friends, like Pierre. Because Pierre was in the Teenage Radio Stars with [him]. James Freud had done "Modern Girl," which we always loved. I still think it's the best thing he's ever done. That appealed to us: "He's just done 'Modern Girl.' Let's get him to play sax on our record!"

The album's working title—suggested by Keith Glass's wife Helena—had been *Two Wimps and a Witch*. *Send Me a Lullaby* came from Morrison, who took as inspiration Zelda Fitzgerald's *Save Me the Waltz*. McLennan, who now considers the album embarrassing and unlistenable, finds a certain

Missing Link promo photo, 1981 *(courtesy of Keith G*

irony in its name, which suggests the kind of irresistible ballads that would later become his trademark. Even at the time the album caused the group no end of anguish—partly because its release was delayed, so the band were forced to live with the suspense of not knowing how the world would judge their debut album. Worse than that, though, Forster and McLennan were unhappy with how it had turned out. The majority of the songs were Forster's, but he no longer liked them; nor did McLennan—who was, however, not yet a sufficiently developed and prolific songwriter to have produced enough substitute material to offset this. True, Forster's songwriting block vanished once the band were settled in Melbourne, but this didn't happen in time to benefit the album, which was finished by the end of July.

The tension was too much for Forster. While on a short trip back to Brisbane, he wrote to Glass to put his case for another recording session, which, he said, would enable him to replace some of his more fragmented art-rock songs with new ones he liked much better:

> FORSTER: A second session [means] a better LP [and] a better chance of a good UK deal. What we'd DO in a second session:
> (1) Replace "Eight Pictures" and "Hold Your Horses"[10]—with two dynamic killer songs.

(2) Re-do "People Know"—a longer version turning a half classic into a true classic (a single?).
(3) Re-do vocal on parts of "Ride" and maybe "All about Strength."
Result—a fantastic contemporary February release.[11]

Back in Melbourne, Forster wrote to Andrew Wilson that "Keith is vague, overworked, and I hate him."[12]—probably because while Glass agreed with Forster that certain tracks on the album weren't that good, he didn't want to foot the bill for more recording. What Glass did instead was to turn the Australian release of *Send Me a Lullaby* into an "8-track $6.99 pop-appeal big seller,"[13] omitting "Eight Pictures," "The Girls Have Moved," and "Arrow in a Bow" (there was a cassette version which featured those tracks as "bonus songs").[14]

The eight-song record ended up not selling too well, particularly when it came into competition with the full-length album released in the UK in February 1982, which contained all eleven songs recorded in the sessions and added the earlier single, "Your Turn, My Turn," to lead off. Australian customers preferred to pay top dollar import price for the full album. This situation might not have bothered Glass in the normal scheme of things, since he was due to receive royalties on the British release. As it turned out, however, problems at Rough Trade meant he would never see any money from them.

Curiously, considering their general feelings about the "art-rock" direction they had taken, and Forster's praise for Melbourne as an inspirational terrain, the next few songs the group came up with were arguably even more indigestible than the harshest tracks on *Send Me a Lullaby*. They included "A Peaceful Wreck," a fast number from McLennan, and "Undo What You Did," a "partly successful dry ballad"[15] of Forster's. Both were added to the live set, which was featuring fewer *Lullaby* songs all the time. In November 1981, the group visited Brisbane, where Forster and Morrison were interviewed by Graham Aisthorpe for local magazine *The Planet*. Their sense of frustration at still being in Australia was, by now, palpable:

> FORSTER: I realize now that Brisbane is a rotting corpse. It stinks. It's terribly infested. It's a town that lacks any sense of sensation. A complete fossil.
> AISTHORPE: We've talked about this town and its people before, and Lindy, I think, formulated the Domino Theory, as it relates to Brisbane bands. Perhaps you'd like to explain it.

Missing Link promo photo, 1981

MORRISON: The Domino Theory is, when one band falls apart in a small town like Brisbane, all the bands fall apart—because when all the bands are incredibly linked and there's only one bass player, who's fairly mediocre at playing bass—he gets to play in all the bands.

Because the scene with the groups is so small [that] when one band falls, the others do too because they're all saying, "Hey, which members are going to play with me?" or "Which members who have left that band are going to ask someone in my band to play?" They fall apart because they get suspicious and they're basically competitive and not interested in anyone else's music but their own.

AISTHORPE: Well, you've decided now to move to Melbourne. Does this mean you've put off the idea of moving to London for a while, or is it just an intermediate step?

FORSTER: See, it's reality, and you can talk about going to England and stuff, but the reality is living in London and . . . I don't particularly want to do that. I see our area more as New York—actually, I see that as the best city in the world for the Go-Betweens to be in.

MORRISON: Yeah, it's like Shakespeare in *Hamlet*: "The dread of something after death—the undiscovered country, from whose bourn no traveller returns—puzzles the will, and makes us rather bear those ills we have, than fly to others that we know not of."

FORSTER: Are you quoting Shakespeare or Peter Walsh?[16]

Around the end of 1981, the group made a rehearsal recording of "People Know" and four of their post–*Send Me a Lullaby* songs, and released them on one side of a limited-edition cassette shared with a group called Pink and Blue, who were "two artists—Jenny Watson and John Nixon," according to Forster. "They started up this group and put out a cassette and they just said, 'Record some stuff on a cassette player, we'll put it on.' And they did. I haven't heard it."[17] The five songs are harsh, though some are enticing. One, "Heaven Says," was

Artwork for *5 New Songs* cassette

eventually recorded for the b-side of the "Cattle and Cane" single; along with 1987's "Cut It Out," it's probably the Go-Betweens' ugliest recorded moment. Others, such as "Undo What You Did," are ungainly yet attractive—Forster finds himself entirely unable to keep pace vocally with his own music, which stops almost long enough for him to catch up and then dashes off without him; the end result is extremely endearing. Another song features the chanted chorus "Cracked Wheat is a meal you eat," probably not an example of art-rock so much as the sign of a Forster work-in-progress, though at this stage in the band's career all was possibility. Some of these songs were later rerecorded in Tony Cohen's bedroom; during the session bikers broke down Cohen's front door looking for money he owed them for drugs—the Go-Betweens hid under the bed.

In Brisbane, the band received praise from an unexpected quarter. John Reid of Razar, the punk group they'd refused to allow on Able, wrote about them in the university magazine *Semper*:

> Brisbane has only one of its original '77/'78 bands intact—the Go-Betweens. Some will quibble about inconsistencies of drummers. They started with anyone who'd stand in on the night and have ended up with maybe the one person more troppo than I am. To me that's intact.
>
> The Go-Betweens were never young, fast and non-boring. I suspect they went to classy private schools, like University, and are thus mature, with savoir faire, and are prepared to pursue a whim to its illogical conclusions.[18]

As old enmities died down, other loose ends were tied up with the official demise of the Able Label. The Four Gods' single, "Enchanted House"/"Restless" was the last release on the label. Andrew Wilson, a fan and friend of the group, had asked for and was granted an Able release.

The Four Gods had a drums/guitar/guitar lineup, but drummer Kerryn Henry was unable to travel to Sydney for the recording session, so, on September 29, 1981, Wilson and his Four Gods partner Peter Morgan were assisted by Lindy Morrison and Grant McLennan on drums and bass respectively. McLennan is credited as "Candice" on the sleeve, continuing the use of one of the fictional girlfriends' names created for "People Say" three years earlier.[19]

Forster with Andrew Wilson in Darlinghurst, Sydney, 1983

In January 1982, despite their uneasiness with Missing Link, the group recorded another single for the label. Two songs were selected: McLennan's poppy and angular "Hammer the Hammer" and Forster's explosive "By Chance." The recording was made at AAV studios during time booked for the Birthday Party's notoriously expensive *Junkyard* album—presumably during session time for which the group had failed to show up. Mick Harvey, who *was* present, realized for the first time the competitiveness that was brewing in the group when Morrison asked him to try and convince McLennan that "By Chance" was clearly the better of the two songs and should be the a-side. Naturally, McLennan and Forster chose to seem aloof from the debate, and "Hammer the Hammer" won.

The *Junkyard* sessions not only produced a great Go-Betweens single, and—eventually—a great Birthday Party album; they also produced a third, rather more bizarre, product in the shape of the Tuff Monks song, "After the Fireworks." As both the Go-Betweens and the Birthday Party were in the studio at the same time, and since the Birthday Party would clearly rather do anything other than record their own album, it was decided that the two groups would collaborate on a song.

The result was one of the few true Forster/McLennan joint compositions. The lyrics are Cave's, and the drumming indisputably Morrison's—as Mick Harvey discovered when he attempted to tell her what rhythm to play. Soon after recording this track, the two groups convened again, on stage at the Tiger Lounge in Richmond, to perform a version of "Ring of Fire." But there was no lasting attempt to forge a creative partnership between the two bands, and "After the Fireworks" remains an isolated if fascinating experiment. Keith Glass released it as a single later that year to recoup money he claims the Birthday Party had squandered in the studio:

> GLASS: [The Birthday Party] were in AAV. It was costing top dollar—$1,000 a night.[20] Despite telling me that all of the tracks were written for the album, they weren't. One night they came up with that track because they had nothing else to do. So I said, "We'll use it as a vehicle to parlay against the accrued costs." They flung it at me: "Here we are, we've come up with this," and I went, "Okay, it'll help." I think Nick Cave came up with the idea to put it out as the Tuff Monks. The general feeling was "put it out." It sold quite a few copies.

In Rowland Howard's recollection, the Tuff Monks name came from Anita Lane, Nick Cave's girlfriend at the time. McLennan agrees with Glass that it was Cave's idea. Wherever it came from, it's a dreadful name. Mick Harvey,

(Jeremy Bannister)

who has nothing positive to say about Glass, denies that releasing the song as a single was the band's idea: "We were over in England and we suddenly heard this record was coming out. I think he must have private meetings where he sits in his living room, imagines we're all there, discusses everything with us and says, 'Right, that'll be okay. I'll do that, then.'"

Glass takes responsibility for the cover picture—of some monks—as well as for the b-side, which consists of parts of the a-side recording reversed, and entitled "After After the Fireworks." The single was released through Au Go Go.

Somewhat earlier, at the end of 1981, with their plans to go to the UK by now firmly set, the three Go-Betweens recorded a confident interview for *Fast Forward*, the cassette magazine published by Bruce Milne and Andrew Maine. The interview appeared in between snippets from *Send Me a Lullaby*, and started with the interviewer, Trevor Block, singing over the top of "Your Turn My Turn," the words "My interview—your interview, my interview—your interview, the Go-Betweens are telling me lies."

(Jeremy Banni)

BLOCK: I'm talking to the Go-Betweens now, Robert, Lindy, and Grant. Where's the rest of you?
MORRISON: That's all it is.
BLOCK: Only three guys?
McLENNAN: Three guys—no, no, it's one guy and two girls.
BLOCK: Right. You've got a new album coming out sometime soon, and it's your first.
McLENNAN: It is indeed our first album.
BLOCK: Is that coming out on Missing Link worldwide?
McLENNAN: No, it's on Missing Link in Australia and Rough Trade in England.
BLOCK: Right. What happened to your deal with Postcard?
McLENNAN: We never had a deal with Postcard. It was just a living arrangement when we were in Glasgow and it was just a one-off thing. None of the bands on the first Postcard[21] had a contract with Postcard at all.
BLOCK: Right. Is your album pretty much material you've been playing live recently?
McLENNAN: No, a lot of the songs we'd stopped doing because the album had been taking so long to get out. But when we realized it was coming out this year we thought we'd better play some of the material off

it. And I think we do seven of the eight songs . . . no, six of the eight songs on the album.
BLOCK: Are you happy with the results?
MORRISON: Yes.
McLENNAN: We're very happy with the sounds. There's a couple of vocal tracks that I think could have been better.
BLOCK: Are you looking forward to going back [to England]? You must have a lot of old friends.
McLENNAN: We don't have any *old* friends. But it'd be good to see some of the people we saw there last time. I think it'd be great to see some of the people from Postcard and see how much they've changed, or if they have.
FORSTER: And also we'll be seeing our good friends the Birthday Party, who we're incredibly close to.
BLOCK: With the Laughing Clowns going across and all, you could set up a rock 'n' roll commune, or something like that.
FORSTER: Well, it'd be great to do . . .
McLENNAN: Certain elements of the bands would look at it as a commune, but some of us would see it as a drug rehabilitation clinic.
[*Laughter*][22]

The last two weeks of April 1982 saw the group play Brisbane, Sydney, and Melbourne in a "farewell tour." It was common knowledge at the time that Australian "alternative rock" fans would always turn out in droves to see groups' "last shows before OS [i.e., overseas]." Forster had almost convinced himself that *Send Me a Lullaby* was so bad that, when released, it would effectively undo all the good work of the previous singles. When the group finally left Australia—they took the same flight as Tracy Pew—it was with a sense of trepidation. They still had sufficient good spirits to lie to Australian music paper *The Record* about plans to invite veteran New York punker Richard Hell to join the band, but they were uneasy about the record they had made and the response they would get on their first journey overseas as a complete group.

12
Before Hollywood

When they arrived in London in May 1982, the Go-Betweens were following a long line of Australian bands who had relocated there in the hope of becoming known to a much larger music scene—one that could hardly be accessed from a base in Australia. The Birthday Party had spent much of the preceding two years in London, and had begun to make quite a name for themselves in Britain and Europe—they had even managed a brief but eventful US tour. The Go-Betweens had similar goals, and in one sense at least they were further along than the Birthday Party had been when they first arrived in the UK—they already had a British record label, Rough Trade, which was about to release *Send Me a Lullaby*.

The Rough Trade label (not to be confused with the Rough Trade record store, by then a separate entity) was a small independent with relatively limited resources, but it had considerable cachet as the home of such key bands in the punk and post-punk universe as the Raincoats, Stiff Little Fingers, Pere Ubu, Young Marble Giants, the Fall, Scritti Politti, and Aztec Camera, and its founder, Geoff Travis, had high ambitions for it, and for the bands he took on. At this stage of the label's development, however, Travis was starting to struggle with the seemingly intractable problem of gaining wider acclaim and bigger sales for the bands he believed in within the independent system of which Rough Trade was an integral part. He would soon despair at the failure of Aztec Camera (the Go-Betweens' former Postcard labelmates) to make inroads on the charts with their Rough Trade releases, and would help arrange their move to a major, Sire, whose marketing and promotion expertise—and money—did ultimately achieve the desired results. Just as importantly, Travis would also soon come up with a band for Rough Trade whose tremendous success would (in Europe, at least) be achieved via the independent system: namely, the Smiths.

Travis hadn't been convinced when Forster and McLennan did their in-person acoustic demo for him in 1980, but he had subsequently become a big fan of their records, and would later recall that the Go-Betweens possessed an "emotional and intellectual maturity" he had never encountered in a band before.[1] When they arrived in England in 1982, he was ready to talk to them about their next album. They, in turn, were keen to work with someone other than Missing Link's Keith Glass. The group were too hard on Glass, who had done a difficult job well, but made enemies of his own artists in the process. Travis, who had after all had the good taste to license the first album from Glass, seemed to be much more the kind of record-company head the Go-Betweens deserved.

> MORRISON: I loved Geoff Travis—incredibly intelligent, Jewish, handsome, gentle, intuitive man. He's just the most stunning man. Very well read, very cultured.

Forster and Morrison moved into the upstairs rooms of a squat in Fulham, West London where their former Zeros bandmate Debbie Thomas was living (members of the Birthday Party moved into rooms in the building as well). It was presumably the commitment to a rock 'n' roll lifestyle, combined with sheer boredom, that was responsible for the widespread heroin use in the squat:[2]

> MORRISON: I used to be the one responsible for cleaning the house because no one else would. I found some heroin of Nick's—I could never afford heroin, I was broke all the time—in an envelope in the kitchen and naturally I just took it. Anyway, Nick came home that night and of course I was really stoned, and Nick said, "How come you're stoned?" because I was the one who was never stoned. And I said "I found some on the kit—"
>
> "You knew that was my heroin!" He went completely berserk about how I'd stolen his heroin, and I said "I didn't know it was yours, I found it on the kitchen floor." But for months afterwards Nick was saying, "You stole my heroin, you took my heroin." And I was *so* happy about it.
>
> Tracy [Pew] was forever having overdoses, always OD'ing. And when they'd hit OD it was like this kind of ritual—that everybody *loved*! They'd fill their syringes with salt water and be pumping him with salt water, they'd be throwing him in the shower. Meanwhile, straight Lindy would be running up and down the stairs *screaming*, "We've got to get an ambulance! We've got to get an ambulance!" and everyone would

say, "Get her out of here! Robert, take her upstairs, get her out of here, don't let her near the phone!" while they walked Tracy up and down the corridor, up and down the stairs, threw him in the shower. It was a regular occurrence. It was an awful scene.

I cooked this fabulous Christmas dinner, and half an hour before Christmas dinner everybody hit up. So when Christmas dinner came, nobody could eat. And everyone was just sitting around, the gravy was congealing in thick lumps over the chicken, the green vegetables were going stiff and the potato was hard. And the plates just sat there all day, it was a tragedy. It was that constant "straight" thing, that constant thing that I was very straight, and I could never move in that other world. Well, I didn't want to. I didn't need to.

Morrison also places McLennan in the middle of this drug culture, partly because she sees him as wanting approval from peers like Cave: "He adored Nick, and, you know, it is a real male-bonding thing—it's to do with that needle, they just love that needle, that ritual of sitting around. It's weird, isn't it? I didn't think it was a particularly radical way to live your life."[3]

Meanwhile the band were on tenterhooks as they waited to see what the influential English music press would make of *Send Me a Lullaby*. The *Sounds* review came first: Dave McCullough gave it five stars in his dense review, musing on the fate of "the Critic," who "rushes off to the toilet almost forgetting to say Go-Betweens are very like Franz Kafka ... Rather amazing, with the emphasis on the 'maze.'"[4]

It was the *New Musical Express* which really mattered, however: at that time, the *NME*'s effect on a group's credibility—in England and Australia—was profound. The anticipated review did not run until the June 26, 1982 issue, and it came as a massive relief to Forster, who had been expecting the worst. Despite declaring that the band were from Melbourne, that the album had been recorded in Sydney, and that its title was *Waiting for a Lullaby*, reviewer Dave Hill delivered where it mattered, pronouncing the album "a record of tremendous depth, a mystery to be fathomed ... edgy, poignant, witty, naked and terse."[5]

But although they were relieved, the group were determined to trust their instincts on their next release, and to return to the kind of music that had originally influenced them, rather than follow the rhythmic or fractured "art" influences that punctuated *Send Me a Lullaby*.[6] One of the newest songs they brought to England with them was McLennan's "A Bad Debt Follows You." Plaintive, bold and almost slick, it was a good yardstick for the

Rough Trade promo photo, 1982 *(photographer uncredited)*

new LP, which would be paid for and released by Rough Trade. Forster soon answered it with the similarly perceptive and crafted "On My Block," and wrote meanderingly to Andrew Wilson:

> We are in rehearsal for an October album, tentatively it has no title. There is a wealth of songs. It's hard to put a finger on what we are doing, I want to make some firm decisions on sound and song style to give the LP some conversational drama.
>
> The weather has been very hot, we've been here four months now. Princess Grace's death is very upsetting, it seemed only a minor accident, all so strange to think this should happen.[7] I think James Stewart could die soon.[8] To know he's still alive and to see his old films from the thirties, that time in between is a wonderful life for him to be able to look back on. But so much of Hollywood is dying, did you see that series *Hollywood*?[9] There was one episode on Hollywood in the beginning, the

Belmondo and Forster, 1983 *(Bleddyn Butcher)*

building of the sets, the sun of California and the people that would have worked [in] early Hollywood. Early Hollywood is a great period of history, a combination that's perfect, of huge casts, stars, intellectual directors and hack directors. The pictures are boring though, even Chaplin, although there has been a Buster Keaton season here that I wish I'd seen.

The Laughing Clowns continue as a miserable soap opera,[10] no doubt [manager] Martin Hardy can tell Sydney all a story, and that can stand.[11]

Forster is here working out the title and, to a lesser extent, the themes of the second Go-Betweens LP. *Before Hollywood* is not a concept album, nor is it related in any way to the days "before Hollywood." But as Forster pursues his rambling train of thought in this letter, we can see the kinds of things that Hollywood might have meant to him. Robin Gold, who directed *Heather's Gloves* and was involved in the early Go-Betweens' social circle in Brisbane in the late 1970s, suggests that they were all familiar with the lively clique of Hemingway's *A Moveable Feast*. Forster might well have been thinking of the Brisbane days before "everyone" left; he might have been thinking about the idea of making history—or remaking history, the way Martin Hardy might do in telling "Sydney all a story" to cover the volatile internal politics of the Laughing Clowns. The days "before Hollywood" were adventurous times. Before the era of sound, films could be made without the hindrance of language differences, in Europe, the USA or Australia (for which claims have been made, with some justification, as the birthplace of the feature film). The ruined European economy after the First World War gave Hollywood the boost it needed to cement its grip on film production; some loose parallels can be drawn with the music business and its perceived domination by Americans. The Go-Betweens, however, with their love and respect for the Monkees, Dylan, the Velvets, Jonathan Richman, etc., would be the last to criticize American cultural domination. In fact, *Before Hollywood* was the first of many albums that the band originally planned to record in the USA, a dream Forster and McLennan would only realize almost two decades later. McLennan explained in 1983:

> We wanted to record *Before Hollywood* in Tennessee with an American producer . . . Jim Dickinson, who has worked with the Byrds and played keyboards with Ry Cooder. We thought he had a willingness to work with us and also he had a great address . . . Route 65, or something like that.
>
> Geoff [Travis] thought we should perhaps record in New York with Chris Stamey. We weren't too sure about that. He played with a band called the dB's. Raucous, melodic sixties band. It just wouldn't have worked. We passed that up and recorded down on the coast in a lazy seaside town.[12]

The "lazy seaside town" was Eastbourne, near Brighton—"like a big retirement home with its very own pier" according to one critic.[13] The producer selected was John Brand, who had worked as engineer and producer to artists ranging from cheap pumping megastars such as Gene Simmons to the snide, funky Magazine and the prog/jazz outfit Brand X.

Brand had apparently contacted Rough Trade in the hope of working with some new groups, and had been assigned first to Aztec Camera (he produced their first album, *High Land, Hard Rain*) and then to the Go-Betweens. Judging by Aztec Camera's singles from that Brand-produced album, "Pillar to Post" and "Oblivious"—folky, yet with catchy, singalong choruses and directly pitched at the charts—McLennan in particular must have wanted the Go-Betweens to move in a more commercial direction. This was going to require both straightening out the wrinkles in Forster's difficult music and convincing Morrison—with whom he was not comfortable at the best of times—that playing "straight" drums was a valid experiment.

It is true that, for various reasons, Morrison's playing on *Before Hollywood* is more conventional. In an interview the following year, McLennan explained it as follows: "I thought there was too much drumming there," he said of her earlier playing, "but Lindy's learnt the beauty of simplicity."[14] In fact, this explanation is not only presumptuous but naïve: the complexity of Morrison's drumming was often a response to the strange timings of many Forster/McLennan songs—timings which previous drummers had simply played through.

> MORRISON: I knew their times were weird. They didn't know how to count. They had no sense of timing. I taught them—I'd sit there going "one and two and three and four." You can understand why they hate me!
>
> When I started in the band, I asked Bruce Anthon what he did about the timing. He said, "Oh, you just play through it, and eventually they straighten it out." I thought, "I'm not going to do that—it's too nice!"

Paradoxically, McLennan's first true pop classic is a bizarre timing experiment, with no chorus: one of the main elements of "Cattle and Cane"—one of the things which makes it so successful, in fact—is the way Morrison so deftly navigates its perilous structure. There is obviously no love lost between McLennan and Morrison, but he pays her the tribute of conceding that "Cattle and Cane" "had a great rhythm, which I don't think any drummer in the world could have played except Lindy Morrison. Never ceases to amaze me, that rhythm thing." Nevertheless, experimentation was not a cornerstone of *Before Hollywood*, and part of the "simplicity" that Morrison had to "learn" the beauty of came in the form of commercial pressures from John Brand. Promoting the album later that year on Australian radio station 2JJJ, McLennan managed to slight the playing of the whole group, including his own, while ostensibly praising Brand:

> John really worked with Lindy's drums. He came to see us rehearse for a whole week, and took notes, and said, "Perhaps you should keep this going and change this beat," stuff like that, and then when we went into the studio he was very strict about singing in tune because Robert and I have a propensity to wander off in directions of sheer anarchic brilliance. And he said, "No anarchic brilliance on this record, just straight melody and in tune." So we did.[15]

The album is certainly very different from *Send Me a Lullaby*. Musically, it is closer to the work of Forster and McLennnan's earlier heroes, such as Television. Lyrically, songs like the poignant "Dusty in Here" and "Cattle and Cane" (both McLennan compositions) initiated an approach, usually perceived as one of innocent sentimentality and nostalgia, that the group would still be embracing (and ultimately perverting) at the end of the decade. "Dusty in Here" was, said McLennan, "the first time I'd ever come to grips—in any writing I'd done—with my father's death. When I wrote that song, it was twenty years ago that he'd died."[16]

"Cattle and Cane," which McLennan wrote on Nick Cave's guitar, also seems to be about McLennan's early childhood after the death of his father—McLennan himself will only say it is "obviously about growing up." Edwyn Collins of Orange Juice, guest singles reviewer for London's *Melody Maker* the week it was released, in March 1983, seized on "Cattle and Cane" as a "monumental record," praising in particular "the line here that's so evocative of childhood ... about leaving his father's watch in the shower. I can't explain what it is about that line, it's just so haunting."[17] McLennan claimed at the time that he wrote "Cattle and Cane" primarily "to please my mother," but that because of the remoteness of the cattle station where she and his stepfather lived, "she hasn't heard it yet. They can't get 240 volts electricity there so I have to sing it over the phone to her."[18] Whether this was true or not hardly mattered: it was a wonderful idea, and summed up the "isolated, rural" idyll promoted by many of McLennan's tracks on *Before Hollywood*. On McLennan's initiative, *Before Hollywood* was dedicated "to our parents."

Marie Ryan, one of the best writers on the Australian music magazine *RAM*, responded immediately to the music and the images McLennan was creating around his past. She wrote of herself (in the third person) on a train, devouring the album's "thick emotional content" as she watched the "dark night drifting by, absorbing the sounds that seem to fit *her* country so well"; the Go-Betweens, said Ryan, draw the listener "into a territory that dwells deep within—*your* past."[19]

Rough Trade promo photo, 1982 *(uncredited)*

Australia is one of the most urbanized countries in the world, and the only New York–style punk group in Brisbane had come to typify, for British and Australian audiences at least, the essence of "Australian-ness" by evoking outback Queensland—not its horrendous racism, its dunderheaded conservatism, or its vapidity, but its beauty, its picturesque fragility—through a screen everybody understood: childhood memory. It made about as much sense as if Tom Verlaine had written a song about the Norfolk and Western Railroad Company's forays into town planning in Roanoke, Virginia, and been credited with thereby exemplifying the American dream; but it also made *perfect* sense. For McLennan's part, he would say (somewhat disingenuously) that he "never really felt Australian"— as if that wasn't a very Anglo-Australian way to feel anyway. Like so many expatriates before him, he had found the perspective he needed in Britain. "Cattle and Cane" also dragged McLennan's personal history into the public fray in a way he might not have anticipated. Clinton Walker conducted the first extended interview with McLennan, in which he celebrated without restraint his friend's arrival as a songwriter. McLennan told him:

> I may have flirted with arrogance and egomania, but I think "Cattle and Cane" is a great song. I don't care what people think, it's one of the best

> songs I will ever write. It was a catalyst for me to hit on a personal yet communicative style of songwriting. Above and beyond everything, it's a great ... and it's an *Australian* song, too.
>
> With "Cattle and Cane" I wanted to write an autobiographical song, and I was aware of that, and I say in the lyrics "Memory wastes." That's perhaps a little clever, but memory can be a wasteland where you wander around and live the rest of your life.[20]

McLennan did not want anyone to think, however, that his "autobiographical" song was a baring of the soul. In 1983 he told Virginia Moncrieff:

> I don't like the word nostalgic, to me it's a sloppy yearning for the past, and I'm not trying to do that in that song. I'm just trying to put three vignettes of a person, who's a lot like myself, growing up in Queensland, and just juxtaposing that against how I am now, and that's the reason why at the end of the song I asked Robert to do four lines, of his impressions, of me and what the song's about and that's why his voice comes in at the end of the song.[21]

There was a propensity for pop songs at this time to include a spoken exultation: ABC's "The Look of Love" was a popular example, and the Human League made it a trademark. Forster had tried singing his small piece at the end of "Cattle and Cane" but couldn't make it work and so spoke it.

Despite Rough Trade's occasional forays into the lower reaches of the mainstream charts, however, neither this or the extraordinary jagged genius of the music of "Cattle and Cane" could make it a hit single, although the response from press and radio was good enough to encourage the band to believe they were getting close. It was certainly considered by many of McLennan's peers to be a classic piece of songwriting, however.[22]

McLennan saw himself as having a distinct musical heritage. He told Walker:

> If my mother had been into John Coltrane and Albert Ayler, I'm sure it would be different. But I come from ... just songs, singalong songs. Scottish folk songs, old war songs, going out to all the properties, and the picnic races ... hearing all the country songs.[23]

This was all well and good, though of course McLennan could not resist overdoing the self-analysis, claiming that the cinema, music, and literature he favored "always in some way [had] something to do with the elements—

Lindy Morrison, 1983 *(Bleddyn Butcher)*

Rough Trade promo photo for *Before Hollywood* (Tom Shee

fire, water, air, earth—men and women fitting into their landscape. That is my prime, great love."[24]

It is testament to the quality and cohesiveness of *Before Hollywood* that these things did not detract from its impact. In keeping with McLennan and Forster's "McCartney and Lennon" dynamic,[25] Forster's songs are far more bombastic, particularly the title track, "By Chance" (rerecorded to make up for it only having been a b-side originally) and "Ask," the album's most charged and powerful song (although "Dusty in Here" is also a strong contender).[26] "As Long As That" was composed by Forster and McLennan in tandem, from an idea of Forster's. "I repaid Grant the compliment of 'Cattle and Cane'" recalls Forster. "We were into this at the time, the two sides of view in one song."

During the *Before Hollywood* sessions, Brand brought in an Australian keyboard player, Bernard Clarke, to play on certain tracks. McLennan says that in working with Clarke, he and Forster were "continuing in our quest to play with very very wonderful pop stars like James Freud": Clarke apparently had a past that included involvement in pre-punk glam cabaret rock, and McLennan remembers him as "looking like Mickey Dolenz and playing absolutely brilliant piano and organ." Some sources have suggested the Go-Betweens were so impressed with Clarke's playing that they actually asked if he would join the band; and he did in fact play some live shows with them. But if Clarke wasn't willing (or was in fact not asked) to become a Go-Between, it was clear that there would have to be someone new to bring to their live performances the texture they'd discovered in Eastbourne with John Brand.

Change continued to be a matter of concern and cause for excitement for Forster, and he was well aware that changing a band for the sake of greater appeal was not without its hazards, as the example of their old friends Orange Juice would show. Forster and Morrison went to see Alan Vega, formerly of Suicide, play in London (they felt the show was "a pathetic joke"), but left halfway through, he told Andrew Wilson, because they'd heard that "Orange Juice were in town at the Columbia Hotel asking after us":

> The Columbia is the visiting pop star place, I spied an air letter to Julian Cope in the mailbox. We found Edwyn's room and there he was, in a boy scout's uniform and listening to an O'Jays album. He was with a New York girl called Cindy who hangs out with Soft Cell and had been on *Top of the Pops* with aforementioned group. Edwyn hasn't changed, as he said of me. Although I detect his wish to be a star. We chatted and then met the rest of the group downstairs,[27] it was a lovely time, sometimes tentative. I heard their new single amongst four tracks that seem to be a patchwork of styles, a bit of funk, Orange Pop, electronic type soul—none of it, in the light of their Postcard work, even strong.[28]

Orange Juice were hanging out with people who hung out with pop stars, and that virtually made them pop stars, too (as opposed to pop musicians). Striving for pop success was also ruining them artistically. Lessons such as these—which had probably been impressed on Forster since he saw the Numbers/Riptides' business practices four years before—were not lost on him. On the other hand, the Go-Betweens were fast approaching the peculiar limbo status of "critics' favorites" who were nevertheless—or consequently—"unable" to sell records.

13
"He's the last to take his coat off"

Dearest Andrew,
Have you heard the news? There's-a-good rockin' tonight. We've been waiting to hear from Robert Vickers, as today was to be his arrival. We'd thought of ourselves as a four-piece, reluctantly I must add, and then Robert offered some new blood, and Grant on guitar so a duel/dual sonic guitar attack from up front.[1]

Forster and McLennan had long been in awe of Robert Vickers: boyishly urbane, he stood out from the crowd wherever he was and whatever he was doing, whether playing bass with the Numbers; playing the male lead in the film McLennan scripted, *Heather's Gloves*; or as a figure in their dreams of a mythical New York. In the late 1970s, they both developed the fantasy that Vickers would not live past his early twenties. Forster said in the 1979 4ZZZ interview that Vickers looked "permanently dead," while in the notes for their unfinished fanzine *Torn Curtain*, McLennan wrote:

Robert Vickers, Brisbane, 1978 *(Tony Forster)*

Rob Vickers—away from it all, the bass seems to be keeping him alive, his sunken eyes cover his pale face, his tongue is pushed into his cheek with endeavor, he is still, he doesn't move, he's the last to take his coat off, he's there and he's rock's next casualty.[2]

As bass player for the band formerly known as the Grudge and Neon Steal but which, on his joining them, became the Numbers, Vickers had been required to wear the mod-style suits that were the group's onstage uniform. What he wore on the streets of Brisbane, however, was far more showy than that forthrightly non-hippie, non-punk wear. Damien Nelson has a memory from the late 1970s of "being with Robert Forster walking down the street in Toowong and we saw Robert Vickers. He'd just bought himself a pair of these suede pointed shoes—he'd started wearing things that if he'd worn them five years before people would have beaten the shit out of him."

Robert Vickers *(Clinton Walker)*

> VICKERS: At the time I certainly dressed a little bit different. I had quite short hair and wore clothing which wasn't really unusual but looked a little odd, I guess. You know, straight trousers, white shirt, jeans—mainly jeans, I guess, or cords, or something. People thought that looked a little odd but not enough that it looked dangerous. But people couldn't really work it out. Wearing school shoes or boots, they just couldn't quite understand it. "Why do you dress like that?"

Peter Walsh believes it was a way of standing apart from the regulation black-leather punk-style outfits of the late 1970s—which were in any case entirely impractical in Brisbane's tropical climate. Local punk band the Leftovers "looked like extras from *The Great Rock 'n' Roll Swindle*," he says. "They had a dress code, everything had to be approved by Sid and Nancy." Vickers' code was every bit as strict, but he was both ruler and subject.

Vickers' initial link with the Go-Betweens was established when he joined the Numbers after returning from a trip to Britain in 1976.

> VICKERS: I went to Corinda High School with this guy Scott Matheson through the last years of high school. We had similar interests in music—the Band, *Star Club* Beatles.[3]
>
> Few things were actually interesting in music at that time. But he went on to do architecture [at Griffith University] and made all these friends, including Mark Callaghan and Alan Reilly and Dennis Cantwell, who were the rest of the band. And they had a guy playing bass, called Tony, who had really long hair and didn't wear shoes and didn't seem to fit in terribly well. So they got me to play bass.

The careers of the Numbers and the Go-Betweens could hardly have been more different, except that they happened in almost exactly the same place. Mark Callaghan—who has gone on to become a well-respected songwriter and music-industry figure—was, according to Vickers, "a really sensible person" who "just knew what to do."

VICKERS: He just put it together, you know, "We're going to have a band, and this is what it's going to be like." And, you know, "we can do it. We'll build a PA." We *built* a PA. That just amazes me now. We got a board from somewhere and went to the university, used their facilities, cut up bits of wood, bought the speakers and put the speakers in. That's what that band was like. We built our own equipment.

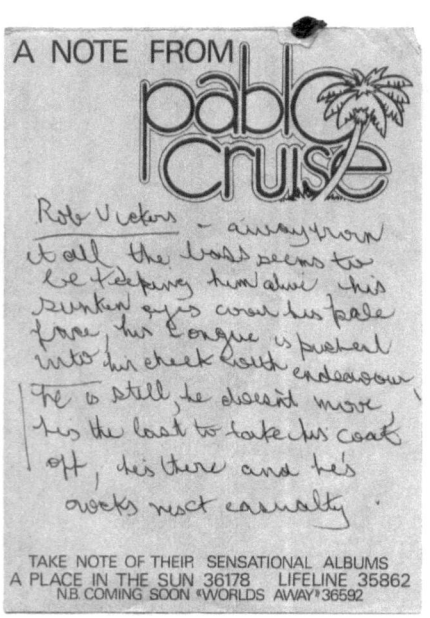

The Numbers recorded three tracks for an Able Label single after the Go-Betweens had recorded "Lee Remick" using their drummer, and the two singles came out at the same time. The Numbers' record—tighter, more conventionally poppy—sold better than "Lee Remick," even before it was remixed and reissued under their new name, the Riptides, to distinguish the Brisbane "band you can count on" from a Sydney group with the same dreary appellation. However, it was soon decided that while Vickers might have looked right, his musicianship was not up to scratch, and he was fired. He left Australia for New York shortly afterwards. McLennan recalls, with no little envy, that "he was a traveler, he just went."

McLENNAN: Stupidly—Robert [Forster] and I have talked about this—we went to fucking *England* first. We should have gone to New York. But by the time I went to New York, at the end of 1979, the scene had gone anyway, had come and gone. Vickers wrote back and we kept in contact and he was in a fucking band in New York. Yeah, great stuff. The Numbers boot you out, man, and you're in a band in New York!

The first night Vickers arrived in Manhattan, he saw a guitar-pop group called the Colors play at CBGBs. They didn't have a bass player. "So I started talking to them," he told a 1984 interviewer, "and went down to the guitarist's flat, which was disgusting but interesting, started playing with him—and joined the band within a matter of a week."⁴ Robert Forster, who never saw the Colors but is obviously familiar with their records and the "buzz," says that they were "in a very nice way, like the Bay City Rollers." The group were sufficiently good-humored to reference their mainstream pop affiliations with in-jokes like a single with a fake Japanese sleeve. But by 1982, after two big lineup changes and two moderately successful independent records, the Colors were in decline.

The Colors' debut EP (Robert Vickers second from left)

Peter Walsh and Michael O'Connell, Walsh's former bandmate in the Apartments (the third group to release a single on Able), periodically appear like fairy godbrothers in the Go-Betweens' lives to aid or inspire them—often to their own ultimate disadvantage. In this case it was Walsh, who was in New York and playing guitar in the final lineup of the Colors. He played Vickers a prerelease tape of *Before Hollywood*.

> VICKERS: I'd heard *Send Me a Lullaby*, it was very good, but unformed. *Before Hollywood* was great, everything had come together. [Walsh] said they were worried they wouldn't be able to do the album justice live, so they were looking for someone else. He said the Laughing Clowns were in London looking for a bass player, too, and he was thinking of calling the Laughing Clowns. He might even have suggested I call the Go-Betweens.

Inspired, Vickers wrote to apply to join the band as bass player. Switching Grant from bass to guitar was an obvious move—he'd played guitar on both albums anyway, as well as bass—but it had not occurred to anyone in the group: the New York bass player they were thinking of was still in that "what if Richard Hell came through the door" fantasy mode. Vickers' arrival in London nearly coincided with Clinton Walker's return to Australia: Walker was around just long enough to take a picture of McLennan ceremonially handing over his bass to Vickers.

The second Robert in the group was to bring a greater pop angle to the Go-Betweens, at a time when they really needed it.

> VICKERS: They knew all about the Colors and what kind of band that was. It was a pop band. They knew what I liked. In fact, I remember Grant picking me up at the tube station the day I arrived in London and going,

The ceremonial handing over of the bass guitar *(Clinton Wa*

"You still like Creedence, don't you? You still like Dylan, don't you?"

The night of the bass handover, Forster wrote to Andrew Wilson:

> It's the end of the party, Clinton's Saturday night farewell: he leaves Wednesday. Rob Vickers turned up this morning—the blond bowlcut hair, looking like someone out of Paul Revere and the Raiders—Geoff Titley, Cameron Allen gang with some gin (I made a damper[5]—very successful—and drank some gin). Ross and Judy Crighton, Aztec Camera and some more people, Biff from the Laughing Clowns.[6] Vickers hit the bottle and is, in Mr. Walsh's words, comatose.[7]

Rehearsals began with the new recruit in the second week of February 1982, but the band could not afford the luxury of easing their new member in gently; the first Go-Betweens show with Vickers was at the Rock Garden on February 16, just over a week before the single of "Cattle and Cane" was released. Short tours of Switzerland, Britain, and Germany followed, and Vickers settled into the group. Within two months, he was fully ensconced and between May 4 and 7, a new single was recorded, with John Brand producing. The two tracks were Forster's "Man O' Sand to Girl O' Sea" and

McLennan's "Newton Told Me," and they indicated new directions for the group, being closer to fantasy pop than reveries about memory and youth. On May 10, a full six weeks after "Cattle and Cane" had been released, the group filmed a drab video for it in an antique shop in Fulham.[8] In the interests of group solidarity, or because the band thought it was somehow the right thing to do, Vickers mimed playing bass in the video, although he had not played on the recording. The minor deception entailed in this, however, succeeded in upsetting everyone involved—including Vickers himself—beyond the point of reason.

Robert Vickers carved a niche for himself in the Go-Betweens, but the effect looked nothing like a niche. He seemed more like a new, self-sufficient planet in the already established solar system of the previous three-piece. In live shows, he usually positioned himself to one side of the stage, and appeared entirely within his own world, tongue firmly—and literally—in his cheek. Vickers never spoke on stage, nor did he do backing vocals. He was always dressed impeccably, in a style he now describes as "Regency . . . Regency *dandy*, perhaps?"

Although he was committing himself to a band that was based on the other side of the Atlantic from his adopted home, and the place where his partner Janie lived, Vickers probably did not imagine the band would be based in the UK for long. The group were at this stage committed to recording their third LP in the US and everybody favored New York. As Vickers told me at the time: "The first album was recorded in Australia, the second one was recorded in England, so the third one should definitely be recorded in America."[9]

On May 16, the Go-Betweens returned to Australia as conquering heroes—on the strength of a few good reviews in the English music press and, of course, a superb second album. Many of the friends they had left behind—especially the Brisbanites among them—had meanwhile raised themselves to positions of relative power in the media, at least in the youth/new wave stakes, and this was to prove advantageous to the band, even though real chart success was not forthcoming.

At Studio 211 in Sydney, July 1983 *(Francine McDouga*

14

"Can you shut your fucking mouth for a minute?"

Before Hollywood and the "Cattle and Cane" single were released in Australia on Stunn, a small label vaguely allied with EMI. The Stunn pressings were of poor quality and their distribution was rather limited, but the Australian press was avidly interested in the group—as were friends and acquaintances. One old friend who recognized the change in the Go-Betweens' fortunes was John Willsteed of Zero, which by this time had mutated into Xero en route to its final incarnation as Xiro. Willsteed designed and printed leaflets condemning the Go-Betweens as traitors, and arranged to have them distributed among the audience and thrown onstage when the group returned to play in Brisbane at Baroona Hall on June 2, 1983. Willsteed, perhaps because of his drug and alcohol use, had a streak of cruel humor that helped him carry out plots most people would just talk about. By his criteria, the Go-Betweens were traitors to Brisbane. Willsteed himself never wanted to leave it—not because he loved it, but because he loved and hated it at the same time. Essentially, although the Go-Betweens drew inspiration from Brisbane, they could feel little loyalty to it—nor to Australia as a whole. Apart from anything else, Australia could not sustain the group financially, let alone creatively.

Willsteed was unusual in believing that a group could betray a town like Brisbane, but many of his peers around the country felt the Go-Betweens had betrayed the cause of punk rock when they agreed to appear on the commercial Australian TV show *Countdown*. Since the mid-1970s, the show, hosted by larger-than-life "talent coordinator" Ian "Molly" Meldrum, had been a national institution, a Sunday night rock show that presented videos and mimed performances from local and international acts. It was extremely influential—it is widely credited, for instance, with Abba's first success outside Sweden, as well as with breaking Australian acts such as Air Supply, Little River Band, Men at Work, and Icehouse. It was of course derided by those outside the mainstream, as well as by those within the mainstream whom it ignored. An appearance on *Countdown* was assumed to signify a group's "arrival," and virtually guaranteed commercial success.[1]

On May 30, 1983, three days before the Willsteed display, all the Go-Betweens except McLennan spent the evening in a 2JJJ studio recording a program called *The Go-Betweens Play Their Favorite Records*. Stuart Matchett, who had once lived with Morrison in Brisbane, was the host of the show, which aired some time later, on July 7, four days after the band played a one-hour live set on the station. Perhaps wisely, they did not choose any of their friends' records to play; instead they showed their extensive knowledge of—and broad tastes in—music, beginning with the Weather Girls' contemporary soul-disco hit, "It's Raining Men." The band sound stoned, but Matchett just sounds happy:

> MATCHETT: Who chose the Weather Girls?—and tell us a bit about it.
> MORRISON: The big fag Robert!
> MATCHETT: You can't say that!
> MORRISON: [*Laughing*] It's all right.
> FORSTER: The reason that I picked that is it's a current favorite. It's a great title, "It's Raining Men."
> MATCHETT: When did you first hear it?
> FORSTER: [*Starts laughing*] When we were doing *Countdown* [*Laughter*].
> MATCHETT: What was that like, doing *Countdown*?
> MORRISON: Fantastic. There's a lot of performance going on while it's being made that I'm sorry a lot of people in the world miss out on. The performance backstage is far more fun than the performance on camera.
> FORSTER: It can get quite out of hand, Molly and Gavin . . .
> MORRISON: We also met Molly in London, and he took us out for four hours of drinking piña coladas and champagne.

Vickers then chose Status Quo's "Face without a Soul," which faded into Morrison's choice, the Carpenters' "Close to You."

> MORRISON: I really like the Carpenters a lot. I was very, very sad when Karen died, and I love their songs, the melodies are always really good, but I really love the way Richard Carpenter arranged them. And the drum parts are always absolutely brilliant. There are always stops in the songs and then the drums lead in to a fuller instrumentation, and they're always

just "plop plop ploplop plop plop," slow rolls, and they're always lovely. Every Carpenters song is arranged the same way, though [*Laughter*].
VICKERS: The secret of success.
MATCHETT: Had you heard that Carpenters song when it first came out?
MORRISON: I don't know, I know I've liked it for many years, but whether or not I'd be prepared to date myself so totally is . . . [*Laughter*]. Funnily enough, I'd just taken a Carpenters record out of the library in London—they have record libraries as you know, Stuart . . .
MATCHETT: We should admit that Lindy and I were once in London at the same time and we used to constantly be running down to the local record library and getting records out.

MORRISON: And is this where I'm allowed to tell JJJ listeners from whom I bought my first drum kit ten years ago?
MATCHETT: Oh, yeah.
MORRISON: It was Stuart Matchett. I bought a Premier drum kit from him ten years ago. For a hundred dollars! But um, yes, I got the greatest hits of Karen Carpenter out of the library and two days later she died, I couldn't believe it. She was only thirty-one.[2]

Morrison was thirty-two at this time, a fact which was usually not mentioned except when she was being baited by the Birthday Party—being over thirty was apparently too old for "new music." Forster sensitively chipped in: "I can remember 'Close to You' coming out, and I liked it . . ."

The next choice was his, a song called "Lost Is Found," by Susan Springfield.

FORSTER: She used to be in a band called the Erasers that came out of New York 1977, 1978. I read a few articles about them, saw a few photos of them, they were an all-girl group except they had a male drummer. I just thought they looked absolutely fantastic and the song titles looked great. Susan Springfield was at one stage Richard Hell's girlfriend. And they just seemed to be the perfect New York loft group of all time. Then I came across this single after the Erasers had split. This is her solo single and I think someone from Television had something to do with it.[3]
VICKERS: Fred Smith mixed it.
FORSTER: Yeah, Fred Smith mixed it. I imagine there's sort of New York semi-celebrities playing on it.

> VICKERS: No.
> FORSTER: And the song I really like is called "Lost Is Found."

This was followed by a Lenny Bruce skit, "White, White Woman, Black, Black Woman." Matchett then turned the conversation to Vickers' experiences in New York.

> MATCHETT: And Robert, Robert Vickers, you were interjecting there because you actually lived in New York for a while, didn't you?
> VICKERS: Yes! Yes! Three and a half years. Awfully long time.
> MATCHETT: What did you do there?
> VICKERS: I had an apartment, and a job, and I was in a band. I just lived there and did everything people normally do in New York. I went to the movies, watched the Yankees . . .
> MATCHETT: You make it sound very easy—I thought they didn't let people stay there very long.
> VICKERS: Well, they don't. You just don't tell them you're there. Once you're in, you're in, and getting you out is the hard problem. They'll never find you in New York.
> FORSTER: It's a jungle.
> VICKERS: If you're prepared to make allowances, you can get a lot out of the city.

It was also during this 1983 tour that I interviewed the Go-Betweens for the first time (though I had exchanged a few friendly words with Lindy while acting the part of doorman at a 3RRR-FM benefit in Melbourne in 1981: something along the lines of "—You can't go in there." "—But I'm in a band, the Go-Betweens"). On this occasion, I had camped out at the Jump Club in Collingwood, in inner-city Melbourne, to get an interview with the group for my fanzine, *Distant Violins*. I had already published, in my "current" issue, a letter I'd received from the executive producer of *Countdown* explaining why he would not ask the Go-Betweens to appear on the show, despite my suggestion; this was enjoyably confusing given that they had in fact been invited to appear on the program soon after the letter was written.

I had wanted to speak to each Go-Between on their own, but McLennan's interview was done in the company of Mr. Pierre, otherwise known as Peter Sutcliffe, who had been a member of Teenage Radio Stars, the Fabulous Marquises, and JAB. Both he and McLennan were drunk, and—luckily for the present-day reader—more interested in taking campy pot-shots at each other than in answering my rather dry questions.

NICHOLS: The big thing with Postcard seemed to be all these comparisons with the Velvet Underground. How do you think you fitted in with that?

McLENNAN: I don't know. I know *NME* said that Josef K were the Velvets [in] 1967 and that Orange Juice were Velvets '69. If we were anything, the Go-Betweens were the Velvets at their first rehearsal. Not quite grasping the songs, but the initial draw was there.

NICHOLS: You hardly play any of *Send Me a Lullaby* any more—what happened?

McLENNAN: Well, we weren't playing that in England because we'd written a whole lot of new songs and we were doing those. But on coming back to Australia, we taught Robert Vickers, the new bass player, "Careless." We do a new version of that, and we do "It Could Be Anyone," as well. We only do that because Pierre—and Clare and Steve from the Moodists—really like that song.

PIERRE: What?

McLENNAN: "It Could Be Anyone."

PIERRE: [*No response*]

McLENNAN: [*Sarcastically*] It's off the first Boys Next Door album.[4]

NICHOLS: Do you think *Send Me a Lullaby* is a good album?

McLENNAN: Not really. The English version is a lot better than the Australian version, because it has four other tracks on. But I don't think it's a *good* album, I think—

PIERRE: Yes, it is.

McLENNAN: You think so?

PIERRE: Brash.

McLENNAN: Yeah.

PIERRE: "Brash" is one of the words you could use to describe it.

McLENNAN: No, no, sorry, I don't think it's a great album, but I think it is a *good* album. There are songs on it which I'm embarrassed about now because I don't think we played as well as we could have. And also, just given the relationship between ourselves and the producer—well, we were the producers—and the engineer, Tony, I don't think we gave full service to the songs. Why, what do you think?

NICHOLS: It's not as coherent as the second one. Some songs don't exactly fit together. I thought it was strange the way you chopped it up for Australian consumption.

McLENNAN: No, no. See, that wasn't something that we wanted to do, David. It was Missing Link, Keith Glass in particular . . . Let's not forget that we recorded in July of 1981 and it didn't come out until about March of 1982, and the original idea was for that record to come out at Christmas. So that's why it was an eight-track record, low-price, with the so-called more commercial songs. But what happened is, it was delayed, and given the initial arguments it should have come out as the eleven-track English record. Of course, we're upset about that—and Robert had more reason to be upset, because Keith saw me as being a more commercial writer than he was. I think that's unfair, because Robert's melodies you just have to absorb more than mine, that's all.

NICHOLS: When you write songs, do you write them totally for yourself, and if other people like them that's good, or do you write them hoping—

McLENNAN: No! I write a song totally for myself. To please myself and to live up to my standards of what makes a good song, completely—

PIERRE: Are you hungry?

McLENNAN: [*To Pierre*] A little bit, not very much. [*To Nichols*] No, completely. If someone likes a song that I wrote, well then that's . . . no, being in the band for five to six years of course I'm aware of what works as a song and what doesn't, but I've always—and Robert feels the same way—I've always written to my standards of what makes a song, and if it somehow connects with people watching, then that's a bonus. What did you think of the Birthday Party when they came out?

NICHOLS: When you go and see a band and expect them to be incredibly wild, you're disappointed that they're not even wilder.[5]

McLENNAN: Nick, Tracy, and Kate, his girlfriend, lived for us . . . *with* us for a while in London, and we'd played with them in Australia and played with them in England and we're quite good friends. And I know how Nick feels about Australia, because the direction they took in Australia, especially the last tour, they were supposed to be the wild, anarchic, Antichrist worshippers, that sort of stuff. Nick hated that, but there's a part of him which also enjoys that sort of glory. This time, coming back, he was worried about the audience expecting him to do the whole Iggy Pop/Jim Morrison death wish on stage. And this time he consciously made a decision not to be like that. A lot of people expected him to, and were very disappointed when he didn't. And that was the big reason why Mick Harvey didn't come back. Because he was sick of coming back and just having a laudatory, wild, easy time in Australia. Australians are very strange, because you go away, and when you come back they just go, "Great, great, they're back!"—which is completely farcical.

NICHOLS: How much do you think being away from Australia and being exposed to—

PIERRE: Methadone—

NICHOLS: [*Mumbles*]—is going to affect what people think of as your naiveté?

McLENNAN: Because we go away and are exposed to the world, we're not as naïve?

NICHOLS: Mmm.
McLENNAN: Well, people who don't know us might think that way, but people who know us, like Pierre, know we're complete dags, wherever we are.[6] All four of us, before we went away, all four of us have traveled.
NICHOLS: No, I wasn't saying . . . I mean, in two years' time you could be writing a song like "Cattle and Cane"—
McLENNAN: Well, I hope in two years' time I'm not writing a song like "Cattle and Cane."
PIERRE: [*Challenging*] Why?
McLENNAN: But I—
PIERRE: Why, is the question. Why?
McLENNAN: [*To Nichols*] Did you ask that?
NICHOLS: No.
PIERRE: [*To Nichols*] Don't you want to know why he doesn't want to?
McLENNAN: First of all, I'll say I hope I'm not writing a song like "Cattle and Cane" because I hope I'm writing a song as *good* as that—but *different*.
PIERRE: Ooh, aren't we sly?
NICHOLS: I can't imagine you writing songs about being jaded or—
PIERRE: Hotel hell?
McLENNAN: When we tour Europe we insist that we don't go into hotels. We get put up in people's homes, in Austria or Switzerland or wherever it is . . . so we can actually write Swiss songs or Austrian songs . . . [*Pause*] Sitting across from the table from me is a faded rock star.
PIERRE: And washed-up has-been.
McLENNAN: Washed-up has-been, one of the has-beens, that was . . .[7]
PIERRE: A *legendary* has-been.
McLENNAN: Teenage Radio Stars . . .
PIERRE: JAB . . .
McLENNAN: He wrote "Shivers" before Rowland Howard wrote it, Mr. Pierre.
PIERRE: My new song is on the next Birthday Party record. "Wings Off Flies."
McLENNAN: Oh, come on, "Wings Off . . ." how *dare* you claim that! You gave Nick the actual phrase "Wings Off Flies," you didn't—
PIERRE: It was a Marquises song!
McLENNAN: I know, I know, he's told me all about it, but it's not your—
PIERRE: It's my chorus, it's the whole punchline.
McLENNAN: See how sensitive he is?
PIERRE: The whole point of the song is the chorus.
McLENNAN: That's how Pierre gets his songs recorded now. All his old friends record his songs.

Conversation turns to the group's *Countdown* experience, their first true encounter with the world of commercial pop. *Countdown* had provided a set that looked a bit like a barn, with hay bales scattered around it, in which the group mimed to the song, and McLennan's earnest straight-to-camera delivery was unusual.[8] Mr. Pierre mumbled something about McLennan hiding in a corner on *Countdown* and looking crass.

>McLENNAN: It's a very good clip, Pierre.
>PIERRE: It's a shitty clip.
>McLENNAN: Pierre, considering *Countdown*, it's a very good clip.
>PIERRE: The thing is, you guys are sort of tasteful. I want to get . . . my country and western single[9] on *Countdown*—I want it to be as tacky as possible. Me singing the first two verses, right, it's "Lost Highway," right?—
>McLENNAN: They wouldn't have you, mate, 'cause you're fuckin' dirt.
>PIERRE: Shut up.
>McLENNAN: They'd know that you'd just think it was a big fuckin' joke and—
>PIERRE: I *love Countdown*. I want to be just drivin' along the road and drinking and have a girl on my arm and stuff—
>McLENNAN: You can't have driving along the road because you've got to appear live before they'll play your clip.
>PIERRE: It's on one of those screens behind me. Then after the middle section when I crash the car because . . . you know, "Lost Highway," I want to have it [so] I'm walking in these clouds—like dry ice.
>McLENNAN: [*To Nichols*] "Lost Highway" by Hank Williams.
>PIERRE: I'm walking in heaven and in the background is my car, turned upside down and burning.
>McLENNAN: He's talking about me being crass in the corner . . . Listen to this! Fuck!
>PIERRE: I could be on *Countdown*. You guys are too tasteful, too aware of not being stupid. I've got a better sense of humor, you know, I've—
>McLENNAN: No, you haven't got a better sense of humor, but you're far more willing to be an arsehole on camera or on stage than we are. We don't take ourselves seriously! We're just aware that when most people think of the Go-Betweens they think: tasteful, nice, scones—
>PIERRE: Beautiful—
>McLENNAN: Jam and cream, all that sort of stuff. No heroin . . . That's what they think.
>PIERRE: And your eyebrows.
>McLENNAN: Listen. Listen. Everybody in Sydney was saying "Grant, how do you do your eyebrows like that?"

PIERRE: I told you, Grant, when I showed you the clip at my house—your eyebrows, you were just too earnest. Too appealing.
McLENNAN: But I looked very nice on the *Countdown* clip.
PIERRE: I was really glad to see you on *Countdown*, I was just—
McLENNAN: But you always say that! You always say that Robert looks so good, and you always run me down. As some kind of competition to make me—
PIERRE: I really like Bobby, right, but he doesn't muck around with me. You do.
McLENNAN: He doesn't muck around with you because I know you far better than he does. He's never slept in the same bed with you.
PIERRE: And also he doesn't really do anything by himself any more. But I'm not running you down. He's so incredibly daggy, right, he doesn't falter—
McLENNAN: And I'm semi-daggy sometimes.
PIERRE: You have doubts, I think, and I don't think he does. You looked so imploring on *Countdown*, I just thought it was really awful.
McLENNAN: [*To Nichols*] He's asking good questions. You should be asking these.

Shortly afterwards, Pierre in fact took over the tape recorder and began asking questions himself:

PIERRE: How has the singing ratio evolved from like, say, seventy-thirty [percent] from Bobby to you, has it been natural because . . . You used to have Bobby singing your songs, right? And nowadays you're singing your own songs. How did that happen? Was it just that you got more confident, was it that he—
McLENNAN: Don't answer your question before you ask it. The reason I didn't sing earlier on was because I was coming to grips with the bass and also I felt doubtful about my ability to sing. But after a while I realized I could do both things at the same time. And also—while Robert, I thought, sang the songs I wrote incredibly well, there was a different interpretation on them, just through the way he sang it . . . As a songwriter, I can write a song and say to Robert, "you sing it," because I think he could do it better, whereas I don't think Robert could ever say that to me. He would always sing his own songs. But we've taken a song to practice and I have said to Robert, "I would prefer you to sing it," because I think he could sing it better than I could.
PIERRE: But that hasn't been the case recently, has it?
McLENNAN: Um . . .
PIERRE: You're furrowing your eyebrows again.

McLENNAN: Sorry. No, there are a couple of new songs which I think Robert could sing better than I could. But when we come to rehearsing them electrically, whether I'll say, "Robert, you should sing them," I don't know.

PIERRE: And is it because a singer always prefers his own interpretation of a song?

McLENNAN: What it comes down to is that Robert, I think, has more—his voice has a lot more character than my voice does. I think my voice is a very AM-type, sweet, melodic voice. I might be wrong. But I think Robert Forster has the capacity to sing a song in a variety of ways. I sing it in a way that is always close to the heart. It's a very intangible thing, I can't explain it in any other way. I'd like to know what you think about that.

NICHOLS: I suppose what it boils down to is why you write songs in the first place.

McLENNAN: I write songs because I'm in a *group*.

PIERRE: Bullshit. Fucking bullshit. Is it true or is it not true that you write songs because you're fuckin' . . . if you were sitting at home, right, and you weren't in a group, you'd be banging away on a guitar . . . and you'd be singing . . .

McLENNAN: If I was singing—sink—sitting at home, and I wasn't in a group, I would not be writing songs, I would be—

PIERRE: You would never bang away on a guitar?

McLENNAN: Can you shut your fucking mouth for a minute? I'd be writing novels or poetry, I would not be writing songs.

PIERRE: But wouldn't you be banging away on a guitar and writing songs to amuse yourself?

McLENNAN: I wouldn't, I wouldn't. Because the only reason I'm in this band is accident. Pierre, look, the only reason I started in this band was because Robert said, "Grant, you should play guitar, you should be in this band with me." I had no intentions of being in a band. My intentions were to continue with my academic career, support myself through tutoring or something, and write. So, at the moment I am writing through melody and lyrics. If this band finishes—and it's going to finish . . . I do not want to do anything in a musical area after this band. I will continue with what I wanted to do.

15

Out of Step

Returning to Britain in August 1983, the Go-Betweens went back into the studio with John Brand to rerecord Forster's "Man O' Sand to Girl O' Sea." At the same time, they recorded a new b-side, with McLennan's "This Girl, Black Girl"—probably the first of his Go-Betweens songs to take on the Australian bush-ballad form that has since become a favored style for him—replacing the earlier "Newton Told Me."[1] It is unclear at this point why it was thought necessary to redo the recording they had done in May, but relations between the Go-Betweens and Rough Trade had evidently become problematical, as Forster indicated in a letter he wrote to me that September. The single was due to be issued in mid-October, he explained, although he wasn't sure it would happen:

> Rough Trade are in severe financial trouble—like before, only this time worse. Probably financial stress had led them to conclusions like, "your music is completely out of step with what's going on." They've changed noticeably in their own enthusiasm towards us since [our] getting back.

The upside, he added, was that "other English companies are interested in us if Rough Trade hit the wall or hit us.[2]

The Go-Betweens had gone back to England with a manager, Clive Miller, in tow. Miller had booked the band's recent shows in Australia, but this was his first foray into the thorny world of band management.[3] His mettle was soon tested as he negotiated the group's difficulties with their English label,[4] for example, the fact that, having invested as much as £5,000 in recording "Man O' Sand" twice,[5] Rough Trade apparently found itself unable to allot more than £40 for its promotion.[6]

Whatever problems the band and their record company were having,

the Go-Betweens were nevertheless in the thick of the Rough Trade "scene" at this time. Sensitive to the isolation foreigners often feel on first arriving in sometimes inhospitable London, Forster and Morrison gave a party at their house for Milwaukee's Violent Femmes, who were visiting after their debut album had been released in the UK by Rough Trade. The Go-Betweens also played a prestigious show at the Venue opening for the label's new hopefuls, the Smiths, a Manchester group some were hailing as "the new Orange Juice."

A European tour followed: Scandinavia, the Netherlands, and Germany. A sneak visit through the Iron Curtain into Czechoslovakia on October 26—on the pretext of giving a lecture on music—was a highlight of the tour. The group played an unadvertised show in a fully lit university lecture theater to an audience attracted by word-of-mouth publicity. Their only amplification was a microphone on a lectern hooked up to a public address system. They were paid by donations in Czech currency left onstage at the end of the show, found a late-night restaurant and spent most of the money on dinner for themselves and anyone who had come with them, then used the rest to buy petrol and returned to Germany the same night.

Two weeks later, back in Britain, they spent time at Pathway Studios recording demos commissioned by Rough Trade for their third album. They demo'd eight songs, but—following the pattern they'd established from the first album onwards—only half of them would make it onto the finished record, the others giving way to more recent material. This practice was not always to the band's advantage; it could be argued that some of the demo'd but then abandoned songs are fresher—perhaps even better—than songs that made it onto *Spring Hill Fair* the following year.

"Unkind and Unwise," "The Old Way Out," and "Part Company" were all deservedly rerecorded for the album. The breezy but slight "Emperor's Courtesan" and "Newton Told Me" (recorded again after originally being slated for the b-side of "Man O' Sand") were indicative of McLennan's new direction, but were not included (although "Newton Told Me" was used as a b-side to "Part Company"). And three quite brilliant songs—"Marco Polo Jr.," "Attraction," and "Sweet Tasting Hours"—remained unreleased until very recently.[7] "Sweet Tasting Hours" is particularly interesting—a duet by Forster and Morrison which might well be a dig at Rough Trade for the

Live ca. 1983 (photographer unknown)

poverty the band were living in at the time.

Other patterns were being delineated just as surely: McLennan was by now writing songs at twice the rate of Forster, who needed the impetus and momentum generated by impending studio recording, as opposed to demo recording, to get his songs finished. Forster later told *Puncture* that "a month before recording" each of the Go-Betweens albums, "he'd have twenty-five songs, and I'd have three and a half." At the same time, he couldn't resist a dig at McLennan: "Grant can write twenty-five songs—and fifteen of them are crap."[8] However that may be, there's no doubt that of Forster's songs on the Pathway demos, only "Part Company" is fully formed.

After the demos had been completed, the band met with Rough Trade to talk about their ideas for recording the third album—they wanted to do it in New York, and they were looking for a more generous recording budget. One Rough Trade employee remembers a figure of £12,000 being mentioned.[9]

It was a difficult time to have such a discussion. As Forster had indicated in his September letter, Rough Trade was having financial problems, and as a result far more preoccupied than before with the bottom line—and with that dangerous notion of "commercial potential." The Smiths had had considerable success in the second half of 1983, giving Rough Trade its first top ten single in November with "This Charming Man," and they were understandably the label's top priority as they prepared to record their debut album that winter. The Go-Betweens, on the other hand, had sold relatively few records (the same Rough Trade source suggests *Before Hollywood* had at this point sold only around six thousand copies worldwide).

With their immediate future in the balance, the group flew to the US just before Christmas for a short tour. Before their New York show at Danceteria, they had dinner with Geoff Travis (who was in New York with the Smiths to line up the US licensing of their future records to Sire, the proceeds from which would allow him to keep them on Rough Trade in the UK). Travis told the Go-Betweens that Rough Trade had decided they could not fund their album—at least, not at the level the band were asking for, and not for a

New York recording. At this point, band and label agreed to part ways.

If Rough Trade truly felt the demo'd songs lacked commercial potential, one has to wonder if they really listened to "Part Company," to my mind one of the most perfect pop ballads ever written. (On the other hand, since it wasn't a hit when it was released on Sire the next year, maybe they were right!) But the new songs certainly did not have that organic, nostalgic feel that *Before Hollywood* brought off so perfectly, and this conceivably posed a marketing and image problem as far as Rough Trade was concerned.

Lindy Morrison, talking to Marie Ryan some months later, had her own theory:

> I think it comes down to our image. Even though Rough Trade pretend they're not into that, they are, and our image doesn't fit. We've never fitted into an English scenario. They just don't know how to cope with the way we look. And also the way we are!
>
> We are different, psychologically and emotionally, to the English bands. For a start we're older, and it makes you more assertive. We tend to be much more boisterous. And all those things mitigate against you in relation to the English because they're a reserved, conservative group of people. And Australians aren't![10]

Ironically, the Go-Betweens' US dates seemed to go better than those the Smiths played:

> CLIVE MILLER: I just loved New York, after the negativity of London, the fact that people resented Australians. New York people were captivated by the idea of the Go-Betweens, an Australian band they'd heard about. It all went extremely well. The Smiths were there at the same time. Our tour went really well, we got great reviews. Relatively speaking, the Smiths' one had been a bit of an anticlimax, the hype just didn't translate over the Atlantic.

One reason for the Smiths' immediate success in the UK was the fact that much of their imagery derived from what seemed to anyone who'd grown up elsewhere to be rather tawdry and unappealing elements of British popular culture. When Lynden Barber interviewed Robert Forster for *Melody Maker* in late 1984, he felt bound to draw Forster out on the subject of the Smiths, whose popularity Forster had obviously given some thought to:

> That interview where he said, "I'd chain myself to Wigan Pier, that's where my heart is"—there's a certain amount of Englishness I can take in, and then it's just a mystery to me. There's a heart to it that I can't get to. I

probably don't like it, as well, because it's a very damp center.

Everything from *Coronation Street* to Terence Stamp to the flowers were all bits that fitted and he could glue them all together and it came over as a vision. I mean, that's something I could probably do in Australia, because I know all the people, know all the things to say that would put us in that position.[11]

Back in Australia, groups like Mental As Anything were in fact doing exactly that—albeit with more straightforward satire and less verve than the Go-Betweens would. But the Go-Betweens were trying to flourish within a foreign culture—one they couldn't tap into in the way Morrissey, to their evident frustration, apparently effortlessly could. If they were to succeed, it would have to be by their music alone, without the advantage of additional cultural props.

Many Australians have felt that they are treated as second-rate in Britain. The Go-Betweens were accepted there despite their Australianness, not because of it. In an *NME* interview late in 1983, Forster remarked that the group incorporated "a few elements of Australia" into their sound: "There are things we could do that English people would find tantalizing, but they're things that we would find rather obvious."[12] Vickers chimed in with a joke about putting Ayers Rock (now known as Uluru) on an album sleeve, something Australian rock group Goanna had done a short time earlier. Rough Trade couldn't afford to "market" the Go-Betweens at all, of course, but even if they had tried to market them as a sort of highbrow Men at Work, with more "Cattle and Cane"–like songs peddling an image of Australia as a rural Eden, the Pathway demos showed that the group weren't in fact heading in that direction at all. They'd got over their homesickness, if that's what it was, or stopped thinking about where they'd come from, and instead were looking at their present surroundings with new eyes.

The other issue at the end of 1983 was whether or not the group would be better off on a major label. Aztec Camera, the Go-Betweens' labelmates on both Postcard and Rough Trade (they would later share a manager, too, in Bob Johnson), tried hard for hit singles on Rough Trade, with disappointing results; Scritti Politti had been in the same situation with "The Sweetest Girl." It seemed Travis might be able to engineer a transfer to another label for the Go-Betweens, as he had done for Aztec Camera.

When it came, the end of the Go-Betweens' association with Rough Trade caused major practical problems for the group. On their return to the UK, McLennan and Forster suddenly encountered immigration problems.

MILLER: We had anticipated that Rough Trade were going to organize work permits for the band. Me and Lindy and Robert [Vickers] were okay, we had patriality,[13] we could come and go as we wanted. But the advice I'd been given by Rough Trade was they'd organized work permits, so when we came back all we needed to say was that we had these work permits, we were coming back to record an album . . .

When we got to the airport, perhaps having not registered the full implications of having been dumped from the label, we were sticking to our story. Robert and Grant went to Customs and said, "We're here to work, there should be a work permit for us." There wasn't. Incredibly difficult situation of saying you don't have a work permit, [but] you said you were going to work . . . Suddenly you want to change your story and say you're coming in for a holiday. So they had a couple of awful days when Customs took them off to wherever Customs take you, and there was a time when they weren't allowed over the line into England. That was a nightmare. We were all very bitter then with Rough Trade.

If anyone feels skeptical about the Go-Betweens' strong emotions concerning their music and their commitment to the band, tribulations like this should dispel any such doubts. Despite personality differences, the group was stronger than the sum of its parts. Peter Walsh noticed this when he was in New York at the same time the group met with Travis:

WALSH: What a way to start the year—dumped by the record company, practically not allowed back into England—but because there were four of them, it was okay. One person feels savaged by these circumstances, another person feels completely oblivious to them. I noticed this with the Clowns: it was never a consensus of doom. No four people all at one time, think, "Oh God, it's finished." There's all these forces going on.

Once Forster and McLennan were finally allowed into England, the group rallied and recorded additional demos for a couple of major labels. Arista got McLennan's new song "Bachelor Kisses" and Forster's dynamic "Rare Breed"; Chrysalis also got "Rare Breed," as well as "The Old Way Out" and "Unkind and Unwise." Clive Miller was having meetings with various record companies; Forster reportedly perceived his role as being to call their offices and ask to speak to his manager—thereby drawing attention to Miller's presence.[14]

Both Arista and Chrysalis were interested in the band, but Geoff Travis had also exerted some influence on the president of Sire Records, Seymour Stein, whom he had earlier convinced to take on Aztec Camera, and who

(Frances McDougall)

had just signed the Smiths for the USA. On March 8, 1984, Forster wrote to Andrew Wilson, who was in New York at the time, telling him "we shall choose this weekend who we sign to"—they chose Sire—and their immediate plans thereafter:

> Late in March is an eight-date Orange Juice tour, we support—mixed feelings about that, but it has helped push through our visa permits to work and will give us a chance to play new songs live which our songs need till they are done for a long player, to be done in May.
> Must tell you to be glad we are rid of Rough Trade. [Their] pettiness plays very hard, the whole "you'll start selling albums in 1990" approach . . . the poor sales of *Before H* and endless other gripes!"[15]

16
Spring Hill Fair

Spring Hill, once Brisbane's "dress circle" suburb, had been under threat of destruction in the name of civic improvement throughout the 1970s. The 1980s saw its heritage status belatedly recognized, and the area began to be developed as a "pedestrianized" period piece, with weekend markets and antique shops. In an odd moment of affection for their old home—and perhaps to celebrate the addition of another Queenslander, Robert Vickers, to their ranks—the Go-Betweens chose to call their next album *Spring Hill Fair*. It was a testament to the close intellectual and cultural colonies that exist in all the inner-city areas of Australian capitals. McLennan—not a true Brisbanite—said at the time that it was "the first time we mentioned Brisbane without being insulting. Everybody from Brisbane I know insults it, and with good reason."[1] Shortly after the album was released, Vickers and McLennan explained the connection to Spring Hill to an English fanzine:

> VICKERS: Spring Hill is a place in Brisbane where we have all, at some time, lived. It's a hip suburb, it's an old suburb very close to the city and like most old places close to the city, it usually fills up with young people, especially bands, artists . . .
> McLENNAN: Junkies, pushers, pimps . . .
> VICKERS: It's a great place, it's a really great place, and it's disappearing slowly because of gentrification.
> McLENNAN: Because the city's expanding. There's some really great old houses and apartment blocks that resemble Mexico City in the 1920s. There's a peculiar type of house in Queensland on stilts, to keep it cool, there's a lot of those sort of houses, all wood with cement underneath. A lot of those houses are being torn down now to make way for office blocks. We all lived there and the main reason was that in September, October of every year in Brisbane, there is, in Spring Hill, a fair, and as

the album came out around then we thought it would be nice to have a parochial mention in a title because we hadn't done that for a long time. Most times, whenever we talked about Brisbane, Australia, it was incredibly abusive, so we thought we'd say something nice for a change.²

The Go-Betweens began recording what was to become the *Spring Hill Fair* album in May 1984. Ironically, although they were now signed to Sire—home of the Ramones and rapidly ascending club sensation Madonna—they were recording not in New York, but in the south of France, at the semi-complete Miraval Studios. Sire had got a cheap rate, and the group were able to record over the luxurious span of a whole month. Once again, John Brand was producing; this time, however, the sessions were fraught, for Morrison probably more than anyone. She and Brand were in conflict from the outset, she claims, because he tried unsuccessfully to seduce her the day she got to Miraval. The problems were compounded by his use of programmed rhythm tracks, which had recently gained prominence in pop music.

Victor Van Vugt, who came to Britain in the early 1980s with the Moodists and knew the Go-Betweens (and would later record them), explains why this was a no-win situation for Morrison:

> VAN VUGT: It was the eighties, and that's the way major labels were working in the eighties—and they still do, to an extent. The idea was you spend a lot of money—you get your flashy machines in, you know. Keep the bloody drummer out [is] production rule number one. And that was hell on Lindy, because of Lindy's pride anyway, but any drummer [would find it hard]. She saw it as a plot to diminish her role. The Go-Betweens would never have been the Go-Betweens without Lindy drumming. The industry people just didn't realize that at all. "Ah, if we get a really slick country drummer and Grant's slick songs, it'll be perfect!"

With synthesized rhythms—about half the drum tracks are programmed— and "slick" sounds, the album sounds the way a major-label debut is supposed to sound. There may, then, be no readily identifiable reason why *Spring Hill Fair* doesn't quite seem to come up to scratch. Perhaps it's that the diversity of the songs prevents it from coming together as a cohesive whole. Nevertheless, the album contains some true gems. Forster's "Draining the Pool for You" is a wonderful look at class and sexual politics, brilliantly evoking a Brisbane-by-way-of-Los-Angeles noir scenario. And his "Part Company" is simply majestic, filled with the beautifully observed details of a failed, or failing, love affair—sentimental but never tawdry, in a way very few groups could bring off. McLennan's "The Old Way Out" is a hoot,

Robert Vickers and Lindy Morrison, 1985 *(Bleddyn Butcher)*

pure and simple; its starting point is perhaps a sarcastic take on the kind of sloganeering the *NME* used to revel in at this time, but with its chanted chorus and bombastic, real drums it harks back knowingly to glam-rock anthems of the kind Chinn and Chapman produced for Gary Glitter, Suzi Quatro, Sweet, and others in the early 1970s. His mostly spoken-word "River of Money" was extraordinarily audacious, almost daring itself to fail—and on balance that's probably what it did. Recorded entirely live, it may owe something to the Velvet Underground's "The Gift," though McLennan claims to dislike that piece. In any case, his opening line, "It is neither fair nor reasonable to expect sadness to confine itself to its causes," puts it in another zone altogether. With typical willfulness and lack of objectivity, McLennan proclaimed the song "just great . . . one of the best things I've ever done. I'm very proud of it."[3] And one critic, at least agreed: writing in *Melody Maker*, Lynden Barber said it was "what Joy Division would have sounded like if they . . . had come from Brisbane."[4]

Chief among the critics expressing disappointment at *Spring Hill Fair* was Clinton Walker, now back in Australia and carving out a career for himself as a prominent music writer. Morrison believes that one reason he felt funny about this album was that one of the songs on it—Forster's "You've Never Lived"—was about him.[5]

> MORRISON: Clinton was critical of our relationship. [He] always used to say to me, "One day he'll open Pandora's box and he'll be gone." Well, I knew that. I was no idiot. I told Robert that story one day and Robert wrote that song, "You've Never Lived." It's really true, Clinton hadn't lived then, and Robert was saying, "We've had a lot more experience than you could ever dream of—together."

It would be McLennan, however, who faced the consequences of Walker's unhappiness.

> WALKER: I was disappointed with *Spring Hill Fair*. Not so much the songs, just the presentation. It strikes me as sort of scrappy.
> McLENNAN: Fair enough. I don't find it scrappy at all. It's a record where we talked right from the start of a *Loaded* or a *White Album*, where there would be different songs on the record, and I stand by that. I deny the allegations of scrappiness . . . It's the best played, best *sung* album we've done. I don't think it's fair to say that because *Before Hollywood* was cohesive the next one has to be equal to it.

"Also," he added, almost arguing himself around to Walker's point of view, "we had a tough time with the producer. He wants to make one record, we want to make another. Or we're unsure."

> McLENNAN: It's misunderstood, I think, our first misunderstood album.
> WALKER: But is it not possible that in the future you might look back on it as a turkey?
> McLENNAN: Oh well . . . I'm sorry—I know you're baiting me—but that's ridiculous, in no way is it a turkey. It's impossible for me to have anything to do with a turkey.
> WALKER: But you do concede you weren't wholly successful?
> McLENNAN: I don't think we were completely successful, no.[6]

Walker, the Go-Betweens' closest friend in rock journalism throughout the 1980s, has never missed an opportunity to denigrate *Spring Hill Fair* since, calling it "a major disappointment,"[7] "disjointed and uneven,"[8] and so on. Even two years after its release, in an excellent "on the road" story about the group, Walker was still worrying at the *Spring Hill Fair* "problem." Forster explained it as "a period in the wilderness. We made a lot of bad moves." McLennan claimed there had been pressure from the record label: "We bowed to a lot of demands we shouldn't have." Morrison's answer makes the best sense:

> The reason *Spring Hill Fair* was such a disaster was due to the relationships in the band at the time. They were fucked. There were little power struggles going on all over the place. We were a neurotic mess. It was a horrible experience, and it shows.[9]

An interview for *Jamming* at the time of the album's release was very much enlivened by these first public signs of rebellion from Morrison. Interviewer Chris Heath took her outburst for "mock fury" when she claimed Forster and McLennan were "the most boring and sad people":

That's why they write the most boring and sad songs. They're moody and sad. That's our day-to-day existence, and it comes out in our songs![10]

A discussion of McLennan's anticlerical "protest" song "Five Words" led her to exclaim: "'Bury them don't keep them! Bury them don't keep them!' They wonder why I'm neurotic . . . I have to hang around with *them!*"[11] On days like this it looked like the kind of situation only commercial success could remedy—and even that would probably only be a band-aid.

The first single released from the album was "Part Company." It made no impact on the charts, but it did give the band the chance to make a nicely ambiguous gesture to their former label. One employee recalls Forster walking around the Rough Trade warehouse and offices with a box of "Part Company" singles, handing out a copy to everyone who worked there.

The second single, "Bachelor Kisses," was the Go-Betweens' first real attempt at a commercial single. McLennan informed the *NME*'s Mat Snow: "Robert pursues a line far more true to his views all the time, whilst I'm quite interested to look at the form, and to work within that form for a while." The form, at this time, was pop music, and the possibility of a chart hit. Forster, on the other hand, never publicly championed the band's chart potential. In the same *NME* feature, he compared the Go-Betweens to character actors: "People like Thomas Mitchell, Thelma Ritter, Ned Beatty. They don't have all the stuff the stars have, but they make a body of work that is often a lot more substantial, a lot more *real* than the stars." McLennan, who so often veered between hoping for more and accepting what was available, agreed at this point, announcing, "No way could I entertain the idea of us as megastars. It's just not that sort of music and we're not that sort of people."[12]

Meanwhile, there is no denying that "Bachelor Kisses" is a distinct attempt at the pop charts. Biba Kopf celebrated it in the *NME* as an "affecting male rejoinder to 'Diamonds Are a Girl's Best Friend.'"[13] Its lush, yearning quality certainly turned Marie Ryan's head. Unlike Walker, Ryan maintained a kind of critical distance; rather than becoming deeply involved in the band members' lives, she became deeply involved in their songs. McLennan knew he could tell her without being challenged that *Spring Hill Fair* was "a brilliant album . . . I'm incredibly honest, so when I say it's brilliant, it *is* brilliant."[14] Of "Bachelor Kisses," Ryan wrote:

> It's sung in a voice imbued with such sad, quivering desire that my stony heart just melts . . . Ana, of the now defunct Raincoats,[15] adds an exquisite backing vocal which augments the haunting, ethereal quality of the song.

When Ryan asked McLennan if he was romantic, however, he replied "No, I'm quite cowardly about it, actually," launching into a convoluted explanation of "Bachelor Kisses" as a response to a number of issues: women he saw in bad relationships ("sexism just didn't come into it, it was just abuse by men"), his feeling that "most men are bastards," and that a woman can be "a slave to the kisses as well." Like any good pop writer, he also insisted that any interpretation of the song was up to the consumer: "It's not my song any more. Whatever people get out of it, I don't mind."[16]

No video had been made for "Part Company," but Sire did front the money for a "Bachelor Kisses" video; it attempted to make the most of the "haunting, ethereal" quality that Marie Ryan and others had detected in the song.[17] Forster commented shortly afterwards:

> My enthusiasm level for the film clip was not on full drive. But the actual basis of the film clip—you know, that black-and-white stuff of the band playing—is actually very, very good, [and] that was going to be the center point of the clip. Then we shot some stuff, down at Brighton, of the water and stuff. And then those two pieces of footage got put together and it was mixed virtually like a single . . . They have this huge mixing desk and they have a couple of screens, and they can just virtually print up colors. And they just went mad. I remember coming into it quite late and we were all quite stunned. The lyric mentions a diamond ring so a diamond ring comes up.
>
> The amazing thing is that the people that did it are these full-on weirdos, into Psychic TV, Cabaret Voltaire—northern industrial avant-gardists. I guess that shows they were a lot more traditional than their haircuts and their clothes made them out to be. I wanted to make a film clip—when we did "Man O' Sand," I wanted to make a film clip like the Doors on *Ed Sullivan*. You know, just the band playing, me right up front.

Forster also elaborated what a "Part Company" video might have looked like:

> It'd basically come from the cover of the single. I just thought with a song like "Part Company," if you were leaving someone, in London, a place where you'd end up would be Victoria Station . . . and it'd virtually be your last look at London before you got on a train and left someone. So it could've been using similar images to that . . . roofs, and stations. I like the idea of baggage, moving, I like the idea of taking the clothes out of the wardrobes, all the physical things that you do when you leave someone.[18]

In October, the group went on a major tour of Britain with Aztec Camera. Along the way they met Gary Glitter (who did not ask if he could cover "The

Old Way Out"). They also recorded a session for John Peel's BBC1 radio show, which was later released as an EP.[19]

The Go-Betweens ended 1984 with a tour of continental Europe and then Australia, in what was becoming an annual Christmas return that combined the advantages of a summer holiday during Britain's winter, the fulfillment of family commitments, and a chance to tour Australia at the time when Australians were most willing to go out.

McLennan's role in the Go-Betweens was mutating record by record, as he sought to find a position he could handle. The image he projected—the man with the most sincere eyebrows in pop—laid him open to ridicule from the particularly "masculine" men whose company he often sought. The rumor at this time among Australian indie-rock stars who knew McLennan was that he kept only books by female authors on his shelves because he could use them to portray himself as a sensitive intellectual and thereby more easily seduce women. Of course this rumor might say more about the Australian indie-rock stars who propagated it than it does about McLennan himself. Another story—which does not come directly from any of the people present; none of them will confirm it—depicts McLennan doing the dishes one morning with his London flatmates, Chris Walsh and Steve Miller, of the Moodists. Walsh was reminiscing about how, as a teenager, it was difficult to come home late at night and conceal from his father the fact that he was stoned. McLennan's quiet response was that he couldn't relate to that because he had been so young when his father had died. Walsh retorted, "We'll cry about that later, Grant," at which McLennan left the room and was supposedly inconsolable for some time afterwards.

This was a young man romanticizing a past that couldn't really stand up to being romanticized: his recasting of his life took schizophrenic forms in bouncy songs like "Unkind and Unwise," which he claimed was the second part of the "Cattle and Cane" trilogy. The song is a testament to ambivalence, the central figure an absent loved one, the absence magnified by the vast landscape McLennan describes. At the same time, his "Five Words"—the refrain of which had resonated with, but aggravated, Morrison so much—is a rejection of memorials, of the lionization of the dead. McLennan was struggling, to no small degree, with these issues.

McLennan insists that his musical output is merely a craftsmanlike approach to "classic" songwriting. Thus he distances himself from the curious position so many songwriters have found themselves in: that it is easier for them to express themselves in song than it is in day-to-day life. Early in his writing career, reviewing Altman's film *Images* for *Gamut*,

Grant McLennan, 1985 *(Bleddyn Butcher)*

McLennan mused on the value of work composed only as an intellectual exercise, asking whether Altman was "just contriving this clever piece of film rhetoric to have us walk out of the cinema, shaking our heads in astonishment."[20] McLennan's ultimate response is that, despite its self-indulgent effrontery, the film is well worth seeing. In contrast, his positive response to Woody Allen's *Annie Hall* a month previously is that the film excels because Allen "has had the honesty to lay down a relationship for all to see." This film—a major success for Allen, in which his former lover Diane Keaton played opposite Allen's character, Alby Singer—was seen by many as confessional. McLennan writes that "although Allen denies it, the events in the film are very similar to the real-life ex-relationship between Keaton and himself."[21]

It might seem somewhat far-fetched to look for McLennan's "real" attitude to creative inspiration in film reviews he wrote years before he ever wrote songs. Yet the value of these writings is that they show McLennan before he became a performer in his own right—and certainly McLennan often seems to regard interviews as performances, too, in which he can blithely remark, "I'm only recording the facts. I'm not making anything up."[22] This McLennan hides his nervousness under anything that comes to hand, whether it is bluster, covert or overt untruths, or a retreat into arguments about "craftsmanship." Few writers try so fervently to cover their tracks at the same time as they produce such transparently personal material. Morrison—no friend of McLennan's—sees him as an artist who is continuing to develop.

> MORRISON: I don't think Grant has found his niche yet, but I think possibly poetry could be his niche. Lyrically, he's really clever—the problem with Grant is he's not been able to overcome his background in the same way that Robert has. Robert's been able to really throw away the shackles of his background.

McLennan, as the commercial pop writer, was to have an increasingly strong effect on the Go-Betweens' sound and direction, with Forster and Morrison—and, in a typically contrary way, McLennan himself—digging their heels in to combat it. By the late 1980s, this would turn the group into a remarkable, amusing, and glamorous pushmi-pullyu.

17

Liberty Belle and the Black Diamond Express

The group returned to London in early 1985 without Clive Miller, who had seen enough of the music industry in action. He was replaced by Bob Johnson, who also managed Aztec Camera and had earlier represented Frankie Goes to Hollywood. But the Go-Betweens were without a record label again, for the second time in less than two years. The band's deal with Sire UK had come to an end, as had seemed inevitable once the label's head office decided against releasing *Spring Hill Fair* in the USA. Again, the band were relieved. In an interview with the London fanzine *Snipe*, Forster hedged his bets with the British public and subtly damned his homeland while discussing where the band stood in the first half of 1985.

> I prefer living here—we've written all the material here, and I find it very hard to write in Australia—we find it very hard to function there at all. And all our gear was here, our accommodation, so we just wanted to stay here. We knew we had four or five months' money to last, to try and get a deal, do a few gigs and rehearse and write a new album, but unfortunately no one here has decided to say, "Yes, we think you're a great group, great songs, you're not going to be top forty next week, but we can see some sort of long-term thing here." We like to tour, you know, we're not the sort of band that doesn't venture out of our rooms, so we thought it all added up to a fairly good proposition, but no one's really bitten.[1]

This was the official position for the British public, and on this day perhaps Forster even meant it, but it had only been a short time before that he and McLennan (whose words to *RAM* readers late in 1984 had rung clear as a bell: "London is a shithole"[2]) had told Australian *Smash Hits* readers a different story:

> McLENNAN: I find living in London intolerable. Through government policies, [there's an] absolutely lousy standard of living, dirt, grime. But it had its purpose. We've just sucked everything we can out of it.
> FORSTER: In London I never felt like entertaining anyone, you just sort of stay in your room.[3]

The despondency was only temporary. On July 9, 1985, they demo'd a new song of Forster's, "Spring Rain," an up-tempo pop piece celebrating difference and spectacle, which functioned almost as (another) Forster response to "Cattle and Cane": Forster was the adolescent outsider here. It was a masterful portent of what would turn out, against all odds, to be the group's best album to date.

In September 1985, the Go-Betweens signed to the newly established UK arm of Elektra Records.[4] This new deal would go badly almost from the start; nevertheless, it soon proved opportune, to say the least.

> FORSTER: Our manager, Bob Johnson, knew a guy, Simon Potts, sort of a hot A&R person—he had signed Simply Red [to Elektra]. Elektra in America wanted to start up an English label so they got Simon Potts to do it. Head of A&R. "You've got your own label now." So as soon as Simon got a job, Bob's saying, "Sign the Go-Betweens!" And Simon—there's a big jump between Simply Red and the Go-Betweens—but he said fine, okay.

Forster wrote—as he always seems to do at key moments in the band's career—to Andrew Wilson:

> We've gone with Elektra Records—start our LP in just over a week. Without any doubt the songs are our best, we are playing our best, and with ourselves producing this unknown masterpiece, it might be great. No South of France and no garbage super technology—an old-fashioned notion of the band out in the recording room and not sitting about in the control room. Strings, piano accordion, Hammond organ, spoons, and bassoons, an exotic melodic jungle album. A few epics, a Prince number,[5] solid gold sterling pop—doing all this in a Kings Cross studio.[6]

It did not take long for the group to begin recording their fourth album. And it didn't take much longer than that for Elektra UK to go belly-up: it ceased trading two weeks into the recording, on October 14. "Simon signed us, we were on the roster," recalls Forster.

Beggars Banquet promo photo for *Liberty Belle and the Black Diamond Express* (Richard Mann)

Bang—money comes through. Bang—Simon leaves Elektra, or Elektra decides not to do it, or something. In the meantime, Elektra pays for the album and don't even know it. We've got an album that's ours, we can sell it to anyone. Free album.

By borrowing some money and utilizing a publishing advance, the band improved on their investment and soon had in their hands a finished album that they could license outright to whoever might want to be the fifth British record company to release a record by the Go-Betweens.

They signed with Beggars Banquet, a well-funded and successful independent label with the additional advantage of access to the major-label distribution system. Beggars had experienced chart success with Gary

Numan, for example, and were also the financial muscle behind 4AD, home of the Cocteau Twins (and the Birthday Party). This, finally, was to be the group's long-term label in Britain in the 1980s and 1990s.

The new album's working title was *Liberty Belle*: this was Forster's idea, and it seemed appropriate, even though it has not been explained. The "Black Diamond Express" came from a conversation between co-producer Richard Preston and the rest of the band on a recording day when Forster was not present. The new LP, like its three predecessors, had a "double l" in its title, a feature which would begin to draw increasing attention from journalists and fans alike. Some groups might have begun to worry that if this was such an interesting aspect of their albums, then there must be something wrong with the content, but the Go-Betweens encouraged the story. They propagated the myth that this was a superstition on their part which took its cue from what was at the time the biggest-selling album ever, Michael Jackson's *Thriller* (and remember, Jackson also had a llama).

At the same time, aware of the reputation they were beginning to acquire for sincere eyebrows and scowling manners, the group took a different tack for the album cover, which showed them smiling and laughing. As well they might: with *Liberty Belle and the Black Diamond Express* they had made their greatest album, and a contender for the best rock record of the 1980s.

The artistic success of *Liberty Belle* derives from a number of unusual and diverse factors. Vickers told filmmaker Fiona Dempster that the group co-produced *Liberty Belle* "with the engineer" (Richard Preston, whom they'd first worked with on the Pathway demos a year and a half earlier):

> Whereas some of the other albums had actual producers, who had their own agendas basically—and producers always have their own agendas—we were really in synch with the person we co-produced it with, Richard Preston. He was great. We did our best work for that reason. It is us."[7]

The songs were unusual, too. As Forster moved back into pop with "Spring Rain" and "Head Full of Steam" (both subsequently released as singles), McLennan took over the role of providing the less obvious songs, such as the rocky "Palm Sunday (On Board the S. S. Within)," with its chamber music overtones in the chorus. He also came up with the classic "The Wrong Road" and the grunge-ballad-before-its-time "Apology Accepted."

On top of all this, there was Forster's perfect ballad "Twin Layers of Lightning," whose line, "Listen, Jack, don't you know I'm a star," heralded a new, flirtatiously grandiose arrogance in his public persona. This reached its apex in the extraordinary video for "Head Full of Steam," a bizarre

At the video shoot for "Spring Rain" *(Francine McDougall)*

pastiche of Prince's "Raspberry Beret" video in which Forster capers around McLennan, who is unrecognizably dressed as a woman.

Forster had been shocking live audiences with his dancing for some time. Sets would begin with Forster standing quite normally, playing and singing, barely moving—until the last few songs. "Draining the Pool" would often be the signal for him to begin dancing in the audience with moves that suggested a combination of eastern mystic and western poseur. "The analogy I make is to the film *Psycho*," he said of Go-Betweens live shows at the time. "Changing before your eyes."[8]

Quizzed about this, as he often was, Forster would combine self-parody and self-aggrandizement. He told the *NME*'s Danny Kelly:

> Bobby Womack himself once told me that I am a soul man, and that as far as modern music is concerned there are only three soul men left: himself, me, and Prince ... Prince came to Brisbane and took the colors, the moves, his whole act, from me. It's true! He's seen my moves!

And, adding to the in-joke:

> I'm a great dancer. Y'know, there's two of us ... myself and James Brown. The only two people in the world who can perform the double flip.[9]

However, he did not always feel it necessary to keep up this pretence, and occasionally came clean about the less enticing reality:

> I think it's incredibly funny, because I always do it the same way. I come on, and I don't really start till about halfway through the set. So people think we're just going to stand there and play. And I like the idea of people following the group and thinking, "Oh yeah, they're just going to stand there and play the nice melodic songs"—and then halfway through it I just start to move and I imagine it must look ridiculous ...
>
> But also, you know, there are all these vaudeville bands around that are quite prepared to leap on PA stacks, and the reason I didn't do it for a long time is that I knew that I could outdance a lot of people.[10]

For someone recently so interested in the days "before Hollywood" to call a rock band "vaudeville" was a curious insult, but it was an understandable one. In February 1985, Forster had told Australian *Smash Hits* readers:

> What I've been saying to people at the last few gigs is, "You're so lucky. You've seen us. We are fantastic! We're opening up a whole museum for these people in one night, and there's only twenty people here! And some vaudeville act down the road is pulling two thousand people."[11]

What these quotes from Forster reveal more than anything, perhaps, is his accumulated frustration with the band's inability to achieve the kind of success that would permit *them* to attract an audience of two thousand people to a show. He may have been able to look back on this period later and remark that "after a while, the lack of recognition was so absurd it was funny." But it cannot always have seemed funny at the time.

Forster always tried to deal with it with absurdities of his own. His interviews from this period (1985-86) are littered with ironic bragging claims such as, "When we walk down the street it must be fantastic to watch us." The real and understandable frustration that underlay the humor in this, however, led him to persist too long with this approach, and some of their existing audience became decidedly fed up with it. *Puncture* magazine, whose editors were longtime supporters of the band, editorialized tartly in 1986: "If they go on talking this rubbish, will we have to revise our high opinion of the band? Or shall we just pretend they're some other band? Say, the Ego-Betweens."[12]

"Relationship" is a thorny word. Forster and Morrison obviously had a "relationship," at least until the breakup of the band in 1989, and in many ways they will always be linked. But the time around *Liberty Belle* marked the end of their romantic involvement.

> FORSTER: We just had to do it. It was strange because it really didn't make all that much difference on the road—you're with each other all the time on the road. Also, in a way we gave everything to the band—first decision, what's the best thing for the band? You're still attached in some way. We didn't really break up. It's not like you break up, "See you, might run into you in six months if we're *unlucky* . . ." It's like . . . you break up in the morning, you're on stage together that night. But it was awful—*Liberty Belle*, making that, we were fighting, screaming in the street. We were a horrible couple to be around. We were explosive, it was dynamite in a bottle. If anything it was a relief—suddenly it was like, "Oh, thank God it's *over*."

As Forster and Morrison disentangled themselves from each other, his public character, and that of the group as a whole, began to be altered. Their next phase would be marked by the addition of the last "classic" Go-Between.

18
Very Quick on the Eye

It took a long time for the Go-Betweens to attain the aura of a marketable commodity that the Birthday Party had managed fairly early in their career. However, in 1985, Keith Glass—who had already released a couple of the Go-Betweens' *Send Me a Lullaby* demos on a cassette ludicrously titled *Rare Trax*, along with early recordings from other Missing Link artists such as the Boys Next Door[1] and Peter Lillie—released the demo recordings of all ten songs as an LP entitled *Very Quick on the Eye—Brisbane 1981*.

McLennan's response to this release is revealing, not just about his attitude to the LP, but about his own work in general: "To me they're just a curio, like the first couple of pages in a photograph album, and I don't like to look at photos of myself when I was a kid."[2] But the real grounds for objection, of course, were not that the recordings were old—after all, the group had recently allowed Beggars Banquet to reissue the Able label singles on a twelve-inch EP—but that the band was being denied any say in the release. When I interviewed Forster in 1985 in Sydney, his response suggested I'd heard of the proposed album before he had:

> It'd be extremely low behavior if he put it out without consulting us.
> I'm shocked and surprised. I wish they'd speak to us, because we've been down to Melbourne twice recently and no one's said anything.[3]

The title of *Very Quick on the Eye* came from a letter Forster had written to Glass about the sessions. An extract from this letter was printed on the back of the sleeve: "What's on tape had to be taped so the volume of songs was the idea . . . at least two tracks sound fantastic and indicate/satisfy a line of thought. So that's great." This is Forster at his most ambivalent in any case, and the phrase "What's on tape had to be taped" has been taken out of its original context, rendering it meaningless here.

Interviewed ten years after the event, Keith Glass still felt he was justified in allowing the recordings to appear (he didn't release them himself, but rather licensed the tapes to Man Made Records, a label run by Nigel Rennard, who had taken over the Missing Link record store). Glass remains convinced the Go-Betweens had effectively done him out of profits from *Send Me a Lullaby*.

> GLASS: I found out that the band had signed a waiver indemnifying Rough Trade against any action I might take to recoup royalties that were in fact flowing from the first album into the second album. So I helped pay for the second album without having any rights to it.
>
> I felt that I'd been shafted on this deal. So I thought, "Well, okay, what have I got to put out? Maybe I can recoup some of this overdue money by putting out this grubby little demo tape"—and the surprising thing was, it actually sold quite a lot of copies, a hell of a lot more copies than the first album did. I'm not sure how many, I'd say between three and four thousand. Of course I was a very popular boy for putting that out. They were pretty terrible recordings.

As an album—that is, competing with recordings designed for popular consumption—*Very Quick on the Eye* is entirely unsatisfactory. Glass even managed to misspell a song title, so that "Arrow in a Bow" became "Arrow in a Boy." To Glass and Rennard's credit, however, there is no attempt to dress the album up as anything more than a document of the band's roots; the back cover clearly states: "Recorded in Brisbane at Queensland Recording Studio early in 1981 as demos for the *Send Me a Lullaby* album."[4] And for anyone interested in the Go-Betweens, it captures a fascinating moment in time. McLennan is starting to write songs in earnest, and Forster is trying to finish off lyrics to songs—for several of the tunes he just sings a wordless melody. Morrison is still feeling her way in what are possibly her first studio recordings, but Colin Bloxsom, who engineered the session, gave her a tremendous, sharp drum sound.

At the same time *Very Quick on the Eye* was released, Glass offered the

Go-Betweens the rights to all their recordings for Missing Link, including these demos and *Send Me a Lullaby*, for a reasonable $1500, telling them, "I hope you can find a buyer and we can both be well rid of each other."[5] He eventually reached a settlement with them a few years later via the band's Australian manager, Roger Grierson, and Grierson's connection with John Foy of Sydney's Red Eye Records led in turn to the 1990 CD reissue of *Send Me a Lullaby* with a redesigned sleeve that evoked Bob Dylan's early album covers.

The five *Very Quick* songs that were not rerecorded for *Send Me a Lullaby* resurfaced in 2002 on the third reissue of that album. Stewart Lee's sleeve notes to this reissue refer to *Very Quick* as a "bootleg album . . . a record so hard to find that the compiler of this album once doubted its existence." In fact, it's not a bootleg—Glass had the legal right to issue recordings he'd paid for, or to license them elsewhere. Nor is the original album that hard to find, at least in Australia.

Still, the irritation the band felt over this whole affair in the mid-1980s is entirely understandable—particularly when, as Vickers recalls, on their next American visit every other interviewer seemed to be brandishing a copy of *Very Quick on the Eye*, which they apparently wanted to talk about more than *Liberty Belle*.

19
Tallulah

When the Go-Betweens traveled to Australia in late 1985, with the classic album *Liberty Belle* under their belts, it was with the intention of staying longer than their usual annual visit. They were planning to reverse the pattern of the last few years: rather than simply tour and visit family before returning to their base in London, they wanted to shift their base back to Australia. Thenceforth, they would only spend time in the northern hemisphere when they were touring or recording.

Robert Vickers recalls "everybody wanting to get out of London and being happy to go back to Australia." Vickers' longtime American girlfriend Janie moved with him, and the band settled into living in Sydney. None of the Go-Betweens had particular ties to Sydney, but it was the obvious place for a group to base themselves if they were to have a chance at a commercially viable career. It was the center of the Australian music industry, and home to the group's new Australian label, Truetone—an EMI affiliate that also had on its roster Ed Kuepper, once of the Saints and the Laughing Clowns, and Mark Callaghan's new band GanGajang.

But although the move was intended to be permanent, on this occasion it lasted only a few months. The volume of overseas commitments was apparently still too great, especially with early talk brewing of an attempt at a considerably more commercial sound for the next album. And for Vickers and Janie, at least, the move wasn't working out too well in any case. "It was fine," Vickers explains, "until the band went on tour and she was there by herself." By the middle of the year the situation reverted to what it had been for the past three years: the Go-Betweens were in London, and Janie was in New York, with Vickers spending as much time back there as the band's schedule permitted.

The group nevertheless underwent a seismic change during this stay in Australia, one that would have an enormous effect on individual and group dynamics. In January 1986, they met and were bowled over by a young musician called Amanda Brown. By April, they had invited her to join the band, and when they went back to London shortly afterwards it was as a five-piece.

Brown had been performing in rock groups since 1983. Her first band, Climbing Frame, seems in retrospect to have been one of the last of the art/improvisational/jazzy groups of the early 1980s: they designed their own posters, played rare and enigmatic shows, and recorded a self-funded, self-titled EP. Shortly before they broke up, they traveled to Brisbane, primarily to play at a party to celebrate the birthday of fellow art-rocker John Willsteed, who had been a key member of Zero with Lindy Morrison. When Willsteed moved to Sydney, he and Brown—who lived near each other—were enlisted by one-time Zero member Michael O'Connell to form a country and western group, Tender Mercies. Willsteed proved difficult to work with, so O'Connell and Brown split off to form a duo, Blood Brothers. O'Connell was doing a masters degree, and Brown, still only twenty-one, had just enrolled in an arts course at the University of Sydney.

Previous Go-Betweens had been inducted into the band largely because they were known to Forster and McLennan, and had a shared Brisbane history. Brown was a very different proposition.

> BROWN: I think they were sort of fascinated by my background. I grew up in the inner city of Sydney, Paddington, Woollahra, went to Sydney Girls' High. My parents are divorced, fairly archetypal seventies parents, fairly bohemian and cultured, experimented with different drugs, well-traveled. My dad did his Ph.D. at a university in America and was a long-haired, hitchhiking hippie. They were all fascinated by those kinds of stories, because all of them are from quite conservative, middle-class, private-school Brisbane families—apart from Robert Vickers.
>
> From the age of about seventeen I always hung out with older people. It seemed pretty natural to me. I was naïve about lots of things in the music industry, but I wasn't naïve socially. And I was certainly pretty cool compared to how they were when they were my age!
>
> [Michael O'Connell and] I had been dating a few months, and he told me that he knew the Go-Betweens, that they lived in London and toured around the world constantly, and did an album occasionally. And I remember thinking, "What a fantastic life"—that seemed like a really ideal experience.

Brown recalls the first time she met Morrison:

> Lindy was really out of it on something—I don't know if she was drunk or . . . She and Robert used to take Rohypnols and drink. That was the first time I ever met any of them and I was really amazed by what an over-the-top personality Lindy is. She started talking to this Kings Cross derro[1] and half an hour later was swapping clothes with him, giving him her suit coat and cardigan, whatever else she was wearing! Then she started taking off her boots, she had these really nice, expensive RM Williams boots and I remember Robert saying, "Not the boots, Lindy, not the boots!" She was going to swap the boots for these horrible brown vinyl Hush Puppies . . .
>
> At Lindy's instigation they invited me to come and play violin, just for a few shows in Sydney and Melbourne. And I did that. I think they were looking for another member, and they wanted a keyboard player. I didn't play keyboards, but they seemed to think I could learn keyboards, and fulfil that function. So anyway, they asked me to join the band after those shows, and I said yes.
>
> I recall them actually calling a meeting, all of us sitting down, and the one thing that they wanted to make clear was that there were two songwriters in the band and I wasn't to write songs. At the time I didn't care about that at all—I was just so excited and flattered that they'd asked me to join the band. All I cared about was being a good violinist, anyway. I didn't think that songwriting was any more special than being a good musician.

Brown was becoming known around the independent scene. The Perth group Chad's Tree, who were living in Sydney and on an upward spiral at the time, asked her to record with them (she appears on two tracks on their debut album *Buckle in the Rail*) and then asked her to join. She considered this while she was rehearsing for the Go-Betweens' Australian shows in mid-February, then rejected them when the more established group made their feelings known. The inclusion of Brown was not put to a vote within the group, a matter that Vickers was particularly unhappy about, though he does not blame Brown. He wasn't the only one made unhappy by the decision:

> O'CONNELL: She was very young . . . and I basically encouraged her to go for it—altruistic of me! Lost my partner in my musical duo and lost my girlfriend. She wanted to be a star. She's an interesting girl. She likes being in the limelight, and this was a great opportunity for her to be in the limelight. I said, "Don't worry about me."

Like Lindy Morrison and Peter Walsh, Brown was stolen by the Go-Betweens from one of O'Connell's bands—he must have felt like an unpaid talent scout. Morrison pushed hardest for Brown; she needed an ally in the group now that her relationship with Forster was more complicated. A year later she sang Brown's praises to *Melody Maker*'s Simon Reynolds:

> It makes so much difference now Amanda's with us. I can say to her that I'm expecting my period and she'll *understand*. Men are so hard. They expect so much from you. And you must never show your feelings. I get *so tired*. The particular three boys we work with are emotionally controlled and stable—they don't *react*.

Brown added: "It's great working with women. I want to have an all-woman band one day. A democratic band, with no individual songwriters."[2] Morrison later told Fiona Dempster that Brown "had left home at sixteen, which was an incredible thing, and at twenty-one had joined this dysfunctional family called the Go-Betweens."

> MORRISON: [She got] taken to London, where we were impoverished, taken from everything she knew—and still managed, in many ways, to teach me, at that age, all sorts of stuff about being professional and about being a musician. For that, I feel responsible to her for the rest of my life. I really do love her and I think she knows that. She was very unhappy for a very, very long time, because of the situation she was placed in overseas, and so lonely, and yet she did so much for me, particularly musically.
>
> *Tallulah* is a real example of a great musical relationship in terms of the rhythms developed between Amanda and me, and the parts worked out between us. Listen to that album if you want to hear great arrangements between strings and drums. Because we really thought all that out, we worked together very closely on that album, that was really the only one we had the chance to do that ...
>
> Because she'd been trained as a ballet dancer, she was always so proper in the way she appeared on stage and her preparation beforehand ... By the time she joined the band in '86 I was beginning to lose it, you know—I was beginning to get sloppy, I was getting tired, I was getting lazy. And Bob had taken over the reins, so I wasn't necessary any more in that role of organizing or managerial duties. So I began to lose it. But she made me pull up my trousers, so to speak, and start to think again about how I was appearing on stage, how I acted on stage, all that sort of stuff.[3]

Living in Australia, Brown was unaware how popular the band was overseas:

The new lineup with Amanda Brown *(Peter Anderson)*

BROWN: I'd heard of them, but about the only song I knew was "Cattle and Cane," and I wasn't a fan of the band by any means. Suddenly, when I arrived in London, everyone I met was like, "Oh wow, you're so lucky, isn't it amazing . . . you're in the band!" and I'd go, "Well, yeah?" It wasn't until we started going on tour that I realized the band was bigger than any band I'd ever played in before.

In general the audiences were early twenties uni[versity] students. More boys than girls. I guess the kind of people that also used to like the Smiths, [and] so-called college bands. They were really sort of adulatory towards Robert and Grant, but it's different when you're a girl, they don't come up and say, "You're wonderful, you're fantastic." It's a different sort of chemistry, the way that girls in bands never seem to attract that blatant groupie-ism that boys do. It probably happened to me a couple of times. But not in nearly such an obvious way as girl groupies. They just hang out backstage and you know they're there for one thing. Whereas the boys try and hide it in other things. They'll say, "Oh, would you like to come out with us after the show and go drinking?"—or go to a bar, go nightclubbing, whatever. They never actually put the hard word on you.

As a new recruit, Brown was in an ideal position to see the Go-Betweens firsthand—and more objectively than anyone else. The band was making a small amount of money, paying themselves a wage from McLennan and Forster's publishing royalties. Unlike Morrison or Vickers in the past, then, she was never likely to be implicitly asked to starve on behalf of the Go-Betweens.

Four months after joining, she fell in love with McLennan.

BROWN: I was desperately lonely, and I think it was one of those things where he was the only person around. Which isn't to say he was the only choice—well, he was—but it was better than that. I really fell in love with him as well. But I was so lonely and started wanting a bit of human companionship—and that's how we got together. I was attracted to him and got on really well with him.

McLennan initially resisted his attraction to Brown for the honorable reason that she was still, strictly speaking, Michael O'Connell's girlfriend. However, once this situation was resolved—messily, of course—McLennan, like Forster before him, entered into his first long-term romantic relationship with a woman who also happened to be a Go-Between. Rumor has it that in the formative days of their relationship he boasted to friends that Brown was a "blank canvas" which he could populate with his own culture, although others close to McLennan dispute this.

Forster claims his response to the new romance was a blithe, "the more the merrier, let's get on with it and make it a total soap opera." And as for Morrison:

> BROWN: Lindy was just *disgusted*. She was disgusted, but she also thought it was predictable and inevitable. Grant had never really had a relationship before—he'd had girlfriends—I think the longest he'd had was about three months. And he'd certainly never lived with a woman and been with a woman for any great length of time, and he was pretty naïve as far as relationships were concerned, so . . . I think she probably just thought it'd last a couple of months and he'd break my heart. That's what he did with everyone else.
>
> What he tended to do was the old musician's "girl-in-every-port" syndrome—on tour he'd get together with the same girl every time he was in a city. In a way, that's the only way, because you're never in the one place for long. If he'd had a girlfriend in London, he'd have been away three-quarters of the year probably, and not seen her and it would've been hard to sustain a relationship . . . So, you know, the fact that we were both in the same band and working together made it possible for both of us to have a relationship.
>
> Robert and Lindy were breaking up when I joined the band. It was a really messy break-up and they would both go off and sleep with other people but then they'd get back together again . . . They both lived in the same flat, virtually, in London and it just dragged on for ages. [They] were quite openly fighting and antagonistic to each other. Pretty much all the time. They had a strange sort of relationship: even after they'd broken up they were still strangely dependent upon one another.

Brown also found herself in the unenviable position of go-between in the tumultuous relationship between McLennan and Morrison, as she recalled later.

> BROWN: Grant and Lindy had never got on, which is probably obvious from talking to both of them. But Grant had actually said something to Lindy, I can't remember the details—perhaps it was something about her drumming being out of time, or playing the wrong thing. She is incredibly defensive. She just cannot take criticism of any kind. And she got in this black mood for days. Her moods, when she's in them . . . it's like, you know, when you're really scared of something, or dreading something, you know this ominous event is looming in the future and you've got that horrible feeling in your heart and in the pit of your

By the Thames Barrier, 1986 *(Bleddyn Butcher)*

stomach. Well, being around Lindy at that time was just like that, twenty-four hours a day. She sort of hated me for ages, too, because I was with Grant and she thought his opinions were my opinions. That carried over into the gigs.

I was trying to be the mediator between those two all the time. I used to make Grant apologize to Lindy so we wouldn't have those constant bad vibes. He didn't like doing it, and under other circumstances he wouldn't have, but he did for my sake and I must say it did improve things. To his credit, on a number of occasions he bit the bullet and apologized to Lindy.

Grant—he's a real gentleman in lots of ways—he hardly ever says anything nasty about anyone. You'd probably be hard-pressed even to get him to say anything nasty about Lindy, and he probably hates her more than anyone in the world. He's never nasty about anyone. He's calm, though not necessarily honest. A very well-mannered, polite person.

Forster and Morrison's relationship had never been given press attention: the band members did not speak about it, and even journalists close to the group did not realize it existed.[4] Lindy Morrison finally revealed it in 1986, to Australian readers in a *RAM* story by Marie Ryan, and to UK readers in an *NME* article in which she also told Danny Kelly that she and Forster occasionally met on the stairs between their separate flats for a "glamorous fuck."[5] Presumably there had been a feeling in the band that the outside world might assume that if a female musician was the girlfriend of a male musician, then she was a member of the group for this reason over any other.

Brown and McLennan, by contrast, celebrated their affair quite publicly. This was most obvious in the video for "Right Here," the first single to feature Brown. It is clear not only that the two are "involved," but also that they are being *sold* to us as a couple. The next five Go-Betweens singles would all be McLennan songs, and in four of the five videos for those singles, the directors clearly foregrounded McLennan and Brown.

In mid-July, the Go-Betweens were back in London, except for Vickers, who was spending some time in New York. In his absence, the other band members, under the name the 16th Century, played some shows at the Enterprise, Chalk Farm, with a new friend, Alec Palao, sitting in on bass. The band debuted a number of new songs, including "The Clarke Sisters" and "Right Here." Forster claimed that "16th Century" had always appealed to him as a name for a group: the magic number 16—possibly another talisman—would appear in the title of the sixth Go-Betweens album.

The sessions for the fifth album, which was to be named *Tallulah* after Mr. Pierre's daughter, began at the end of 1986 with the recording of the two singles, "Right Here" and "Cut it Out," both McLennan compositions. "Right Here" is funny and spirited; its title derives from the chorus of Forster's "You've Never Lived," but the concept—of a fact, or a person, laid bare, glaringly obvious and tangible—had always appealed to McLennan.

The rationale for the attention paid to the production of the new singles was as follows: since Forster's songs "Head Full of Steam" and "Spring Rain" had been minor commercial successes (the latter had even made it into Jonathan Demme's comedy *Something Wild*), then the highlighting of the more commercial songwriter, McLennan, plus some slick production, should increase the group's chances of a hit single by two hundred percent. The two songs were recorded with producer Craig Leon in London, in between Christmas and rehearsals for the rest of the album.

The Craig Leon sessions were intense, according to Alec Palao:

> PALAO: Let me set the scene. Tony Visconti's studio, there's this big control room [and] mixing desk there, Grant, who wrote the song, and Amanda . . . Craig Leon, and this other guy, Simon Fisher-Turner, this bizarre English eccentric. Meanwhile, Robert and Lindy are sitting on a couch at the back of the control room, arms crossed . . . they were *not* into it!

B-sides for the singles were recorded in the second week of January; Steve Miller of the Moodists and, once again, Simon Fisher-Turner (who recorded under the name of the King of Luxembourg), contributed guitar and backing vocals respectively. Victor Van Vugt was producing, and remembers that Forster insisted on recording his vocal without any headphones: "he kept going, 'this is the future. This is the future. Everyone will do it like this one day. I feel good. I feel good.'" The songs were "Don't Call Me Gone," which featured lyrical contributions from Brown and Morrison; Forster's jokey "A Little Romance," and the intriguing "When People Are Dead," with lyrics from an Irish fan, Marion Stout. They were mixed on January 11, and both singles were cut the following day. As if this was not enough activity, three of the Go-Betweens—Brown, Forster, and Vickers—also rehearsed and recorded a radio session as the backing band for David Westlake of the Servants, who considers the band "the sweetest, sharpest, most life-affirming people you could hope to meet." The Servants had been discovered by Morrison when she saw Westlake's classified ad for band personnel, listing the Velvet Underground and the Go-Betweens as influences. The band went on to support the Go-Betweens on tour, and Brown played violin on their EP *The Sun, a Small Star*.[6]

A week after the Westlake session, the group shots were taken for the *Tallulah* cover, even though—or perhaps because—it was becoming increasingly clear that Morrison's position in the band was rather tenuous. Vickers recalls a rehearsal at which it seemed to him that Morrison was treading very thin ice, her position in the band under threat. "There were moments like that, it's true," says Forster. "It did reach extreme points. Her own volatile nature—she is that kind of person. It was never serious in terms of having meetings without her, or, 'Have you seen any good drummers lately?' Never."

Vickers also remembers a rehearsal at which Morrison, in the middle of an argument with Forster, told the rest of the band that Forster had been secretly planning to record a solo album. This took the other members by surprise, and with the group dynamic thrown into disarray, Morrison's position became more solid again. At any rate, Vickers' diary for January 23, 1987 records succinctly—in between drinks with the group Microdisney and time spent watching Derek Jarman videos—"Lindy not sacked." Forster later explained that the idea of a solo album would come to him at times when the band was going through troubles; he also claims that he actually quit the group for a short time during preproduction for *Tallulah*.

A week of recording, this time with Richard Preston again, started on February 2. During the second week of February, a day was spent filming the "Right Here" video; the single was released on February 23. By this time, the rest of the album was virtually done, although some tracks were later remixed by yet another producer, Mark Wallis. In the meantime, it was becoming clear that the Craig Leon treatment had not set "Right Here" alight commercially, a development that disappointed Brown particularly. She had been in the group for over a year when she told *Melody Maker* "We've been shamefully ignored for too long . . . I can't see any reason why the masses shouldn't take the Go-Betweens into their hearts."[7] Once again, the masses managed not to do this, something she now recalls philosophically:

> BROWN: The first single I ever played on was "Right Here." It was produced really well and it sounds great. It was a pretty hooky song, and I thought we had a hit on our hands, for sure. I thought, the band's finally going to sell some records. I really believed that because it was a good catchy song it'd be a hit. I just didn't know about things like payola and the narrowness of radio stations' choices of programming, and when we

couldn't get the song played on radio in England, I was disillusioned and disappointed. I remember being really heartbroken about it and the rest of the band being what I thought was blasé. I now realize that they were just used to it.

"Right Here" was a sumptuous package, from the cover painting (by McLennan) to the excellent video, which sold the band not as brash or sarcastic like "Spring Rain" or downright weird like "Head Full of Steam" but as attractive individual personalities. This would become the pattern of their future videos, and Forster would have a decreasing visual presence in them—when it came to the commercial sphere, he was seen as being too difficult. While video directors had to appreciate that, as far as the band was concerned, Forster was as much a part of the equation as McLennan, every promotional video from "Right Here" onwards shows Forster completely backgrounded. Morrison, too, was being pushed aside, as she told *Sounds'* Ralph Traitor in publicity interviews for *Tallulah*:

> MORRISON: Our management are asking us right now to try and attain a greater pop sensibility on recordings and to be much more aware of eighties production values. I find it sad that a lot of music is sounding the same today, which is a technical thing of standardizing sounds. I don't like having to make records that sound like everybody else, just because we live in the eighties.[8]

She also told Bernard Zuel of Sydney's *On the Street*:

> Craig Leon—who did that Dr. and the Whatsits'[9] "Spirit in the Sky"—it seemed to the record company [that he] had a pop sensibility. I thought that record was a pile of shit, but he goes back to Blondie and Richard Hell, too. He's done a lot of American punk bands of the mid- to late-1970s and we thought it could be the marriage of the American side with this pop sensibility. He was chosen to make this single accessible to people, to get us to crawl out of our cult corner. No, of course it wasn't successful. It's never successful. I don't know why the record company bothers.[10]

The second single, "Cut It Out," released in May 1987, represents very neatly what striving for commercial success was doing to the Go-Betweens. It is disjointed, mechanical, and trite, and while in some cases such attributes can combine to make winning pop music, "Cut It Out" is just a slender tune battered to death by studio effects. This was not entirely Leon's fault—the song was too new and the group were unable to spend enough time working it up, or out. A few months later, "Cut It Out" actually began to flow in live performance. This was too late for the single, which sounds like the usual Go-Betweens pastoral idyll being periodically invaded by bad funk. Everyone in the band has subsequently disowned it.

"Bachelor Kisses" exemplifies McLennan's decision that pop—which he usually called "simplicity" or "directness"—was his strength. He saw this as a way in which he would complement Forster's work rather than swamp it or cancel it out. Go-Betweens albums continued to feature five songs from McLennan—in the case of *Tallulah*, "Right Here," "Cut It Out," the sumptuous and yearning "Bye Bye Pride" (which was a single in some territories), "Hope Then Strife," and "Someone Else's Wife." Forster's five songs this time were the powerful "I Just Get Caught Out," the throwaway

Brown and McLennan in Japan *(Courtesy Amanda Brown)*

"You Tell Me," the hilariously testosteronal "Spirit of a Vampyre," the broken but masterful "The Clarke Sisters" (which, according to Forster, is not about his old university friend Virginia Clarke, although it is named for her), and the dramatic "The House Jack Kerouac Built."

The initial plan had been to make *Tallulah* a double album. McLennan was writing four songs for every one that Forster wrote; at this stage, Forster was forcing out songs in the belief that he had to keep pace with McLennan—*not* because he secretly planned to make a solo album. The double album concept was abandoned early on, but the various power struggles in the band were clearly taking a toll on Forster, who needed to redefine his role. He was certainly unhappy with the way so much of the attention was now focused on McLennan and Brown.

> BROWN: I suppose as I became more well known as a member of the band and my contributions to the band became a more integral part—my melody lines, and my violin and oboe parts and my backing vocals became major hooks in some of the songs—I attracted a bit more attention. Also, when I joined the band—I'm not saying it had anything to do with me—but the band's popularity was steadily going up all the time; each album would sell more than the last one. When the band broke up we were actually quite popular for the first time in our lives, we were drawing a decent wage, we could actually buy material possessions like

televisions, and stereos, and clothes, for the first time ever.

So, my profile grew as the band grew, but Robert was really—I'm sure Lindy would say this—he was really threatened by my presence. He was used to being the star. Even though Grant and Robert perhaps were perceived as being equal, Lennon-and-McCartney–like contributors, Robert was really the star.

I never realized the extent of Robert's animosity, and the venom that he had been storing up about me, until one gig in Frankfurt. It was a really weird gig because it was in a nightclub—it was quite crowded, but most of the people were there for the nightclub afterwards, they weren't the typical attentive Go-Betweens audience. The set went over really cold, people were barely clapping. [But] the band had a few really entrenched, ingrained policies that they adhered to through thick and thin—and doing encores was one of those. The encores were always completely unspontaneous—they were usually the same songs, and there would always be two encores. And I said, "Look, let's not do any encores, no one's clapping." Disco music was pumping out and everyone was getting into that. And no one wanted us back, it was obvious to me. But Robert was insanely persevering and wanting to go out and had this idea, I suppose, that he could win them over. I just thought, "After a whole set, if they're not won over, why bother?" So I said, "Let's not do it." And there was all this confusion. Everyone went out except me. I stayed in the dressing room because I thought it was stupid. And they were confused about what song they were doing. Half the band started playing "Cattle and Cane" and half the band started playing something else. It just sounded really awful, it was one of those really embarrassing moments, and the crowd just went silent and hostile. They all just ended up coming off and Robert just screamed at me. Something like "You fucking arsehole"—really horrible, I'd never heard him swear at anyone like that before. It was a real outburst, I was so shocked I was shaking. It was so awful I couldn't believe it.

Another time we were doing a gig in Queensland and there was someone videoing it—you know, they had a video camera in the pub, television screens all around—they were filming the band and it was on the telly for people to watch. The cameraman had the camera on me all the time. And I knew, and I was really embarrassed. I kept trying to walk away from it. And Robert said to the cameraman, "Hey, stop it, put it on me." [He] went really over the top, went out in front of the stage and really hammed it up, trying to attract attention back to him. That's a minor example, but I think that's the way he felt.

Forster's response to the latter story is that he would conduct himself in this way not for self-glorification, but to protect Brown. This sounds logical enough, but does not explain why his response to the new glamorous Go-Betweens image was to dye his hair silver before the promotional appearances for *Tallulah*. He told the *NME*'s Donald McRae:

> I walked into the hairdresser's and, very coolly, I said two words... "Blake Carrington." Of course, everyone looked at me as though I was mad, so I said, "Well, it's more the *shade* than the style of Blake's hair that I'm interested in." It's that sort of silvery-gray color, y'know... At first they refused to go for gray because they said it couldn't be done. But I knew that it was possible. The reason I wanted to go gray was so that I could look like a respectable older man. Like, I dunno[11] if you've taken much note of Eric Clapton and Iggy Pop's hair color lately, but those men must have a lot of gray in their hair because they're dyeing it black—so I just thought it was time a younger man reversed the process.[12]

The mid-1980s in England were the heyday of the inept "C86" groups (most of whom simply churned out an ignorant rehash of the "Postcard sound" combined with the Buzzcocks) and apparently groundbreaking diversions like the Jesus and Mary Chain, the first real post-punk–youngster punks. Robert Forster was now thirty, while the competition was ten years younger, or at least could get away with pretending to be. Since the Go-Betweens were on their fifth LP, and since the press were still provoking them with the same old nonsense—why weren't they pop stars yet?—it must have seemed to Forster that the best course was to accentuate their age rather than deny and ignore it. It was also, of course, a completely perverse move—and it worked.

Hair was a dominating theme of the time. Forster embarked on a haircare column for the magazine *Debris*, which explored his interest in style as substance:

> Now Redken Deep Cleansing Gel Shampoo or Mild Protein Shampoo is expensive (£3 to £5 a bottle or tube), but it's worth it—your hair will look and feel wonderful. It is available at certain hairdressers, generally the better ones. The main problem with getting Redken is having to put up with the bored supercilious staff that frequent hairdressing salons. You shall immediately disarm them by asking for Redken. They will realize that you know the hidden secret of hair care; this will hurt them, as they wish to keep Redken for themselves...

> The Robert Redford look is one of my favorite hairstyles. Redford is possibly a Redken user. He lives in the hills of Colorado, so he has access to clear, clean mountain water. This helps hair. Redford is natural and unforced, a slight layered cut falling just short of the eye but over the ear. I have yet to decide if he uses dyes to get his reddish/blonde hair colour. As he gets older we shall find out. He has a magnificent hair-line; I suspect that just after washing his hair, he combs it back when it's wet, and just lets it fall naturally on his head. Redford does not use a hair dryer.[13]

The hair obsession was also a retreat from, and a canny reaction to, image-obsessed London. Although the band's initial attempt at shifting their base back to Australia had not worked out, the idea was very much still in the forefront of Forster's mind, at least. In mid-1987 he told the British magazine *FSM:* "At the end of the year, when the tour's over, I want to spend some time there without working." Australian film and music, he commented, had "a total lack of introspection, touching on naiveté, which I find quite funny"— a common expatriate reaction. But, he stressed, in Australia "there's room to move, and a feeling of freshness."[14] Clearly that freshness and space was something he felt he—and the Go-Betweens—needed at this point. And at the end of 1987 the band did indeed decide to move back to Australia again, planning at the very least to stay long enough to write and record their next record there. But the decision would cost them one of their number.

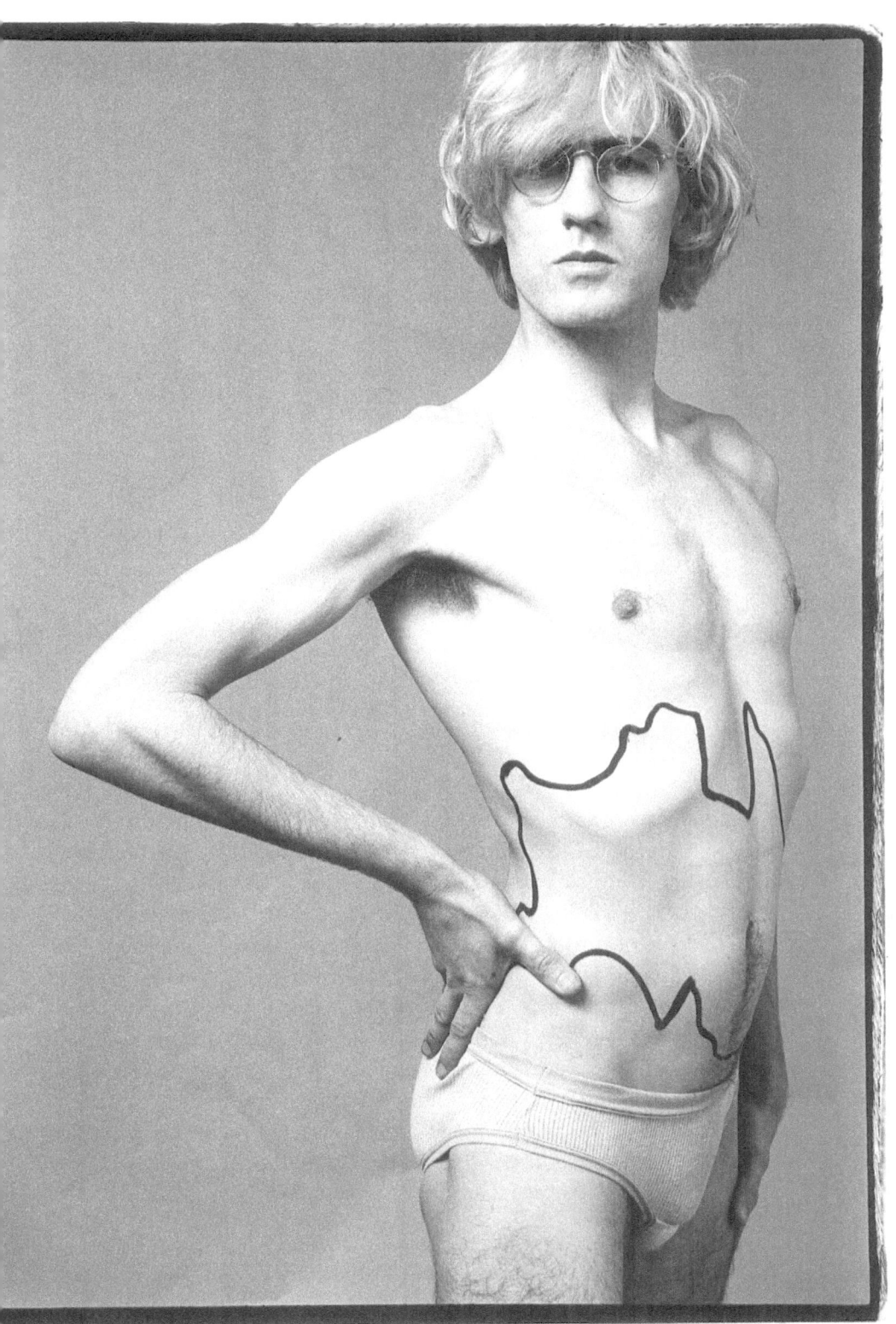
(Bleddyn Butcher)

20
16 Lovers Lane

The Go-Betweens have said farewell to bass player Robert Vickers, who has left the group to move to New York.
He has already linked up with other musicians to form a band in the Big Apple, and has stressed that he left the Go-Betweens because of "geographical differences as opposed to the time-honored 'musical' ones."
The rest of the group, meanwhile, have found themselves a replacement and have returned to their native Australia to work on material for their next album. They will also be playing some live shows down under in the company of Nick Cave and the Bad Seeds.
(*NME*, February 27, 1988)

Robert Vickers' understanding with the other Go-Betweens had always been that during the extended periods when the band was not touring or recording, or rehearsing in preparation for either of those, he would be free to go back to live in New York with his girlfriend, Janie. He had already made plans to do this again once their 1987 touring schedule was completed—and then "Lindy insisted that we had to keep rehearsing on a weekly basis even if we weren't preparing a record or a tour." Her motive was a perfectly reasonable one—she felt she got out of the groove during long periods of inactivity—but it created additional strain within the band. After the Go-Betweens played the last date of a short US tour, supporting the dB's at the Ritz in New York on Friday, October 2, 1987, Vickers remained in New York, his future with the band uncertain. Then came the renewed discussions about moving back to Australia, and working on the next record there.

VICKERS: I made a two-night trip back to London from New York at the end of 1987 for a meeting about what became *16 Lovers Lane,* and we discussed the idea of moving to Australia at that point. I was in favor of it.

Then I went back to NYC and thought about it more. Janie and I had tried the move to Australia the first time and it didn't really work out. A few weeks later when Robert called to find out when I was coming back I told him I wouldn't be.

On the same day that the Go-Betweens played their last show with Vickers, McLennan and Brown had met with a potential manager for the Australasian end of their business affairs. The new figure on the scene was Roger Grierson, who had once played in Canberra punk band the Thought Criminals, and subsequently ran the Green record label and management organization together with journalist Stuart Coupe. Coupe was in fact competing with him for the position of Go-Betweens manager, but Grierson won out.

Grierson had always been unhappy with the people the group had previously chosen to arrange their tours, and thought he could do a much better job for them in Australia. But his responsibilities soon became much greater than he had foreseen.

> GRIERSON: One day a fax turned up, "Hi, it's Bob Johnson, Southside Management—you've got the guernsey" [i.e., the job]. And that was it.
> "And the band's coming back to Australia to live . . ." Double whammy! "They're all yours. They're arriving in three weeks."

The group did not choose their new bass player nearly as carefully as they had chosen their manager. In a bumbling manner that some might find lovable, they picked up John Willsteed, who they knew was a funny, intelligent, ex-Brisbanite like themselves. He was also a very good musician, and he knew it. Willsteed claims that memories of the late 1980s come back to him through a haze, but he seems to have fair recall of the circumstances at the time.

> WILLSTEED: I was doing a lot of graphic art, living with a guy called Andrew Leitch who used to be in the Riptides and Catchcry. We started doing some little film collaborations, and I got into a band with Michael O'Connell and Amanda Brown, a country covers band called Tender Mercies. I'd been doing some bits of radio comedy on Triple J and . . . just fucking around, really, too many drugs and way too much drinking, just trying to figure out what to do in Sydney. Because I was just a fish out of water here.
> Then I joined this band from Brisbane, Let's Go Naked, girl drummer, boy singer, three-piece. They lost their bass player and me and this boy, Tony Nolan, joined. He was playing guitar and I was playing

In-store performance, San Francisco, September 1987 (Erik Auerbach)

bass. They really idolized the Go-Betweens—even though Murray [Power, the band's lead vocalist] would hate for me to say that. But they were like a Go-Betweens tribute band, only they played original songs. So I had a bit of grounding, you see. And I'd probably seen a bit of Lindy, because I always liked to see her when she was back.

BROWN: He was really manipulative in getting into the band. He can be incredibly charming when he wants to be and he endeared himself to everyone in the band in Sydney when we needed someone to join. We all thought he was such a nice, fun person to have around. And I had known him before, too, and I'd never had a problem with him. So we all thought it would be plain sailing.

Willsteed, who had never liked the band—only the people in it—and was often heard expressing the opinion that they "couldn't play," accepted the position unconditionally.

WILLSTEED: I was very lucky, I was really fortunate, because they'd put in an enormous amount of work to get to that point, whereas I just walked into it. And fucked it up!

They asked me [to join] at Christmas time in 1987. We started work on the album virtually straight away, so I really didn't have to jump right into some solid touring schedule or something like that. It was all fairly easy, preproduction for an album and then recording at 301 in Sydney, which is a lovely studio.

It was all quite luxurious from my point of view and there was a wage, and there was *time*, it wasn't really fuckin' full-on or anything, it wasn't shows six nights a week. It was a fairly lush lifestyle. I had been making a fair bit of money [just] before that, but I'd been on the dole for a long time, so it was quite a change in lifestyle for me.

Willsteed seemed perfect for the job at the outset, especially once he began working his magic on the sixth Go-Betweens album. *16 Lovers Lane*, as it would be (semi-ironically) titled, was recorded in April 1988. The group had chosen as producer Mark Wallis, who had remixed some of the songs on *Tallulah* and subsequently worked on U2's *Unforgettable Fire* album. The day Wallis touched down at Sydney's Kingsford Smith airport, a single he had produced for the Primitives ("Crash") was number one in Britain.

The new album was to be the group's first for Australian label Mushroom, at that time riding high on the unexpected success of Kylie Minogue and lesser pop lights such as Jason Donovan, another Stock/Aitken/Waterman success story. Mushroom was also the Australian home of the Triffids. Meanwhile, in the USA, the magical figure of Simon Potts—who had got them on Elektra long enough to record *Liberty Belle*—had re-emerged to sign the band to Capitol Records.

In a significant departure from previous LPs—and probably to avoid the tensions of *Tallulah*—the two songwriters worked on the songs together, coming up with suggestions for arrangements, then bringing them to the band and Wallis when they were reasonably complete. Forster was living with Grierson and a Melbourne ex-musician called Phil Grizzly in a huge Woolloomooloo terrace house, within walking distance of the city center and Mushroom's offices. Grizzly claims the main thing he remembers about Forster was that he wore dresses around the house and had a large poster of David Cassidy above his bed (Forster denies both claims). Lindy Morrison may also have lived there for a while.

> GRIERSON: The house we had at Woolloomooloo, the front door opened straight onto the dining room/kitchen thing. It was a bald-faced terrace and I remember the postman coming round and Robert and Grant sitting there and doing nothing but drinking endless cups of tea and writing songs together and the postman came in and said, "Excuse me, saw the door was open, got some mail for you. Christ, you're my favorite band!" They were impressed, of course, to be recognized.

Though he was hired as bass player—and that is what he would do live—Willsteed is responsible for the proficient guitar playing that embellishes much of the album. Brown recalls that "he was probably the best musician in the band. The intricate, beautiful guitar work you hear on 'Streets of Your Town' and 'Love Is a Sign' and 'Dive for Your Memory'—most of that is John Willsteed."

Brown, the other "real" musician in the Go-Betweens, claims to have found the demo method no impediment to her work on *16 Lovers Lane*, but then, living with McLennan, she was probably more connected to the work in progress than Morrison, who saw it as a challenge to her ability as an arranger and interpreter. She feels she is only half there on *16 Lovers Lane*: Wallis's approach, like that of John Brand and Craig Leon, was to use programmed drums. Willsteed recalls of Morrison: "Mark Wallis threw a lot of stuff in there, she was pushed to the outer [edge] and he was allowed to do that by the band." This was not a new problem. But, more seriously, Morrison's time and attention during the recording of the album was taken up by her father's ill health. He died during the recording, and she was often unable to attend sessions. "It breaks my heart," she now says of the album. "I just wasn't there for it. You can tell. The drums aren't there, there's nothing there."

The finished *16 Lovers Lane* is the slick pop record the Go-Betweens had always promised to make, and to Wallis's credit he did not feel it necessary to enforce the sterile environment adhered to by Craig Leon. For the vocal track of "Clouds," Forster and Brown sat in a circle of candles and roses, wrapped in blankets. Grierson recalls of "Dive for Your Memory":

> Robert came in to do the vocal and said, "You're not set up."
> Mark said, "Yeah, I'm ready."
> "Well, where's the mike and stuff?"
> "It's on the roof."
> The roof of EMI, the sun was setting. He stood on the roof watching the sun set and getting his vocals right for the song, which I thought was really neat.

The jewel in *16 Lovers Lane*'s crown is undeniably the first single, "Streets of Your Town," possibly the closest the Go-Betweens ever came to capturing that "striped sunlight sound" they had once talked about so much. McLennan belies his professed wish for simplicity in this song, which is a vibrant tune combining lush Spanish guitar with paranoid, bitter lyrics. The shafts of sunlight, in this instance, are glints from a butcher's knife. It may

Lindy Morrison, 1987 *(Bleddyn Butcher)*

not be about Brisbane per se—it is about "your town," not "mine." In the line "this town is full of battered wives," "battered wives" also sounds like "bad advice," and both readings fit the Go-Betweens' attitude to Brisbane at this time. Morrison was happy to offer her own reading of it to the *NME*, in terms that recall her days as a social worker: "Gradually all the inner city where the black and poor people live has been taken over by the council. Brisbane was partly taken over—the government was moving out all the poor and redeveloping these areas for business. Consequently, when people are uprooted, there's a lot of domestic violence."[1]

McLennan had brought "Streets of Your Town" to the album relatively late, during preproduction.

> BROWN: Grant wrote it at home, at our flat in Bondi Junction. It was one of those songs, like all melodically really good songs, that came out almost instantly and I knew when he played it that it had a nice melody. I started singing the vocal counterpoint and the harmonies at home and then we brought it in to the band at one of the rehearsals. I remember Lindy getting really shitty about it, she thought it was a conspiracy because we'd worked out the hook at home. But it was nothing as intentional as that, it was just like, "Oh, this is a nice song, I'll sing along to it." I liked that song a lot.

Willsteed, who will only grudgingly admit to finding anything at all appealing in the Go-Betweens' oeuvre, is less effusive:

> WILLSTEED: "Streets of Your Town" only came up late, presented as a fait accompli almost. It might not have passed the audition if it had been examined with more scrutiny at the time—I have no way of knowing. It was democratic, in that we voted on the songs, but "Streets of Your Town" bypassed the weeding process. I found it somewhat vacuous, but reasonably appealing. Mark Wallis thought it was a goer. I don't know. It all seemed a bit neat.

In essence, the new album was user-friendly, highly produced pop. McLennan told the Australian edition of *Rolling Stone* that the group's ambition was bigger than it had ever been. "Moving to Australia is to try and consolidate a lot of the good feeling that we've had here over the years. And working with Mushroom, it's the first time we've worked with a company that does have some say in records being on the radio."[2] In the same feature, Forster explained that he had toned down his outrageous persona:

A lot of that boasting came from London. I felt like screaming and stamping my foot a lot over there. I now feel that I just want to play and sing the songs. I'd much prefer to be singing "Dive for Your Memory" and know that I'm getting to the heart of something. That I'm really saying something and I can feel it inside me, as opposed to "I'm a star!" or "I'm a sex god!"[3]

In fact, he was speaking prematurely. Around this time he started wearing a dress onstage.

> FORSTER: I just got interested in it. I was wearing dresses offstage. I had one made—dresses are very comfortable. Maybe it was time . . . or my own sexuality. I knew it looked visually good. It was just something I was interested in, something I felt comfortable in. The band didn't mind, it was fine. I was doing it before that, not ones I'd had made, I'd bought them from shops. *16 Lovers Lane*—that was like "Operation pop star, going off." That was, "What airport am I in?" Within this juggernaut, the dress was part of this . . . I was never in a dress in band photos, I never commercialized it, like Robert Smith with his red lips and his hair. It didn't become my trademark, and I didn't want it to, that cheapens— "Oh yeah, that's the band with the guy in the dress." It just came out occasionally—that was its power—a click of the finger, a *turn*, then it might come back two months later, for one encore. Then it goes away again.
>
> It was a man in a dress, there was no drag connotation. It was like extreme *natural* drag, if you like. I wore the dress in Sydney [when we supported] R.E.M. and Gudinski[4] came up to Grant and said, "You run the band, don't you?" and Grant looked at Gudinski and went, "Yeah." He said, "Get rid of the guy in the dress."
>
> The dress actually became a career killer [when] I wore it in LA—we were dealing with Capitol, we'd spent three days working like dogs. We're the new Aussie group. We met everyone, from the president to the person who opens the front door. Us photographed walking around the top, LA, everything. And in three days' time we were going to do a gig down the road. And our manager wasn't there, and Simon Potts wasn't there, so we had to deal with the record company all by ourselves. They were nice people but there was a bit of teeth-crunching by the end. We'd spend hours doing video IDs—"Hi, we're the Go-Betweens" . . . "This next one's for KLBP in Detroit" . . . "Hi KLBP!"
>
> The last time I'd worn the dress was in Sydney a month before. Everyone at Capitol's going to be at this thing. And I'm at the hotel and I get a phone call from Grant. Grant goes, "Are you going to wear the dress

tonight? I think you should." And I go, "Yeah, I am." And so we get down there, we go onstage, *16 Lovers Lane* just out—everyone from Capitol, about a thousand people there—and jaws dropped. People that we'd been with just didn't talk to me after the show. It was like, "You can't do this. It's not going to work." It was like, "We've never seen photos of you in a dress. We've been with you three days and we've never seen you in a dress. Okay, it might work in San Francisco, they'll love it in New York, [but] you can play nowhere in between." I got calls from various people in the business the next day, it was like, "What the fuck are you doing?" And I just went, "It's done. That's the type of band we are."

We finished the tour. Of course, Kurt Cobain and that chap from the Lemonheads, they do it a couple of years later and it becomes the statement of 1993 or something. It didn't really go down well. Although certain people really liked it.

Bob Johnson, recalling these events later for Fiona Dempster's documentary, has an additional perspective on the matter:

JOHNSON: I wasn't at the show. I don't know whether it made any difference but Robert came out and wore his calf-length, kind of olive dress, very attractive, evidently—satiny, I do believe. And, the head of promotion took one look at him as he walked onstage and turned to the A&R guy who was running the whole show and said, "I'm not going to prioritize any faggots or their music"—and walked out of the venue. And the band played, you know, went down very well, except the A&R guy phoned me the next day and said, "I'm afraid it's all over, the record's off promo." You know, "It's off priority, it's not going to happen." He told me the story about the dress. It killed the record.

I phoned the band the next day to tell them what had happened and couldn't get hold of Robert so I told Grant, "It's all in the dumper, you know, it's not going to happen." Grant assumed it was not because of the dress, but because Robert's shoes didn't match the dress, that was his main concern, that Robert had done some kind of styling error . . .

Robert just couldn't believe it, he didn't understand it all and many months later, around my house, appeared in the dress, to explain to me what a very, what a very attractive piece of clothing it was. And it was. He wore it many times over that tour, but it was the last tour the Go-Betweens ever did, so maybe the dress had more importance than we all put on it at the time. He got away with it for many years, but, you know, he's a well-dressed man.[5]

It was a provocative, anti-commercial move, and it pushed Forster further to the outer margins of the Go-Betweens' pop career. His clothes weren't the main factor, though. "There's no doubt," agrees Roger Grierson, "that Michael Gudinski and the people at Mushroom felt Grant's songs had more potential." McLennan fell into line with this thinking when, after "Streets of Your Town" had scraped the outer reaches of the top forty in Australia, it came time to pick a second single from the album.

> GRIERSON: Grant was humbly suggesting... He didn't want anyone to be upset, but in Grant's inimitable style he suggested that the record company were saying that his songs had more commercial potential than Robert's. And even though he didn't want anyone to think he was hustling it, the overwhelming evidence was that the Mushroom people thought his songs had more commercial potential, and he reluctantly went along with them.

McLennan was pushing for his driving, anthemic "Was There Anything I Could Do?," an excellent song, but hardly a strong candidate for chart success. Morrison now describes it as "a fuckin' shitty song." Everyone else in the band now claims they wanted Forster's lighter, catchier "Clouds." Grierson claims the single would have been chosen democratically, but he is unclear on whether anyone outside the band had a vote.

It is curious that though the Go-Betweens were never backward in criticizing the regular pop market and would point out to journalists—who invariably agreed with them—that their work was immensely superior, the competition they felt most strongly was with their peers. The Triffids' success in Britain was galling to Forster, despite the friendships that existed between members of the two groups. The Triffids had taken a very different career path to the Go-Betweens. Although both bands had started in the late 1970s, the Triffids had spent a lot longer in their home town, Perth, as a hobby band, but then rose very quickly in the credibility stakes in the mid-1980s, first in Sydney and then in Europe. Some observers certainly thought they were riding on the Go-Betweens' coattails, in that both groups had the same fan base and played the same places. On a more critical level, Forster and McLennan might have felt ambivalent about the kind of genre songs the Triffids' primary songwriter, David McComb, was writing. Although the Go-Betweens always wore their influences on their sleeves, their albums did not change direction and sound from track to track as the Triffids' did from *Born Sandy Devotional* onwards.

> GRIERSON: Every time the Triffids scored some small victory, it seemed to cause some consternation amongst the Go-Betweens. I'd say, "Oh, the Triffids got *NME* single of the week" and they'd say, "Would you leave the

room?" and they'd all go into a little huddle. Once I came home and said to Robert that David McComb had got [Smiths producer] Stephen Street to produce something. Robert just went "Oh really? Really?", got up and walked out the front door, closed the door, and screamed and screamed his guts out. Opened the door and came back in.

Forster says now that the Triffids were "friends and competition" and that "If at times I had to walk out a door and scream, I was still always aware that someone on the other side of the door was watching me scream."[6] And certainly, if the Go-Betweens resented the Triffids' success, and the lives of relative luxury they lived in London—arguably after bands like the Go-Betweens had paved the way for them—they didn't resent their parties, renowned as oases of culture and conversation for Australians suffering for their art in bleak England. It is perhaps a mark of the respect the Go-Betweens had for the Triffids, or Ed Kuepper, or Nick Cave, that they considered them as their rivals, rather than, say, Kylie Minogue or INXS.

With the release of *16 Lovers Lane*, the group threw themselves into far-ranging and intense touring. The first major show was billed as a "Night of Miracles," a kind of Rock 'n' Roll Circus for the late 1980s, at the Enmore Theatre in Sydney. The group and their support act, Died Pretty, were interspersed with magic acts. They started the tour proper in July in

Hotel room in Athens, November 1988, with Steve Miller (second from l Victor Van Vugt (center), and John Willsteed (right) *(Courtesy Amanda Bro*

Melbourne, then went to London to play the Astoria; short stints in Germany and Italy followed. 1988 came to a close with more Australian shows.

1989 was to be similarly hectic, largely because of the link-up between the group and R.E.M. After supporting R.E.M. on their Australian dates, it was suggested that the Go-Betweens might want to continue the connection on the North American and European legs of the tour.

> GRIERSON: R.E.M. came along, did the shows, everybody hung out. They got on famously, turned out they were *extremely* happy to have the Go-Betweens on board. They had all their records, because they're the trainspotters that they are—particularly Peter Buck. Had a couple of parties, one at Gudinski's place. They just started talking about "come and do these European dates." Suddenly everybody moved heaven and earth to make it happen.

The tour ran to August 1989, with the Go-Betweens usually putting in a half-hour set before R.E.M. A stadium tour is usually a baptism by fire for a support band, but for the Go-Betweens—apart from the obvious frustrations of being forced to play such a short set—it was something of a success. R.E.M.'s audiences were, as one might expect, the most polite and gracious that a support band on a stadium tour could hope for. The two groups were from similar backgrounds, despite being from different continents, and had similar interests: there was a healthy degree of socializing. During the tour, McLennan and Forster managed to put together their track listing for the planned *Go-Betweens 1978-1990* compilation.

When the rest of the Go-Betweens returned to Australia, Forster did not go with them. Over the past couple of years, he and Grant had got to know the members of a German band called Baby You Know, from Regensberg in Bavaria. Erhard Grundl, the group's singer, recalls that after seeing the Go-Betweens at Glastonbury in 1986, he and violin player Karin Bäumler "became diehard fans immediately," and kept in touch:

> GRUNDL: My second [Go-Betweens] show was in 1987 in Linz, Austria—another remarkable show, maybe the best Robert Forster performance I have seen, maybe the best performance I have seen by anybody. I talked to Grant after the show and then he invited us to the show the next day in Nuremberg.

For Forster, the Baby You Know connection developed into a romance with Karin Bäumler, whom he regarded as a much more serious and interesting proposition than the aimless and listless Go-Betweens. He and Bäumler spent the summer of 1989 together in a house "an hour out of Munich" (later immortalized in his song "German Farmhouse").

> FORSTER: It was a really golden summer for me. I very much enjoyed it. I had been running on full with *16 Lovers Lane* for a year and a half, touring nonstop. Suddenly—bang, I just stopped and I found myself in a country house in Germany.

By the end of the summer, when he returned to Sydney to meet up with the other Go-Betweens, he had amassed a number of new songs that would give him fresh ideas about where the band should go from here:

> Lots of songs. I had about seven or eight. I'd had a very happy three months. I thought these songs had taken me in another direction.

When they were in Sydney for any length of time, McLennan and Brown would play shows as a duo. Their first performance was as the support act to the Roger Corman–produced film *Cockfighter*, at the Mandolin Cinema. Their duo performances included covers, some Go-Betweens songs, and songs of McLennan's that had been deemed unsuitable for the Go-Betweens, either by him or by group vote (some of these songs would later appear on his first solo album).

Brown was also able to engage in other extracurricular activities in Sydney. Via the Grierson connection—he managed both groups—she played violin on *The Great Gusto*, the exceptional fifth album by Tactics; she also played live with the band when schedules allowed. She was part of the Reels' ill-fated *Neighbors*, an attempt by the pop extremists to recreate the success of their earlier *Beautiful* with an album of Reel-ified covers of Australian songs. Brown played on their rendition of Cold Chisel's "Forever Now" and appeared in the video when the song was released as a single.

It had become increasingly clear throughout 1989 that Willsteed was unsuitable for the Go-Betweens. In his year and a half with the group, he had caused them all—starting with Brown and Morrison—considerable anguish. On the group's first European dates to promote *16 Lovers Lane*, Willsteed and Brown had been interviewed by a German journalist who told him he should be very happy to play in such a great group. Willsteed's response was that the "boys" were all right, but the "girls" were crap, and couldn't play.

Brown feels that Willsteed's attitude was that he was on a free ride, and should get as much out of it as quickly as possible.

> BROWN: From monopolizing the rider,[7] to when we'd do an in-store, [when] he would shamelessly scam as many free CDs and records as he could. When it came to picking up girls from the audience, he'd come to a gig and just go out and cruise the audience, basically. He was certainly driven by drugs and alcohol a lot, too. When we were touring America he was madly consuming everything he could get his hands on.
>
> I remember when we played at the Ritz in New York, which was [a] big show—a terribly important gig—he got so out of it before the gig that he was playing the wrong notes, in the wrong places, completely out of tune and out of time, and the mixer just ended up tuning him out of the mix totally. It was a band playing with no bass. That's how bad it was.

Willsteed had performed drunk many times since the 1970s: he and Luckus used to have drunken fights onstage in the days of Zero when, Luckus says, "He'd tell me to get fucked and I'd tell him to piss off and get fucked himself—people in Brisbane accept that sort of thing." And he was certainly not the only Go-Between to play drunk: critic Eric Weisbard recalls a post-R.E.M. show during which Morrison fell off her stool, unable to play. She confirms that she too was a "mess" at this time.

Brown feels that it was a long time before she and Morrison could convince McLennan and Forster that Willsteed was a liability.

> BROWN: Robert and Grant didn't believe it because he was still being pretty charming to them. I always used to call him the Iago of the band. Like Iago, he used to play Robert and Grant off each other. He'd go to Grant, "your songs are much better than Robert's, we should really be working on your songs, your songs should be the singles." And then he'd go and say the same thing to Robert. He'd say how crap Grant was to Robert. Eventually they realized, and at that point he was fired. But it wasn't until he'd caused quite a lot of havoc and damage.

When the decision was made to sack Willsteed in August it was McLennan, who presumably did not relish such tasks but was taking on this kind of responsibility more and more, who called on him with the news. Willsteed says he was surprised, but does not believe his alcoholism was entirely the reason for his banishment. He was also, he says, alienated by preexisting group dynamics.

WILLSTEED: I was always, and still am, quite happy to admit that I did awful things. I would never try to cover up—I would say at the time that the bottle was a reason. There were lots of other reasons as well. I felt isolated, I think, towards the end. Lindy Morrison says to me that I would never support her when there were conflicts, she would probably say that I would side with the boys when that's not so, in fact I know of occasions when I sided with the girls. Suddenly there were three people, Amanda, Lindy and I, who were quite capable of making decisions about the band, and Robert and Grant were being made to do things that they might not have wanted to do, or weren't allowed to do things they did want to do.

This sounds like a backhanded insult to Vickers who, for his part, thinks the choice of Willsteed as his replacement was foolish on personality grounds. There is, however, some sense to what Willsteed says. Vickers had traditionally trod the middle ground to keep everyone happy, and would put the interests of the band first: he was conciliatory in a way that Willsteed could not begin to be.

WILLSTEED: I really enjoyed the [R.E.M.] shows and got a lot of pleasure out of it. I came back to Australia and we were on holiday. Grant came back about a week later and came around to my flat and sacked me.

He came round and said, "John, we've decided we're only going to have four people in the band." And I thought that he meant he'd sacked Lindy. And he didn't mean that at all. That's how my mind worked. I don't know why I assumed that. Christ, I don't know . . . I was just sitting around waiting to buy some drugs, it's as simple as that.

While he was talking to me a man rang me up and said, "This is Michael from the Plug Uglies, do you want to be in our band?" and I said, "Yes, I'll talk to you later." So from my point of view it was, oh well, that's a shame, but here's something else—a band I really love, and they want me to be in them. That's cool, that's a good swap.

But I was never given a reason—and if I assume right, they must have been talking about this for some time to come to this decision. I had no inkling that that's what they were going to do, it was a real surprise. I said, "Oh well, that's a shame . . . shall we buy some drugs then?" I just sort of left it and worried about the details later. There weren't many details, I wasn't part of the songwriting, I had no financial interest in the band, it was very easy to cut me off. It was just: "That's the end of your salary."

I don't hate any of them. Some of them hate me though.

21
Parting Company

FORSTER: If I hear the enactment of the breakup of the Go-Betweens at one more dinner party I'm going to go crazy.

The band broke up in Sydney, which is a media town gone haywire and we were always a very public band in a way—we weren't four guys in duffel coats, living in some squat in Newtown,[1] do you know what I mean? We were a little bit more flamboyant than that, we knew people in the media, and so the breakup of the band was sensational—and had an afterlife. I mean, people loved the band, and so it was talked about.[2]

The Go-Betweens did not release a record in 1989, although an old Peel Sessions recording emerged as an EP on the Strange Fruit label; the group had no control over this release.

For the first Go-Betweens album of the 1990s, Forster hoped to seize back the reins and carve a new future. He had new songs he was excited about, for one thing, but he also wanted the band to record in a radically different way from their recent albums. A few years earlier he had visited Hansa studios in Berlin, and now he wanted to make an album the way Nick Cave and the Bad Seeds had done when they worked there—it would involve recording live for the most part, accentuating the quality of the group's playing.

FORSTER: I had a very clear idea of how this album was going to be. I didn't want to make a produced, super-commercial album. I wanted to go in another direction. I wanted to go into a big studio with a big budget and a really good engineer and—"Let's play," looking at each other . . .

16 Lovers Lane was done with virtually [just] one person in the studio at a time. I adore *16 Lovers Lane*. As time goes on I adore it more.

> A perfect-sheen pop album. But I had ideas of us playing together. Not in a crappy studio but in a big studio.
>   Lindy was talking about drum machines. Lindy was also talking about Amanda playing keyboards on some kind of violin synthesizer. Which was totally what I was against. To me, that was so 1985. That's finished, that's dead. You've got one of the best violin players in the world. I thought that we should make a stand and say, "This is an organic, long-term band, we're going to turn, we're going to twist, we're going to grow, the way a great rock band does." And not panic.

With Willsteed dismissed, a new bass player had to be found. Accounts differ as to Robert Vickers' role at this stage. Forster claims that Vickers told him at this time that he wanted to return to the band, but that Forster and McLennan had decided that their credo should be "don't look back." Brown denies that bringing back Vickers was a consideration. Vickers, however, claims that on a trip back to Australia towards the end of 1989, McLennan asked him back for one last album and tour.

> VICKERS: Sydney was just great. I really liked the summer, it was just beautiful. I was thinking, "This is really nice," and I was thinking, "Maybe I shouldn't have quit the band. Could have come back here, lived here, it's really nice . . . Now I've missed out on doing this album with Capitol. Maybe it wasn't the right decision." Grant actually asked me, he said, "We've talked it over and decided we would like to do another album, the final album, and we would like you to come back and play bass." So I said, "Yeah, why not, seems like a good idea."

But before he could officially reclaim his position, Vickers had commitments with Yo La Tengo in Japan. And while he was away, auditions were held for a new bass player. Roger Grierson's list of potential new Go-Betweens, dated October 10, 1989, is topped by "John Fell" (Fell was an English lover of Morrison's, and this is most likely a joke) "or Rob Vickers" and goes on to list Tony Robertson, previously of the Hitmen; Helen Carter, who had been in political pop group Do Re Mi; Michael Armiger, a friend of Grierson's who had been a member of the Johnnys, a good-natured "cowpunk" group Grierson had managed; "Mick [Michael Couvret] from Ed Kuepper's band" and Nigel Harford, of Perth-via-Melbourne band White Cross. Brown recalls yet another contender, Phil Hall, who'd been in the Dropbears.

> BROWN: We auditioned about eight bass players in one or two days. It was down to Michael Armiger or Phil Hall—he's a great bass player

and a really nice guy, too, he's played in the Lime Spiders. And those two were the best musicians—and both nice people, so it was a tough choice between them. But there was also one really young, really pretty boy that came along to the audition . . . He wasn't very good, though, and there was no way he'd have got the job, but Lindy and I were going, "Let's vote for him, let's vote for him, we want him"—so Robert and Grant will be threatened that there's this really handsome, pretty boy in the band. They'll be really opposed to it and it'll be really hilarious because straightaway they'll go, "No way." And sure enough that's exactly what they did!

Michael Armiger, on the other hand, believes that the competition was between himself and Helen Carter. Carter was a friend of Clinton Walker's and Grierson's. Her band Do Re Mi were a group many would have placed in the same league commercially as the Go-Betweens, although, in common with so many other groups, their one big single, "Man Overboard" (an Australian top ten hit in 1985), alienated their old audience without giving them a lasting new one. The idea of Carter joining the group is intriguing, not just because of her playing style but also because of the way it would have altered the sex ratio in the band. It was to combat Carter, Armiger recalls, that he honed his style for the audition.

ARMIGER: She was still playing in a fairly funky way at that time. I knew the way Helen played, and I thought, "If they're going to go in that direction, then they will pick Helen." So I decided not to go in that vein at all: "If I keep everything really simple then that makes the choice really clear." I knew the Go-Betweens, and had gone to see them a couple of times, but I didn't actually own a Go-Betweens record, so I had to borrow other people's, learn the tunes.

According to Grierson's documents of the auditions, Armiger was actually only Brown's first choice, but he was the second choice of the other three members, all of whom had different favorites. Grierson—evidently a seasoned hand at resolving group conflicts—pointed this out. The group opted for Armiger, and though being a Go-Between immediately put him on a wage of "three hundred a week" he was canny enough not to give up his day job at the Mambo design firm.

Forster continued to feel unhappy. McLennan was not too excited about his plan for the new LP, for which two possible titles were being considered: *Freakchild* (the favorite) and *Perfumed, Poisoned and Damaged*. But he was willing, for a time, to support it, whereas neither Morrison nor Brown had any interest in Forster's concept.

> FORSTER: Amanda said, "It's your record, it's very much your record." [But] we had to reinvent ourselves, we had to come up with a new push. And making eighties-sounding records wouldn't help us. We went into a state where we were rudderless. We didn't have a [producer] daddy figure. It was a very dangerous thing to do, because we were going to do it ourselves. We didn't have that camaraderie. We couldn't do it. I was trying to do something that couldn't be done.

On Forster's initiative, and in keeping with his desire for a more basic approach, the Go-Betweens had lined up five shows for December—four of them in smaller inner-city Sydney venues. These would serve to break in their new bass player and give them the chance to play the new songs. Then, in early 1990, they would begin work in earnest on the new album.

In preparation for this, Forster and McLennan recorded demos of twenty-one songs, the so-called "Botany Street Sessions," on October 24. There followed two weeks of rehearsals, during which the new songs were introduced to the group. As well as the songs from the "Botany Street Sessions," the group also learnt "Baby Stones" and "Buy More Time." Armiger recalls one "Botany Street" song, "I've Been Looking for Somebody":

> ARMIGER: [It] had a nice little syncopated rhythm part, and I worked together with Lindy [on] getting a rhythm together on that. It seemed really obvious to me, the way Robert was playing guitar, where he wanted it to fall. But when Lindy played it, it was just one of those things, I played my part and then just tapped out to her where I thought the kick should fall. That worked out all right, in fact that's about the only one of the songs that actually sounds like it's together.
>
> Grant had the song he [later] released as a [solo] single, "Easy Come Easy Go." And I think at that stage they also wanted to pull a couple of really old ones out of the hat—"People Say," which I don't think they'd played for a while.
>
> I could sense complications sometimes. It was mainly taken out on Lindy, the way she played. I don't know whether she'd taken a break for a while, was just a little out of practice or something, but sometimes you spotted frustrations, nothing huge.
>
> Looking back, it's easier now to see the way the dynamics worked than [it was] when you were actually there. We'd run through a few songs and then halfway through the night we'd have a break. Lindy and Amanda and I would go out and have a coffee and a bit of a chat, and they both

made me feel very much at home, which was really great. I ended up spending a lot more time in the presence of Lindy and Amanda, just because we'd hang out together during the breaks. It was strange, I hadn't actually played in many bands with women before, and it was surprising how much interest they took in your personal life, and they'd say, y'know, "Who you goin' out with?" y'know, "What sort of man are you? Are you a tits man or a bum man?" That sort of stuff . . . they took an interest, which was really very nice of them.

Grant and Robert would sit up in the rehearsal room and just talk or work out bits and pieces. I felt cut off from them but at the time I just assumed that was the way they worked. It was hard to gauge at that stage.

Armiger's first show, at which the Go-Betweens starred alongside Ed Kuepper, Died Pretty, the Ups and Downs (all Brisbane acts), and New Zealand band the Bats, was an artistic disaster for the band. The event was a BlockAIDS benefit at Selina's (in the Coogee Bay Hotel) on December 1, arranged by their former manager Clive Miller, who was working for the AIDS Trust. The group were only expected to play a half-hour set, and this was probably a good thing, since they couldn't hear each other on stage and the sound for the audience was poor. Unfairly, Armiger copped some of the blame for this from fans, much to the amusement of his co-workers at Mambo.

ARMIGER: They've got JJJ playing the whole time, and they'd have people ringing up on Mondays saying what shows they'd been to on the weekend. Someone rang up and said they'd been to the Selina's show and said, "I didn't think much of the new bass player." All these musicians coming up and saying, "Bummer, Mick."

The schedule the group had planned for 1990 was the most luxurious of their career. January and February were set aside for preproduction and recording of *Freakchild*, possibly with Mick Harvey producing and possibly at Hansa in Berlin, although by then it was looking more likely that they would be recording at EMI's Studio 301 in Sydney, where they had done *16 Lovers Lane*. Armiger recalls a budget in the region of A$200,000[3] being discussed, rather a different proposition from the previous occasion on which the group considered Harvey as a producer, for their first album. The reason so much money was available is that Capitol were still interested in the band, despite the dress fiasco—they were willing to pay a decent advance to license both the *1978-1990* compilation and the new album from Beggars Banquet. Even the initial response Grierson recalls from Beggars Banquet to the new demos—"They got the comment back, 'You're not ready to make the album because half of these songs are just old songs that didn't make the last record'"—wasn't going to derail the project, apparently.

After recording, the group were to have March and April off except for a small amount of Australian press; May would see *Freakchild* released around the world, followed by a tour of Australia. In June and July the group would focus promotion on Japan, and tour Europe; August and September would be another tour of Australia and New Zealand. The *1978-1990* compilation album would be released in Japan, and October and November would be a tour of Japan and then Britain again.

It has been suggested in some quarters that while McLennan might have supported Forster's desire to make the Hansa *Freakchild* from a technical standpoint, he was above all motivated to avoid going overseas at this point. He was convinced that if the band returned to Europe, Brown would end her relationship with him. Typically—and understandably—he does not factor this into his official version of the decisions he and Forster made that led to the breakup of the Go-Betweens. He presents them as entirely artistic ones.

> McLENNAN: I wasn't looking forward to rehearsing the new album. Teaching Michael new songs, the whole thing.
>
> I spoke to Robert about it and said, "I don't think I can come into this room any more. It's not in my heart. I don't know what to do—except, if you want to continue, keep the name, it's yours."
>
> And Robert said, "Look, Grant, I feel the same way. If you're not doing it, it's not the Go-Betweens. When do we tell people?"
>
> We waited a while, carrying around a secret which other people should have known and I honestly, truly, regret that. It should have been more of a band thing—discuss it, maybe walk away for a while, put the band on hold, do some different things—but that's only in hindsight. It was, "Okay, let's get out of the car." It wasn't, "Drive on till the gas runs out." It was "Get out of the car *now*." Unfortunately, we were parked on the outskirts of town, which meant a lot of people had to walk in, and they weren't quite prepared, and that's a serious regret.[4]

In addition to these artistic and personal factors, it seems clear that there were important economic factors at work.

> GRIERSON: Robert and Grant had made this decision that they didn't want to continue with the band. They didn't want the pressure of the band and the overhead—they got themselves in the situation where unless they sold a zillion records they weren't going to recoup their

royalty account. The only money that was really coming through was the publishing money, obviously songwriting was keeping them alive.

Grierson says it was a "subject of some discussion" between the songwriters and the other band members as to "whether the band were on tour to generate publishing royalties or whether Robert and Grant were using their publishing royalties to subsidize the band when they were on tour."

> GRIERSON: I think they were all wrong. There was no point in having an argument, the girls had their position, the songwriters had their position and the bass player was feeling superfluous to the equation. If you take a contrary position to Lindy it's very difficult to convince her she's wrong, but they were *all* wrong. Anyway, the boys then decided they didn't want the overhead of having a band, they wanted to keep it simple—I don't know, they wanted to turn into fucking Simon and Garfunkel. At that stage they were talking about getting Hal Willner to produce.[5] Capitol had given them carte blanche. They got to this point where they could do whatever they wanted—and they decided they didn't want to do it. At that point it all started to unravel.

This songwriting debate led to Morrison and Brown making plans for an interesting side project, in which the two of them would write songs, not for the Go-Betweens, but for their own group. Brown recalls she and Morrison had agreed to "try and write some songs of our own and just demo them, do something with them. We weren't particularly serious about it, we just knew we wanted to try our hand at songwriting."

Meanwhile, Forster and McLennan were still trying to decide for sure whether to break up the band, but not for long:

> FORSTER: I said to Grant, "I'm going to go to Brisbane and think about it, I want to get out of this cauldron of Sydney." I went up, I talked about it with my parents, I thought about it and called up Grant just before Christmas and said, "Yes, let's break up the band."
>
> I was also very very much missing Karin. I realized then that I'd found a different life. On the next album, there wouldn't be much touring. I'd found something else.

Whether fueled by insubordination, arguments over publishing money, creative tensions, a feeling that the group was becoming too big or ungainly, or even McLennan's belief that he could be a pop star on Mushroom Records in his own right—and all of these possibilities have been mooted by Go-Betweens insiders—the decision to end the band had been made. McLennan and Forster had not completely given up on the idea of continuing to work with one another, however. According to McLennan, at this time they were talking about recording "a sort of *Blood on the Tracks* acoustic album" together.

When the five Go-Betweens played their two nights in December at Max's Petersham Inn on Parramatta Road, a busy shopping street in Sydney's inner west suburbs, only Armiger, Morrison, and Brown still believed they were leading up to recording a new album in January and touring throughout 1990, although Forster was in typical form:

> ARMIGER: I was having a nervous crap before the gig at Max's and Robert came into the toilets. He didn't know I was in there. A punter was in there too and he goes, "Wow, this is really great seeing the Go-Betweens in Max's, this is fantastic! I'm kinda surprised that there aren't terribly many people here." There weren't many punters there—two hundred, two hundred and fifty, which for the Go-Betweens was a small gig. But it was the fifth small gig we'd done in as many weeks, so it wasn't that surprising. And Robert said, "Yes, I'm kind of surprised too, because if I wasn't in the Go-Betweens, they'd be my favorite band."

The last Go-Betweens show for a decade—a momentous event, and the last time Morrison would play with McLennan and Forster—was far from lackluster, but still full of mistakes and problems. The group looked back over its entire catalog, including "People Say," "That Way" from *Before Hollywood*, three songs from *Liberty Belle*, five from *Tallulah* and four from *16 Lovers Lane*, along with five new songs. Stage banter was awkward, revolving around repetition of the supposed story "behind" a number of the songs: a woman who has a car accident wearing nothing but a bra and a towel.

Forster introduced the group before the next-to-last song, "The Wrong Road": "I'd like to introduce the band as they come onstage—on drums, Lindy Morrison," an announcement which met with applause and cheering, rising and swelling until Forster halted it with, "Save something for *me*. On bass guitar—Michael Armiger." The relatively unknown Armiger received less attention. Next came, "On violin, oboe, guitar, vocals, Amanda Brown," also receiving uproarious applause. Forster concluded with, "On guitar and vocals my partner . . . Grant McLennan. And he starts this song."

In an almost poignant mishap, Armiger had to stop the final song—"Streets of Your Town"—because McLennan was playing it wrongly.

ARMIGER: He had the capo on the wrong fret, so it throws everything out, it's totally in a different key. Because I'd just spent all this time learning these songs, I had to be really definite where I was. I knew what key it was in. I had to make him stop and change his capo position on the thing.

It's funny, he starts playing, I start playing and think, "no," so I sort of said, "whoah, Grant, you've got it wrong, you've got it on the wrong fret," which is really weird shit to do live. And he turned round at first and said, "come on, I *wrote* the song." And I said, "dead set, you've got it on the wrong fret." Then he played [it] and . . . "ah, yeah."

A few days after the Max's show, as the group prepared to go on a brief Christmas break, McLennan and Foster decided they would tell Morrison, Brown and Armiger of their decision to end the group at precisely the same time—or as near to that as possible, given that it was Forster's job to tell Morrison, and McLennan's to inform both Brown and Armiger. There is a boyish, grandiose element to this scheme that recalls their early days of definitive statements and "happenings."

BROWN: All they did was tell us separately, Grant told me, Robert told Lindy. They said to us that they were going to make an acoustic record together and that they wouldn't need the band. At first I thought, "it's just a sideline project for them, they're doing this and they'll come back to doing the band." But then I realized it was a pretty clumsy way of breaking up the band. They just didn't know how to say it, I think.

Armiger was in South Australia with his parents at the assigned breakup time, but his recollection is similar:

ARMIGER: Because Amanda was living with Grant, he got to their place and he had to say—bang, it's five o'clock—"I have to tell you something. We're breaking up the band." I really felt sorry for Amanda in that instance, because having a relationship with Grant at that time, having someone just dump you in the band, that caused the end of their relationship. I can imagine being in that kind of position, I'd just feel betrayed.

So Grant told Amanda and Robert told Lindy. And it was Grant's gig to ring me. I was still in South Australia at that time, he left a message on my answering machine. I gave him a ring the next day. By the sounds of things they [had] planned to tell me at the same time, which I found very surprising. Obviously Lindy and Amanda had been there for years and years, [so] planning to tell me at the same time . . . Rather than raising me to the level Amanda and Lindy enjoyed, it brought them down to the level of me, only in the band for a month and a half.

GRIERSON: Lindy rang me, and said, "What do *you* know?" It was like, was I in cahoots with them and did I know? And I didn't. But it kind of got weird. And I said, "Do we get together tomorrow and have a discussion about it? Let's not break up, list all the reasons why you should stay together for six months, two years, whatever?" And Lindy went, "No, no, forget it, it's over, it's over, don't even try." So I didn't. I just let it work itself out. Of course, a week later Lindy's like, "You never even *tried* to keep the band together." A little unfair. And then Amanda turned around and said to Grant, "Well, if I'm not in the band, then I'm out of here." And she walked out on him! He—God knows why, the thought hadn't occurred to him.

You've got to understand that this was a band where everybody was emotionally dependent on everybody else. With the possible exception of Grant and Lindy. But Robert needed Amanda, Robert needed Lindy, Robert needed Grant. Grant needed Amanda, Grant needed Robert, Grant didn't necessarily need Lindy, Lindy needed Amanda, Lindy needed Robert.

Everybody needed everybody else.

22
Danger in the Past

McLENNAN: I just did not wanna be in a democracy any more, and the rules of the band—they were sort of unwritten rules. We were all too close, and it all came down too quickly, and I perhaps did things [for which] no one understood my motives and that's probably my fault. And it snowballed . . .

I remember Johnny Marr telling me how people were saying he was a bastard for breaking up the Smiths, but sometimes groups run their course, and there's nothing worse than a band soldiering on and making garbage, the name being dragged through the streets. If we were going to break up, it was the perfect time.

This was how McLennan described the demise of the Go-Betweens in 1991, when he was promoting his first solo album, *Watershed*. The album's title—and much of its lyrical content—clearly relates to the breakup of the band and to the collapse of McLennan's relationship with Brown. One can trace similar links on Forster's solo debut, *Danger in the Past*; many of the songs on it, including the title track, were written during his Go-Betweens days.

Both these records were almost two years in the future, however, when the group ceased to exist at the end of December 1989. Roger Grierson recalls a period of confusion, with McLennan and Forster at first clinging to the acoustic duo idea.

GRIERSON: It was going to be a folky duo. Robert's dramatic swing of his arm: "Sell my amplifier! I don't want to see it again. Get someone to go round to the rehearsal room, get it and sell it and send me the money." He didn't ask me to sell the [electric] *guitar*, though.

McLennan, meanwhile, tried to salvage his relationship with Brown, who, feeling betrayed, had immediately moved out of their Botany Street flat in Bondi. Trying to undo the damage, he suggested that she should play on the mooted Forster-McLennan acoustic album—or that he and Brown should record an album as a duo.

It is quite possible, as Amanda Brown thought, that the idea of recording a "sort of *Blood on the Tracks* acoustic album" together was only ever a device that gave Forster and McLennan some kind of excuse for dismantling the band. But even if there had been a realistic chance that they would make such an album together at this point, it soon evaporated:

> GRIERSON: [Grant and Robert] went, "Okay, fine, that's it," and Amanda went, "I'm out of here." And then Grant said, "Oh, I didn't necessarily say I wanted to make a duo record, I always said I wanted to make my *own* record, and I want Amanda to play on it."
>
> Suddenly Robert's going, "Well, what am *I* doing?" They've just broken the band up so he and Grant can make a record together, and then Grant's saying, "I don't actually want to make a record with Robert, I want to make a record with Amanda." For obvious reasons.
>
> [Robert] thought they were going to do one thing and a week later the whole thing had changed. So Robert said, "Fuck it, I'm off to Bavaria."

Brown was understandably unwilling to make a record with Forster and McLennan that would effectively have been a Go-Betweens album without Lindy Morrison, but Grierson recalls that Morrison was keen for the songwriters to make an album without her under the name the Go-Betweens—provided she received the share of royalties from it to which she was legally entitled. "Maybe they didn't want to because they didn't want to pay her any money," Grierson muses. "Maybe there was a smidgen of that."

> MORRISON: By 1990 I was a mess. My father had died. I was desperate to have a baby. I had it tattooed on my forehead, *desperate to have a baby!* The best thing that could happen to me was the band breaking up, so I could find stability and have a child before I was too old. I was out of my brain. Everybody was out of their brain.

Grierson and his London counterpart, Bob Johnson, saw great potential in continuing to use the group name as an umbrella for McLennan and Forster as a duo. Indeed, Johnson had long advocated the route along which he steered Roddy Frame of Aztec Camera after his first album, which involved hiring musicians to be "Aztec Camera" only when needed to record or to play shows under the band name. If Forster and McLennan could be induced to take the opportunity, there was another "Go-Betweens" album contracted to Capitol in the US, and a lucrative seam to be mined with Beggars Banquet in the UK, as well as a strong relationship with Mushroom in Australia.

While it seemed unlikely that most diehard Go-Betweens fans in the early 1990s would warm to the idea of a Go-Betweens without Morrison or Brown, who were integral parts of the band's public face at the time, diehard fans are only a small percentage of the people who buy the records. But in any case, Forster and McLennan had envisaged the abandoned *Blood on the Tracks*–style acoustic album as a "duet" project, to be released under their two names, rather than as credited to the Go-Betweens. Their attitude to what the Go-Betweens meant as a brand name would remain resolute for six years, and they each went into their solo careers with firm resolve.

Tracing the "solo years" of musicians strongly associated with a group's output is difficult from anyone's perspective, including that of the artists themselves. In rock music, a group is about dynamics and negotiating individual personalities within a group; a solo career is about recreating oneself for each new release. Forster and McLennan tried valiantly to carve out solo careers in the 1990s with diminishing commercial—and variable artistic—returns. As usual, the commercial success of their work bore little relation to the quality of the work produced: McLennan's 1997 album, *In Your Bright Ray*, is easily his best solo album, but coming as it did after the excessive and rambling *Horsebreaker Star*, and amid mounting interest in his renewed association with Forster following the 1995 "Australian Go-Betweens Show," few people wanted to hear a new Grant McLennan solo record, and many critics (and most of his audience) dismissed it.

Having said that, much of Forster and McLennan's solo work continued to be complementary throughout the 1990s: while there was no overt call-and-response between the output of each of them, it was clear that—just like their songs on the Go-Betweens albums in the 1980s—each regarded the other as the most important gauge of how he was doing. They continued to support each other, playing live together on many occasions and collaborating in other ways, and there does not ever seem to have been any acrimony between them.

In other respects, the ripples from the breakup spread very widely. Throughout the 1990s, and to some extent up to the present day, it was almost impossible to remain on friendly terms with every ex–Go-Between; only Robert Vickers seems to have managed it.

July 1990 saw the release of *The Go-Betweens 1978-1990* on double LP,

CD, and cassette (each with a slightly different track listing) in a number of key territories. This collection marked the first album release of several tracks Forster and McLennan clearly thought of as important to their story, including "The Sound of Rain," which they had recorded for Beserkley twelve years earlier, and which featured Peter Walsh during his very brief tenure with the band.[1] Clinton Walker, for whom the Go-Betweens were enormously important, wrote a review of *1978-1990* for Australian *Rolling Stone*, which, he claims, editor Toby Creswell reworked to make Walker's considered theories read like sharp, bitchy attacks. Walker (and Creswell?) effectively condensed the history of the group into a paragraph:

> Any band formed by two naïve boys effectively claiming homosexuality wasn't just for poofters, who then recruited a feminist female drummer (and "older woman") who became a lover to one of the boys, and then recruited a naïve young girl who became a lover to the other boy, by which time the first affair was well and bitterly over, is bound to run into trouble . . . (sort of like an Antipodean Fleetwood Mac; sure made for some good material though . . .).

The review went on to criticize the band for their lack of technical ability, saying that both Forster and McLennan "played the same guitar solo for ten years!" Its point was, however, that the group was a platform for the songwriters' songs. He ended with the provocative "They were a great band. It's just a shame they couldn't play"[2] (to which Forster retorted: "It's called punk, Clint"[3]). Morrison took issue with Walker's assertions as they appeared in *Rolling Stone*, and the two have not been on friendly terms since.

Within two years of the breakup of the Go-Betweens, Lindy Morrison had realized her goal of having a child. Amanda Brown, too, had become a mother. The two women stayed in contact, and soon followed up on their desire to have a band in which they wrote the songs. They formed a duo they called Cleopatra Wong. The instrumentation was hi-tech, in the vein that Forster had claimed Morrison wanted to follow on the planned Go-Betweens album, and Brown was the primary songwriter. Aside from the free jams of her earlier band, Climbing Frame, and a partial credit on the throwaway "Don't Call Me Gone," these were Brown's first songwriting forays.

Cleopatra Wong played around Sydney—and even toured Southeast Asia—in the early 1990s and released two EPs: *Egg* (1992) and *Cleopatra's Lament* (1993).[4] Old and new friends of the Go-Betweens rallied around them: both Colin Bloxsom and Michael Armiger played with the group.

Cleopatra Wong was abruptly terminated by Morrison in 1993, in a surprise statement at a business meeting called to discuss packaging the two EPs together as an album for US release. Understandably, record-company backing for the project fell through, and Morrison and Brown did not speak to each other again for some time. They are now reconciled, and play music together again as Square, which they call a "garage band."

Amanda Brown, who played a few shows with Forster in the mid-1990s, spent most of that decade completing two degrees, playing with a broad range of rock bands from Silverchair to R.E.M. (she appears in their video, *Road Movie*) to the excellent Sydney-based country band Love Me. She graduated in screen composition from the Australian Film Television and Radio School in 2000 and has composed music for numerous films and events. In 2003, she released a solo album, *Incognita*.

Since Cleopatra Wong's breakup, Lindy Morrison has become involved in two different fields: working in music therapy for the disabled, and as an advocate for the payment of royalties to arrangers and recorded musicians. She is also on the board of several music-industry–related groups. As well as playing in Square, she has been involved with the Bondi Senior Swing Band and the Junction House Band, a group of musicians with intellectual disabilities. She is also a noted media commentator on feminist and music-industry issues, which of course frequently intersect. In 2003, she stood as a candidate of the Democrats (a small but occasionally powerful Australian party) in Sydney local elections, but was not elected.

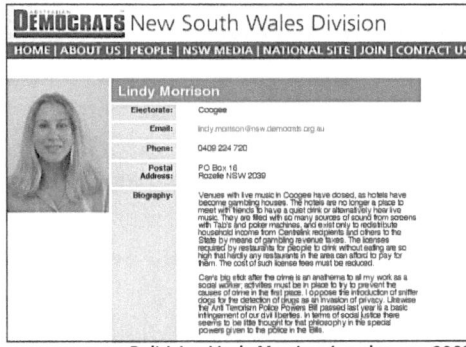

Politician Lindy Morrison's web page, 2003

Morrison's involvement in the issue of royalty payments for non-composers is rooted in her own experience: she—and, subsequently, Brown—sued Forster and McLennan for unpaid royalties due to them for arranging and playing on Go-Betweens records.[5] Not surprisingly, these factors—the original refusal to pay, and the subsequent legal action—have soured relations between members of the 1980s lineup.

Of the two Go-Between songwriters, McLennan seemed the most likely to abandon rock for his original career goal, literature. Instead, he continued to play music—solo and in group situations—throughout the 1990s, often in partnership with other male songwriters. The first such collaborative project to see the light of day was the Jack Frost project; for McLennan, it was an almost instant return to the songwriter duo format, with Forster replaced by Steve Kilbey. Kilbey's group, the Church, had enjoyed their biggest commercial success in 1988 with "Under the Milky Way," which had made the US top forty; the group members had long done low-key solo projects and extra-group collaborations in addition to their regular activities. Jack Frost—celebrated as a "marriage" by *B-side* magazine's Marci Cohen[6]—recorded their self-titled debut over a two-week period. Cohen recorded McLennan's views on the record:

> It took on a life of its own. It deserted us. It controlled us. We didn't have anything to do with it. We just went along. We just got on the Ferris wheel and just kept on going round ... It just started as a lark, as a gamble. And at the moment, it's racing down the street ahead of us. We're trying to catch up. It's a proud, defiant little critter. It's running around saying, "Listen to me. Listen to me."[7]

To another interviewer, McLennan described the record as a "complex mess."[8] Still, it generated sufficient enthusiasm for the duo to discuss the possibility of a tour, and for a second album, *Snow Job*, to be recorded in 1993 (it was not released until 1995).[9] In retrospect, the hurried nature of the project meant that for all but the most ardent fans (these are usually Kilbey/Church fans), initial excitement over the Jack Frost recordings has given way to the view that the songs are shallow and throwaway. This may also, however, be related to disillusionment as the often-expressed (quite possibly false) rumor sinks in that McLennan introduced Kilbey to heroin during the Jack Frost sessions. The persistence of this belief may well say more about public impressions of McLennan and Kilbey at this time than anything else. Certainly it was something McLennan was willing to "play" with; during a mid-1990s Jack Frost performance in Melbourne to promote *Snow Job*, McLennan told the audience that Kilbey's physical appearance was testament to Sydney being a den of evil and debauchery: "This is what you'll end up like if you live in Sydney for too long!" Since moving from Sydney back to Brisbane, McLennan has often given it a "sin city" profile.

In the meantime, Forster married Karin Bäumler in Germany and set about recording his first solo album there. Using songs he'd written originally for the projected Go-Betweens *Freakchild* album (he would later claim that one of the problems facing the group in its last days was a surplus of songs) as well as some new material, Forster recorded *Danger in the Past* at Berlin's

Hansa Studios—where he had wanted *Freakchild* to be recorded—with Mick Harvey and Victor Van Vugt producing.[10] His backing band were Harvey on bass, his fellow Bad Seed Thomas Wydler on drums, and guitarist Hugo Race, a Melbourne icon in the early 1980s, whose bands were Plays with Marionettes and the Wreckery.[11]

Danger in the Past was issued in December 1990 to critical acclaim; it is probably the most realized and cohesive of the solo Go-Betweens outings. Forster apparently believes it is still his best solo work: he has referred to it as the product of "a full flood of energy that lasted about two years."[12] The title track and certain other songs on the record allowed Forster to take a new approach, which runs through his solo material, that involves rambling and funny monologue-songs; usually, a slight but enticing melody will provide the backdrop for a series of musings which he can elaborate on further in live performance.[13] This, it is clear, is the Forster persona that the Go-Betweens had prevented flowering. Other songs celebrate his new relationship and denigrate older ones.

Soon afterwards, Forster assembled the first of a series of German backing bands to perform the *Danger in the Past* material live. The band included drummer Matthias Strzoda,[14] who would play a brief role in the reformed Go-Betweens ten years later.

> STRZODA: I got to know Robert when he was looking for a German band for the *Danger in the Past* tour of Europe in early 1991. Through a friend of his, Thomas Meinecke of FSK, Robert heard of a hip C&W outfit, Oklahoma Lone Star Heartbreak Institute, consisting of members of several Hamburg-based bands. We jammed for one night. He was impressed and booked us straight away. In London, Grant was there to watch our show. One of his rare comments: "Very subtle."[15]

Forster also played with McLennan again not long afterwards, for the first time since the breakup of the Go-Betweens. The pair toured as "Robert Forster and Grant McLennan," opening for Lloyd Cole on his 1991 tour of Europe (Robert Vickers, incidentally, was playing in Cole's band at the time). Strzoda recalls that after the Hamburg show on this tour, Forster's touring band "backed Grant and Robert at a small club for a rocking and legendary secret late-night show remembered as 'the Clarke Sisters in session.'"

McLennan had long been teased by friends about his seriousness (not to mention his sincere eyebrows). In 1991, he was ruthlessly parodied by a Sydney group who knew only his reputation: Smudge's first single, "Don't

The Robert Forster band, 1991: Christian Dabeler, Frank Schmiechen, Detlef Diederichsen, Matthias Strzoda *(Ronald Sawat*

Want To Be Grant McLennan," was an independent hit in Australia.[16] Its release coincided with McLennan's first solo album.

Between 1989 and 1991 McLennan had decided that he should make a determined attempt at the charts—a wish that appeared, incidentally, to necessitate wearing a baseball cap to project a more youthful image (and conceal a receding hairline).[17] His first proper solo single, "Easy Come, Easy Go"—another ex–Go-Betweens track from the final year of the group—was issued in February 1991, and the album, *Watershed,* credited to "G.W. McLennan," followed in May.[18] The album was dedicated "to Sweetpea, always,"[19] and its listed players were major figures in the Sydney rock scene, including Amanda Brown; Phil Hall, who might almost have been the replacement for Willsteed in the Go-Betweens; Stephen Phillip, Helen Carter's partner and the cofounder of Do Re Mi; members of the Cruel Sea, who would become one of Australia's biggest groups of the 1990s; Kit Quarry, who had been the drummer in one of Australia's best groups of the 1980s, the Craven Fops;[20] and Paul Kelly, who has long had the reputation of being one of Australia's finest singer-songwriters. What all these people actually did on the album is, however, not specified.[21]

The album's producer was Dave Dobbyn, who first rose to prominence in the 1970s as a member of New Zealand pop-rock group D D Smash, and had a number-one hit in Australia in 1987 with the single "Slice of Heaven," recorded in conjunction with reggae band Herbs as part of Dobbyn's soundtrack to the animated film *Footrot Flats*. Using Dobbyn as producer was an industry-friendly decision, and it produced worthy results: the album has a light, airy pop feel throughout.

Watershed was not a huge success, but Mushroom had sufficient confidence in McLennan to go in with Beggars Banquet on funding a second solo record, *Fireboy,* this time with Dobbyn arranging, producing, and playing guitar. They were joined for this project by drummer Michael Barclay, who had previously played with Paul Kelly. Backing vocals were provided by Penny Flanagan and Julia Richardson of the band Club Hoy, for whom McLennan had produced a single. *Fireboy,* released in 1993, was accomplished and mature, but lyrically very bleak: McLennan had used up his lighthearted Go-Betweens songs, and was now turning out very stark, sad material. And the single "Lighting Fires" was, in musical terms, virtually a rewrite of one of his earlier songs, "Was There Anything I Could Do?"[22]

The McLennan/Dobbyn/Barclay team also played live shows, using taped backings which led to awkward situations such as Barclay miming to female backing vocals (at least, if he was not miming, he made the audience feel awkward by failing to explain that he sounded exactly like Amanda Brown when he sang).

By this time McLennan had swapped the management services of Grierson—whom he retained for a short time after the Go-Betweens' split—for a different Roger, Roger King; but the failure of *Fireboy* to make a great impact on the charts necessitated a rethink, and a scaling down of the McLennan pop machine.

Meanwhile, Forster produced an album, *Clear Water*, for his Regensburg friends, Baby You Know. His previous forays into record production—for English group the Corn Dollies, for instance—had not fared well with the critics, but this time he was able to devote himself to a role that involved him becoming almost a member of the group.

> GRUNDL: Robert and Baby You Know share the same musical taste. We agree on what sounds good and what doesn't. Robert could have been a member of our group if he'd been born in rural Bavaria.
>
> Being on a small label, we had little studio time at hand so a lot of attention went into preproduction. Robert was brilliant in arranging the songs with us and getting the best out of our songs. He liked what we had and we liked his approach.
>
> We played a fifteen-date European tour, [which we] called "the Rolling Thunder from Bavaria and Down Under Tour" in 1992 to promote *Clear Water*. Those were very nice shows, structured a bit like Dylan's Rolling Thunder Review shows.

By the middle of 1992, Bäumler had finished her university degree, and she and Forster moved to Brisbane to live. One major reason for this was clearly so that Forster could develop his solo career. "I'm known in Australia," said Forster at the time:

> I can get things done quickly, and there's a certain amount of respect, even love, for what I do. Being amidst those warm feelings, that familiar stuff—and seeing what people were up to—was very exciting to me.[23]

Looking to put together a band to perform his new songs, Forster acted on a suggestion of Warwick Vere, of Brisbane's leading "indie" record store Rocking Horse, and went to see a show by local indie-country group, COW (an acronym for "country or western"), whose members included drummer Glenn Thompson.

THOMPSON: He came and saw us at the Queen's Arms Hotel. He asked me what kind of drumkit I had—the kind of question that Robert would ask! He was very pleased to find out I had a Ludwig.

I wasn't a huge Go-Betweens fan—I'd heard one of their albums, *Liberty Belle,* and I'd seen them once—but yeah, I was up for anything musical.

He seemed to have all the songs, he'd been rehearsing them in Regensberg, with some of the band called Baby You Know, so he'd kind of rehearsed them up with them, I think he'd even done some demos with them, we just went into a practice room and just went through the songs. That was it.

"The band knew who I was, of course," Forster remarked of COW at the time, "and they had a sort of healthy disrespect for me. They had a practice room and enthusiasm, and they were ready to go on songs, ready to bite into something different."[24]

Forster and COW booked into Sunshine—the same studio, although now with a different name, in which the Go-Betweens had recorded their earliest singles. Forster later claimed he wanted to make a "more Brisbane, let's put-a-couple-of-mikes-up-around-a-lounge-room record."[25] Thompson recalls that Forster brought along "an album called *Saddlebags of Wine*—by Tony Joe White, I think—and he sat it on the glass between the control room and the recording room, cover [facing] in—'that's the vibe for the album.'" An EP, *Drop,* was released in May 1993, and the album *Calling from a Country Phone* followed soon after. Though Forster described it in retrospect as "the dark star, sort of like the *Tallulah* of my solo albums,"[26] it is in fact a gem, an unpretentious, beautifully played song-based classic.

Glenn Thompson—graciously rising above being miscredited as "Glynn" on the album[27]—soon became a recurring character in Forster's musical life, as well as a personal friend. He toured with Forster for *Calling from a Country Phone* in both Australia and Europe. On these tours, Thompson reports, Forster's eccentricity showed no sign of abating:

THOMPSON: Robert Moore, David McCormack, Robert Forster, and myself are driving south to play our first Sydney show of the *Calling from a Country Phone* album tour and Robert Forster has a crook back. He's been complaining about it. Then we stop at Goondiwindi for a food break. We pile out of the Tarago and Robert, wearing what looks like a Coles New World[28] assistant manager's uniform—white shirt, thin, acrylic-looking V-neck jumper (red I think), black slacks and his favorite Bata Scout–style school shoes—gets out, tall and crooked, and immediately lies down on the concrete footpath of the main street, mid-morning. After five minutes he gets up and takes the lead up the street to the take-away, with the top half of his body vertical but ten centimeters to the right of the bottom half—and big bed hair.

We arrive at the Annandale[29] and it says on the chalkboard outside: "Tonight: Robert Forster, ex–Go-Betweens (the tall one)"!

I was the only one that went overseas. That was about an eleven-week tour of Europe and the UK. The rest of the band were the Germans, Mickey Schott and Robert Pöschl, who were in Baby You Know.

Matthias Strzoda was also on this tour, this time as a guitarist, and Forster had no qualms about throwing him in at the deep end:

> STRZODA: I joined him as a drummer, [then] on 1993's *Country Phone* tour as a guitar player. Which was an honor—and a risk, as I had never played a professional show carrying a guitar before until I was facing Roddy Frame, Tracey Thorn, Ben Watt, and Edwyn Collins in the crowd for that sold-out London show at the Garage.

On returning to Brisbane, Forster decided to form a permanent backing band, using Thompson and a double bass player—perhaps inspired by McLennan's work with Phil Kakulas, who played double bass on *Watershed* and in concert with McLennan in the early 1990s. The double bassist Forster had in mind was Brisbane-based Adele Pickvance. Pickvance's extremely musical family[30] had relocated from Manchester in the early 1980s, when she was in her mid-teens.

> PICKVANCE: 1982 was a terrible year in England, Thatcher was in. We were in the north of England, in Bury . . . and she came in and basically closed the whole of the industrial north down. Dad was made redundant. We had a cousin who'd moved to Australia and he'd always send us photographs of him bronzed with his gold chains and his Baileys in the pool, sunshine and blue skies. Mum and Dad would be looking at the photos, it'd be pissing down outside.
>
> We'd never moved in our lives. It was either Australia or Canada. So we went for Brisbane. We thought if we were going to move to Australia we may as well have the surf and the sunshine. We arrived and Dad supported us on his music. We lived in Bracken Ridge. It's one of those places where you've got your big garden and it's about twenty-five minutes from the city. Big garden, big house, it's a seventies housing estate.

By the early 1990s, playing double bass in the Natives of Bedlam, she was part of a new Brisbane folk scene. She had never heard the Go-Betweens, though she had seen Robert Forster play live. Then he called her and asked her to come and "jam."

> PICKVANCE: I think he called me on the recommendation of Glenn. I'd never met Robert before, or even heard too much about him—I'd just seen him play that night when we supported him. And I don't even think he was around to see the support band, so I don't think he would have seen the band! But he was interested in the idea of a female double bass player, that was what he was visualizing.

Forster's backing band was called Warm Nights, though it had no autonomous existence; usually, they would be billed either as "Robert Forster" or "Robert Forster and Warm Nights."

While McLennan kept a low profile in late 1993 (following the lukewarm reception of *Fireboy* he embarked on a trip to the USA and announced that he expected to live there indefinitely), Forster quickly got started on a third album. The only thing he lacked was songs: he had precisely one, "On a Street Corner." His next project was, therefore, a covers collection. *I Had a New York Girlfriend,* named for a Jonathan Richman track that wasn't on the record, was released in September 1994. Once again, Forster and McLennan were paralleling each other: McLennan had recorded a covers collection in miniature with the three songs he'd recorded as extra tracks for the 1992 single "Surround Me."

Forster selected the songs for his album, flew to Melbourne for a few days' rehearsal with a hand-picked band of local luminaries, and recorded the album under what turned out to be rather difficult circumstances. These included a last-minute cancellation by the scheduled producer, and Forster's refusal to use a computerized mixing desk. He later described the record as "madness. I don't know what I was doing."[31]

While *I Had a New York Girlfriend* has a number of high points—including a version of Grant Hart's "2541," Neil Diamond's "Look Out Here Comes Tomorrow" (McLennan's single had featured a Mike Nesmith song, while "Look Out" was originally recorded by Nesmith's old group the Monkees[32]), and a reading of Heart's "Alone"—it is hard to escape the sense that Forster wasted an opportunity to record a wonderful album with his Melbourne peers, who included such exceptional creative musicians as drummer Clare Moore (once of the Moodists, and at that time a member of Dave Graney and the Coral Snakes), violinist Warren Ellis of the Dirty

Three, pianist Conway Savage of the Bad Seeds, the Triffids' Graham Lee, Mick Harvey, and more.

The Warm Nights band toured the album, featuring Thompson and Pickvance; she soon switched from acoustic to electric bass because it sounded better.[33]

McLennan released his difficult third album, *Horsebreaker Star*, two months after *I Had a New York Girlfriend*, in November 1994. Whereas Forster's problem had been a shortage of original material, McLennan was bogged down by a surplus. Recorded in Athens, Georgia, at a studio often used by R.E.M., *Horsebreaker Star* was released in Australia and Europe as a double album and CD. For the US release (on Beggars Banquet, through major label Atlantic), six songs were dropped to allow a single CD release that also included "Lighting Fires" from his previous album. Neither version was a huge success; McLennan's attempts at pastiche (his forays into rap, for instance, and his occasional Dylanesque vocals) sound less like a great songwriter stretching his wings than like a desperate man clutching at straws. Robert Christgau wrote in the *Village Voice* that the album "gives up its pleasures gradually, mmm by mmm and aha by aha. But if at times it seems virtually inexhaustible, at other times it seems virtually boring."[34] Though its countrified backing sounds great and there are several high points, *Horsebreaker Star* is surely the least successful of McLennan's solo works. Disconcertingly, it was followed by the long-delayed release—into obscurity—of the second Jack Frost album in 1995.

Perhaps surprisingly, given his emphatic criticisms of the city in previous years, McLennan moved back to Brisbane at this time—and embraced it wholeheartedly. He discovered that the city he had once reviled for its closed-mindedness, violence, and lack of inspiration, had become a vibrant and exciting place.

McLennan and Forster now found themselves living in the same city again for the first time in six years, and soon began collaborating—on a script for a romantic comedy thriller. The central character of *Sydney Creeps* is a man in his early thirties who leaves Sydney to return to Brisbane in interesting circumstances—a person who from that brief description might seem to have some similarities to Grant McLennan. McLennan himself said of the script—from the stage of the Mercury Lounge, New York, in 1995— "If I say these four words, immediately all the producers and studios are going to *not* be interested: no sex, no violence."[35] This may not have been the problem with selling *Sydney Creeps*, however. Though there was a concerted effort on the part of the duo to get their completed script to filmmakers and studios, no one has yet taken the bait, and Forster now feels the material itself is not strong enough.

It is not an uncommon occurrence for an apparently infertile couple to adopt a child and soon afterwards conceive one of their own. The experience of touring *I Had a New York Girlfriend*, it seems, brought forth a number of new original songs from Forster. A number of these were "groove" numbers, in which the band allowed Forster to extrapolate over a simple backing.

> PICKVANCE: Yeah, it's a groove thing, three chords, I think. On *Warm Nights* there's a song with two chords, "I Can Do." The kind of song you can stop, start, slow down, quiet—and we've played it live so many times that it turns into something different. You can sit back on the simplicity of the groove, and the two chords. All this weird stuff was going on too, different lyrics, a bit of a dance, he'd even walk over to a piano that was onstage and try and play something to the chords—so it was great. I was into the folk thing, so playing kind of simple stuff and making it work was quite an education for me. For me, music had become something busier: everything had to have some tricky thing in it. Robert brought it back to basics.

In their live sets, Warm Nights also played a range of Forster's Go-Betweens songs, which made Pickvance and Thompson the obvious choice of personnel for the 1996 "Go-Betweens reunion" shows in Brisbane, one of which is described in chapter two.[36] The idea was originally proposed by French music magazine *Les Inrockuptibles*,[37] which asked Forster and McLennan to re-form the Go-Betweens for a show in Paris. Instead, Forster used the Paris show—which, like the Brisbane shows, was Warm Nights plus McLennan, only this time performing under the Go-Betweens' name, which they had not done in Brisbane—to launch a Warm Nights tour of Europe. Thompson and Pickvance agree they felt very uncomfortable playing as the Go-Betweens. According to Thompson, the ironic name he had coined for the shows—"the Australian Go-Betweens show"—was a way of "deflecting" potential criticism. "It was hard doing a Go-Betweens reunion because it felt a bit like you were an impostor, being the replacement drum and bass players."

Forster and McLennan were adamant that the Go-Betweens "reunion" in Paris was a one-off, and each returned to their solo careers immediately afterwards. Forster's album, *Warm Nights*, and its single, "Crying Love,"

Paris, 1996 *(Bleddyn Butc...*

were released the following year, in August 1996. Recorded in London with production by Forster's old Orange Juice acquaintance Edwyn Collins, the album did not feature Pickvance or Thompson, purely for financial reasons—Forster could not afford to fly them to London for the sessions. Thompson says that he and Pickvance were "disappointed, of course."

> The funny thing is he took a tape over of all Adele's and my versions. The three of us, Warm Nights, playing together.

And the songs on the finished album, he says, "came back pretty much sounding the same, which is nice."

Forster himself gave Collins credit for influencing him in both songwriting and playing on *Warm Nights*: "Especially watching him play guitar—he did a few things on guitar that I just nicked straight . . . He played a couple of things to me and I just took them."[38] *Warm Nights* included a new version of an old Go-Betweens track, "Rock 'n' Roll Friend," a classic Forster song that had been a b-side to "Was There Anything I Could Do?" in 1988. It probably deserved to be revived as an album track, though the original version had been included on the *1978-1990* collection, and Forster's 1996 rendition did not really add anything new to the song.

After *Warm Nights,* the world would not hear any further recorded work from Robert Forster for four years. He and Karin Bäumler returned to live in Germany, where he continued to work occasionally with Baby You Know: members of the group would do short tours backing Forster as Robert Forster and the Rockin' Boys. Forster carved a niche for himself in Germany, according to Grundl: "Robert speaks very good German. He can impress people from northern Germany with Bavarian phrases."

Back in Brisbane, Thompson and Pickvance involved themselves in a number of diverse projects, some of which included McLennan. Thompson also joined a Brisbane group called Custard. His experience with that band should be borne in mind by anyone who still wonders why the Go-Betweens weren't commercially successful.

> THOMPSON: At about the time I joined, Custard began to have more expectations on their shoulders. BMG had just bought [would-be cutting-edge record label] RooArt and so there was money behind them. They got a new manager. There was a lot of expectation, you couldn't help but feel that Custard were pretty keen to please. And of course keen for success. Not at any cost, we didn't want to be ridiculously polished . . .

We were into indie bands still, and we wanted to keep ourselves happy on that front. And so we tried to compromise and achieve both things, not really succeeding at either. At that stage, the indie people got pretty sick of Custard. We never sold any records.

The fact that Custard were, like the Go-Betweens fifteen years before them, an independent band from Brisbane hardly explains their lack of commercial success. Most independent bands, whatever their origins, would be likely to have similar experiences in making the next step up from moderate studio budgets and mid-sized venues to chart success. Custard's story is a reminder that the Go-Betweens were not unique in their lack of commercial success.

Members of Custard—Thompson, David McCormack (who had also been in COW), and bass player Paul Medew—played shows as McLennan's backing band at a bar called Rick's, in Brisbane's Fortitude Valley. At approximately the same time, Thompson, Pickvance, and McLennan recorded demos in Brisbane for McLennan's next album *In Your Bright Ray*. This effectively amounted to McLennan replacing Forster in Warm Nights, although Pickvance and Thompson did not have the time to develop the same sense of ownership over these songs as they felt over the songs of Foster's they had played so often.

In the middle of 1997, another odd event in the history of the Go-Betweens occurred with the publication of the original slapdash incarnation of this book by Allen & Unwin.[39] Not unnaturally, McLennan, Forster, and the majority of other former Go-Betweens remained aloof from the book, though their attitude was for the most part gracious. They found themselves the subject of renewed interest—both because of the book's existence and the publicity for it in Australia, and because at around the same time Beggar's Banquet reissued—worldwide—the six Go-Betweens albums in special uniform CD editions with new sleeve notes. This was especially important with regard to *Spring Hill Fair*, which because of its checkered label history had been out of print since soon after its release, and had never been available on CD.

Submitting to my interviews for the book had required the original Go-Betweens to reassess their 1970s-1980s output, behavior, and attitude. The book's publication was purportedly one of the factors that led Forster and McLennan to consider a Go-Betweens future. One of the first consequences was to contemplate the release of the early "Teeki tapes," the home recordings of their very early material made in 1978 and 1979 by their friend Gerry

Teekman. Forster gave me a cassette of the complete Teeki tapes in 1995, and said he hoped to resurrect the Able Label, for one release only, to put them out as a vinyl LP (no corresponding CD was planned).

Soon after the book and the reissue series, McLennan's fourth solo album, *In Your Bright Ray*,[40] and the single, "Comet Scar," were released. By far the best of McLennan's solo works, the album is consistent, upbeat, and extremely strong musically and lyrically. It was produced by Wayne Connolly, who had been recommended to McLennan by Brett Myers of Died Pretty. McLennan was interested because he had enjoyed Connolly's production work for the Underground Lovers.

On the last day of tracking, McLennan announced that he would not be present when the record was mixed.[41]

> CONNOLLY: I never really figured out why he did that. I always prefer to bounce ideas off the artist when I'm mixing, but he just said, "I want it to sound really beautiful." I took that to mean he wanted it quite lush. My sensibilities would probably have seen me make it quite direct and dry, to go back to the approach they favored on the first Go-Betweens album, and maybe I made it a little too lush while I was second-guessing his ideas of what made a beautiful album.
>
> The album is good because he had a collection of great songs. The demos were excellent. They obviously came from a happy period in his life—a very prosperous songwriting period. The originals had a slightly more folksy sound to them, but we opted for more electric guitar sounds—I played a bit of electric as well as Brett. Grant left it to us to pick the band, so I engaged the services of Maurice Argiro, who was in the Underground Lovers, probably the most fabulous bass player in Australia. He played a lot of melodic bass parts, [that sounded] like the bass on those early Go-Betweens records.[42]

For the most part, the attention focused on McLennan at this time was because of his involvement in the temporarily revived Go-Betweens, and the excellent *In Your Bright Ray* did not receive the attention it deserved. In fact, it was at this time that both McLennan and Forster, who had done so much together throughout the 1990s despite their unwillingness to record together, were dropped from Beggars Banquet as solo artists, even while the label was promoting the Go-Betweens reissues series.

Robert Forster did not record again until the new millennium: instead, he and Karin Bäumler, living in Germany, concentrated on bringing up their son, Louis, born in 1998. McLennan, still in Brisbane, was undeterred by the diminishing returns of his music career outside the Go-Betweens. He decided to collaborate with other musicians again, in what would turn out to be a new group with yet another important male songwriting partner.

Invited to perform as part of an art event in Brisbane, he set out to create the perfect pop group. This was to include McLennan himself, drummer Ross McLennan (no relation), singer, songwriter and guitarist Ian Haug from the highly successful Brisbane group Powderfinger,[43] and Adele Pickvance. The group called themselves FOC, a deliberately vague name intended to suggest a range of possible notions, including "Fear of Commitment" (or "Children"), "Face of Concern," "Friends of Carlotta," "Fuck Off Cunt,"[44] and "Far Out Corporation," the last of which was ultimately adopted as the name by the time the group's album was recorded with producer Tim Whitten.[45]

> PICKVANCE: It was visual art, photographs and images from Julianne Lawson—she set up this show, it was called *Occipital Hammerings*, at the Metro Arts in Brisbane—and two photographers, Kino Ruin. The idea was when we got into the rehearsal room, the boys'd come along with their photographs and we'd play to the visual side of things—it's very jammy music. And Grant wrote lyrics. We had a great time and it sounded really good, so we thought we should record. We paid for everything ourselves, but having Ian and Grant together was a great way of getting a licensing deal pretty easily, with Powderfinger's record company, and through their management. It was like, "Ooh, big time!" We did a few shows, we did a video clip, we got played on JJJ—high rotation—and that was fun, and we did a tour. We were all co-songwriters, which was a nice thing. Grant did write the lyrics. It was a nice, special thing, it was a generous band.

McLennan's presence, and the group's status as a Powderfinger side project, gave FOC some sway in the late 1990s, but Powderfinger of course had much greater pull on Haug, who was called back to his main group soon after. This meant there was little to keep Pickvance in Brisbane, particularly after Dave Graney called her from Melbourne and invited her to play with his and Clare Moore's new band, the Dave Graney Show.

> PICKVANCE: I thought, there's not really much of an opportunity for FOC to play regularly. I felt the urge to move, so when Dave rang me up,

Forster backstage at CBGB's, 1996 *(Michael Galinsky)*

I thought, bugger it. There was no reason to stay in Brisbane—I'd been hanging around waiting for the Go-Betweens to get back together, and that took too long!

Pickvance made the move, and has since played on three Dave Graney Show albums[46] and toured numerous times with them; she also played with Clare Moore and her Speckled Band, which for some time had a similar lineup to Graney's band,[47] as well as working on her own songwriting side-project, Cape Cod.

The Go-Betweens' profile was boosted further in 1999 with the release of two compilation albums. The first of these was a version of the previously mooted "Teeki tapes" album. Forster had given up the idea of a vinyl-only Able Label release, and instead produced a CD on his new label, Tag Funf. *The Lost Album: '78 'til '79* incorporated the four Able Label a-sides, plus "The Sound of Rain" from the Beserkley sessions, and a small selection of the many songs recorded by Gerry Teekman in Forster's bedroom. The album's packaging and sleeve notes urged the listener to approach it with the awareness that sound quality and professionalism were not the hallmark of these recordings, but the tapes were clearly a revelation to many, and make a very worthy addition to the group's oeuvre.

There may have been other motives for the release of *The Lost Album* at this time. For one thing, it might have been meant to pave the way for fans' acceptance of a Go-Betweens without Lindy Morrison, since she had not played on the Teekman-recorded material.[48] Even so, the album would seem not so much an anti-Morrison judgment as merely a reminder that she was not the first Go-Betweens drummer.

Bellavista Terrace: the Best of the Go-Betweens followed the (by now thoroughly irritating) "double l" scheme; the name simply comes from the street where the cover photograph (by Peter Fischman under McLennan's guidance) was taken. The songs were chosen from almost all the Go-Betweens albums to date.[49] Only *Send Me a Lullaby* was not represented, and Forster's sleeve notes advised newcomers to the band not to buy it "without at least owning three others. It'll make no sense otherwise."[50] What makes even less sense, however, is the decision to begin *Bellavista Terrace* with "Was There Anything I Could Do?," an unrepresentative and comparatively undistinguished up-tempo number. But the rest of the album is undeniably an appealing and seductive selection.

Forster and McLennan embarked on another of their duo tours to promote the album, with an extra, unusual twist: there would be a smattering of new songs in the set. What's more, rather than appearing under their own names, this time they were going to tour as the Go-Betweens.

A transcript from the Australian Broadcasting Corporation's nightly current affairs TV show, *The 7:30 Report,* answers the question of why this seemed like a good idea in April 1999.

> MAXINE McKEW: Finally, one of Australian music's most eagerly awaited comebacks—the Go-Betweens.
> Ten years after breaking up, the cult Brisbane group has re-formed, or, more correctly, a duo has emerged made up of Robert Forster and Grant McLennan. Tonight, they're launching their world tour in Sydney.
> The Go-Betweens have been described as the quintessential critics' band. They made an art form of commercial failure. But as Bernard Bowen reports, they're happy to have earned the industry's respect, even if the dollars didn't follow.
>
> [*Excerpt from "Streets of Your Town"*]
>
> BERNARD BOWEN: Ten years after the Go-Betweens broke up, the two musicians who formed the band's songwriting core are re-forming, touring Australia and then the world, having one more shot at commercial success.
>
> FORSTER: And still I believe that not enough people know about the band and we're still relatively unknown in a way, and so the opportunity to draw as much attention as we can to the work that we did, we'll take.[51]
>
> BOWEN: Robert Forster and Grant McLennan were friends before forming the Go-Betweens in the late 1970s. By the early 1980s, they were considered the cutting edge of Australian rock. But the band's influence far outweighed its record sales and they wear the tag of commercial failures.
>
> [*Excerpt from "Lee Remick"*]
>
> McLENNAN: Ultimately, what it comes down to is the work, the songs, to me. So if, after twenty years of writing songs, I can still listen to them and find some beauty or some—yeah, some glory in them, you know—I'm very happy and I can face myself in the mirror.
> I'm fortunate I don't have to put on makeup and be like Mick Jagger, you know, so I think in a way the fact that we never had the commercial

success that you're alluding to has worked to our benefit really, because it hasn't dated us.

[*Excerpt from "Cattle and Cane"*]

CLINTON WALKER: The Go-Betweens were important, I think, because they came through in the 1980s as a sort of a pioneering alternative band, but the Australian ideal was, and still to such a large extent is—it's a hard rock thing, it's macho... Back in those days, it was Jimmy Barnes... now it's Silverchair—it's still hard boys' rock. And "the Go-Betweens"—Robert and Grant—have continued with something that's more introspective, more poetic—more feminine, dare I say.

BOWEN: Their sound was more attuned to European tastes and the group had more success after leaving Australia.

[*Excerpt from TV show* Countdown, *1983*]

MOLLY MELDRUM: *Well, this is a pleasant surprise, coming to London and finding the Go-Betweens. I find it almost ridiculous that I have to come to London for you to come on* Countdown.
LINDY MORRISON: *That's exactly what we said before we came.*
MOLLY MELDRUM: *And I don't blame you.*

BOWEN: But while commercial success didn't match critical acclaim, the decade since the Go-Betweens broke up hasn't diminished the band's international cult following. Two years ago, a writers' poll conducted by one influential French rock magazine[52] voted them the best band of all time.

[*Excerpt from "Bachelor Kisses"*]

BOWEN: Prominent local writer Nick Earls, whose novel *Bachelor Kisses* was named after a Go-Betweens song, credits the band with putting Brisbane on the cultural map.

EARLS: Those people come from here, they've created things, they've written things, they perform them and they're taking them anywhere. That's the first time that I got a sense that you could come from Brisbane and write something and take it places.

BOWEN: Now Robert and Grant are taking their music back to those places they played in the 1980s. Together again after all those years, it hasn't taken them long to strike a harmonious chord.

McLENNAN: Over the last couple of days, it's just coming together quite beautifully, I think. He's also a gas to tour with.

FORSTER: Yeah, it's fun.[53]

As noted earlier, McLennan and Forster had toured together periodically since the early 1990s. But this was the first time that they had talked about recording together again since the aborted "duo project" of 1990. McLennan later told Franklin Bruno that three weeks into the 1999 tour, "I just said to Robert, 'Why don't we make another record?' And he said, 'I agree.'"[54]

In the course of the tour, Forster and McLennan made important connections, such as meeting the members of a group that is in one sense miles away from the Go-Betweens but in another sense utterly compatible: Sleater-Kinney.

CARRIE BROWNSTEIN: I was the only Go-Betweens fan in Sleater-Kinney—I mean *then*, we all are now. They were one of my favorite bands and we were flying back from Japan and were going to play two shows in San Francisco. And they happened to be playing, just Robert and Grant, that night. We went backstage and met them, and we were just so shocked that they knew of our band—it seemed like two totally different worlds.

Reunited onstage with Robert Vickers, New York, 1999
(Talin Shahinian)

More generally, by the end of this tour the two founding Go-Betweens had consolidated their intentions for the new millennium. They had reinforced their rights to the Go-Betweens as a brand name, as well as educating a whole new audience to the idea that they—Robert Forster and Grant McLennan—were the *real* Go-Betweens, and all others who had played under the name were at best temporary, even peripheral. They had also forged an excellent working relationship with two talented musicians—Adele Pickvance and Glenn Thompson—who could not only support their new plans skillfully, but also had considerable respect for their work and its history.

PICKVANCE: I met up with Grant in Brisbane in 1999—I go back there quite often, every couple of months—and he said "I've got something to tell you." We sat in Rick's and he said, "We're going to get an album together. Robert and I are going to record some new songs. We're going to call it the Go-Betweens—and we want you to be in the band and play for this album."

I was like "Great, fantastic!" That was pretty exciting.

I was surprised it took them so long. To play acoustically together for so long, to do those little tours that were so successful in Europe—wherever they went it was a full house. It was a long time coming.

23
Unfinished Business

> McLENNAN: There are some people who wanted Picasso to stay in [his] Blue Period, too. I can understand that some people are passionate about the band but I ask them—what band are they talking about? Are they talking about the two-piece Go-Betweens that made the first three singles? Are they talking about the Go-Betweens when we were a three-piece? Or the Go-Betweens when Robert Vickers joined the band or Amanda Brown joined the band? If I thought that Robert and I were going to fuck it up, I'd be out of the door straight away—because I'm a big fan of the band too.[1]

With their comeback record, Forster and McLennan achieved one goal that the original Go-Betweens had always sought: they recorded in the USA. Not in New York, as they had hoped to do back in 1984, but in another thriving hotbed of musical innovation, one that would barely have registered with many pop fans the last time a band called the Go-Betweens existed: the Pacific Northwest.

Forster and McLennan, along with Adele Pickvance, traveled to Portland, Oregon in January 2000 to record *The Friends of Rachel Worth* at Jackpot Recording Studios because of two chance meetings that occurred during the west coast leg of Forster and McLennan's pre-"reunion" US tour the previous year. In Seattle they had met Jackpot owner/engineer Larry Crane, and in San Francisco, as we have seen, they struck up a friendship (and established mutual admiration) with the members of Sleater-Kinney. As Forster explained to *Puncture*:

> I announced from the stage that night that Grant and I were going to make a record. When we came offstage we met Sleater-Kinney for the first time and Janet immediately said, "I'll play drums!"

Well, *Dig Me Out* was such a great record—it knocked me sideways. So I knew she could do it."[2]

McLennan later told Melbourne writer Sophie Best: "Coincidentally, we'd just been in Seattle the night before and met Larry Crane who owns Jackpot, and Sleater-Kinney were just about to record their album there."

Crane had arranged to meet Forster and McLennan to interview them for *Tape Op*, the music-recording magazine he edits:

> CRANE: We went over the recording scenarios for their previous records and weighed the pros and cons. Robert was great to talk to and we hit it off. He started asking me what I did, and Jackpot Recording came up. I mentioned that I had worked with Elliott Smith and Quasi. He asked if that [i.e., Janet Weiss] wasn't the same drummer from Sleater-Kinney and went off on how much he adored them, which really surprised me.

Soon afterwards, Forster called Crane and told him that the group were planning to record either in Portland or back home in Australia. The decision was perhaps made easier by the newly formed Sleater-Kinney connection—since Glenn Thompson was apparently unavailable because of other commitments, McLennan and Forster were no doubt happy to be able to take Janet Weiss up on her earlier offer.

> CRANE: As far as sounds, and how they saw the record coming together, I remember Robert and I talking about Dylan and the Band's *Basement Tapes*, and keeping a loose vibe. I really enjoy *16 Lovers Lane*—but I don't make those kind of records! Jackpot is a very low-key studio with a smallish live room. I even had to rent a twenty-four-track two-inch tape deck to do the session, as my main deck then was a sixteen-track two-inch which sounded great but was far less compatible with other studios.
>
> From the beginning it was understood that they would be mixing in Germany with Mario Thaler at Uphon. That was fine by me; I was already a bit nervous working with a band I liked so much. I was very excited to be able to record them in a manner I felt fitting. I never felt that any of the previous records were captured in the kind of straightforward, honest way, with full sounds, that I wanted to hear. There wouldn't be any drum machines or gated drum sounds here.

McLennan said later: "We didn't want to go back into a big studio, because the last time we did a record was *16 Lovers Lane* at EMI in Sydney, with a producer and budget. We didn't want to put that pressure on ourselves. We wanted it to be simple. Just go into a studio and record live—which [is what]

Outside Jackpot Recording: Janet Weiss, McLennan, Pickvance, Forster *(Bob Johnson)*

we did. *Before Hollywood* was recorded like that too."

The ill-fated *Freakchild* concept had collapsed, Forster once suggested, because the Go-Betweens had too many songs. Now, however, having too many songs was seen as a positive thing: he said at the time that whereas previously he had sometimes struggled to complete five appropriate songs for Go-Betweens albums, the fact that he had recorded nothing since the *Warm Nights* album four years earlier meant he had plenty of material this time:

> FORSTER: I brought eight songs to this record that I thought were good. That was a really nice thing. That's why I felt confident going into this record because ... it wasn't like, you know, I had three and the recording was coming closer and you know, then I might get a fourth ... I felt confident right from the start.[3]

The credited group for the album is Forster, McLennan, Pickvance, Janet Weiss on drums, and Sam Coombs (of Quasi) on keyboards.

CRANE: Sam Coombs attended all the rehearsals and it seemed like he would be more involved in the final outcome than he was. Much of the rehearsing was done at the studio the week before. I was mixing an album for Sugarboom during the evenings, so the Go-Betweens could rehearse during the day.

When they rehearsed I was working on *Tape Op* in the office and listening to them—which was a great way to hear the songs and think about how I would record them. They only worked on the twelve songs; nothing else was rehearsed. Very efficient. Janet's a great drummer and got parts for the songs very fast. Adele seemed to have practiced most of them before and already had many parts written.

Forster and Pickvance at Jackpot *(Janet Weiss)*

Pickvance had in fact played some of the Forster songs before. His critique of Patti Smith, "When She Sang about Angels," for example, had been in Warm Nights' live set. A newer song, "German Farmhouse," recalled Forster's life immediately after the demise of the original Go-Betweens.

FORSTER: ["German Farmhouse"] goes, "I was living in seclusion for a couple of years in a German farmhouse and drinking beer/Every day I'd wake up with a smile from ear to ear." And that's what I'd think. I'd wake up happy—[rather than] knowing there was a band meeting and I had to be somewhere, or worries about who's producing the record, tours, getting money for wages, all that. I was very happy that was over.[4]

Why he felt a new Go-Betweens album ten years later was the appropriate forum for this celebration—which was also combined with a further renunciation of Morrison (an "ex-lover's eyes")—is hard to know. But it was a sign of confidence, and of a very different Forster. It also signaled that Forster and McLennan were picking up where they'd left off.

CRANE: There didn't seem to be any doubt that this was a Go-Betweens record. All it took to be that was the fact that Grant and Robert were there. I felt some of the songs were a bit different than any Go-Betweens I'd heard, but I think that's okay. "German Farmhouse" is more of a rocker than they had in the past, and I encouraged that.

The only song that gave the group any real trouble was Forster's pièce de résistance, "Surfing Magazines."

> CRANE: There was a slower, acoustic version we recorded that Robert didn't like the feel of. The one on the record is version number two, and the music is actually slowed down in tape speed, though the vocal isn't. It seemed to be a hard song to get the feel of. If I had been in a "producer" capacity I would have put that on the "Going Blind" CDEP and put "Woman across the Way" (a b-side to "Going Blind") on the album . . . Subject matter–wise it didn't fit into the Go-Betweens' style as much. Then again, "Cattle and Cane" has a similar sentiment, looking back.[5]

Steve Miller recalls that once the group had agreed that the album would come out in Australia on the W Minc label, which he runs together with former Triffids guitarist Graham Lee, there was concern—on the part of both Forster and Go-Betweens manager Bob Johnson—over the poor quality of the songs McLennan intended to bring to the album. Miller was assigned the job of speaking to him about this, and though McLennan appeared unwilling to listen to Miller's advice,[6] the songs McLennan finally brought to the Jackpot sessions—including "The Clock" (the best song on the record) and "Orpheus Beach"—were very recent compositions, postdating their conversation.

Professors lecturing on the Go-Betweens in the future might wish to direct their students' attention to the fact that many of the songs on *The Friends of Rachel Worth* are "about" the Go-Betweens—either about past and present members of the group, or the concept of the group itself ("Spirit" is an example of this latter category).

The album was preceded by a promo-only CD of "German Farmhouse," a bold—if repetitious—track, but the single from the album was McLennan's "Going Blind," another putative "rocker" which—although this is not McLennan's field of expertise—possesses a certain charm. All three members of Sleater-Kinney contributed to this track.

> BROWNSTEIN: I played guitar on "Going Blind" and Corin sang on that song. I had a really great time but I was there so briefly that it was all work, I just went in and did it and left. My part on that record, which they loved—"Oh, that's perfect!"—that was so funny because basically what I did was listen to all my Go-Betweens records, and just write a Go-betweens part. And they were like, "it's great!" I said "well, thanks, but that's because it's exactly what you do on your records." But I was glad they liked it—I was scared they wouldn't.

After recording the album, Forster and McLennan took the master tapes to Germany some weeks later to mix them with Mario Thaler at Uphon Tonstudios in Weilheim. The goal, as Forster explained to *Puncture* at the time, was "to add a little European crispness to that warm organic sound" they'd obtained at Jackpot. In fact, though, they ended up keeping four of the rough mixes Crane had done for them in Portland:

With Larry Crane at Jackpot *(Janet Weiss)*

CRANE: I was surprised how many of my rough mixes they kept on the final record—the mixes I did on the last day of recording, taking one hour to do each of them. They were just for reference. I don't know why they couldn't better them. They feel okay, but I hear stuff I'd change. I still don't enjoy the mixes for "German Farmhouse" or "Going Blind"; I think the vocals are too loud.[7]

Forster and McLennan would not be making use of the Capitol records deal that had been extended to them as a carrot in the early 1990s to induce them to continue recording as the Go-Betweens. Instead, their record would be released on various smaller labels in different countries. Given the improvements in low-budget recording equipment, the recognition that 2000 was a very different time to launch a new Go-Betweens record than 1990 would have been, and the adoption of a fresh approach to the whole enterprise, this did not necessarily mean starting further down the ladder. Forster told the *Portland Mercury* in 2000 that he and McLennan did not want to deal with a major label: "You see, then you're dealing with people who don't like music. They stand in back at your shows and they're just tin-eared."[8] There is also a perception that a good-selling independent record can earn more money for the artists involved than a higher-selling major-label release. In the USA, at least, an additional factor was involved in their choice of label: the publicist at Jetset Records was their former bandmate Robert Vickers.

The Friends of Rachel Worth received very favorable press coverage for the most part. Few critics were concerned about the niceties of old and new band lineups, preferring to see the album as fitting "with the rest of the Go-Betweens' oeuvre, a bittersweet, adamantly melodic match of McLennan's overt pop songs and Forster's more eclectic and arty exercises."[9] The

Sleater-Kinney connection proved important for reviewers (and possibly consumers) in assessing the group's relevance or interest value in the new millennium.[10] Sleater-Kinney (who have interesting Australian connections themselves)[11] were depicted as being as far removed from Forster and McLennan as humanly possible, an assessment which ignores the fact that both groups use melody and hooks, have two songwriters, are often identified with post-1970s "the personal is political" ideas, and are clearly and unabashedly intelligent people, and so on.

Forster certainly thought there was a connection:

> I hate claiming any kind of influence, but when I first heard *Dig Me Out*, I heard faint little echoes of *Before Hollywood*, and I thought, "That just can't be. These young women from Portland are not even going to have heard of the Go-Betweens." But when we met them, they mentioned that record, and they mentioned Television, and it was amazing. This hunch I had turned out to be true.[12]

What is perhaps more surprising is that reviewers could not agree on what they did and did not like about *Rachel Worth*. Some, for instance, thought Forster's humorous "Surfing Magazines" was the worst track on the album; others (myself included) felt it was one of the best. Most agreed that the unflashy production was highly appropriate, particularly in relation to very 1980s-sounding Go-Betweens albums like *Tallulah* (though by the same token some of the keyboard sounds on *Rachel Worth* are very 1970s-via-the-late-1990s faux-naïf–sounding, and may well end up dating this album just as damningly within a few years).

Whereas in the late 1990s interviewers would persistently ask the Go-Betweens about the "double l's" in their album titles, the new album gave them a new dull question to ask: who was Rachel Worth? Forster and McLennan had a number of answers, none of them very compelling. McLennan told Irish journalist Paul Malone that the name was "made up" but added, "I get a kind of picture of kids sitting in a tree-house, smoking cigarettes behind their parents' backs—or she could be some kind of movie star. It's just a feeling that comes out of that name. It's almost like a book title."[13] The name signified nothing directly; it was just mysterious, with a "friends of Dorothy" (or, for that matter, "friends of Carlotta") air to it.[14]

The Go-Betweens played live to support the *Rachel Worth* album throughout most of 2000, but the tour of Europe and North America that began in October 2000 turned out to be a classic disaster. The best interpretation that can be placed on the events is that the revived group was suffering teething problems; less charitably, it could be argued that Forster and McLennan had not learned how to overcome the standoffish approach and unwillingness to engage in discussion that had made the original band's 1989 breakup so unpleasant.

The problems that occurred were rooted in, or at least aggravated by, the reluctance of Go-Betweens' manager Bob Johnson to fund things adequately, several informants suggest. Steve Miller, in addition to being their current Australian label boss, was also drafted into his old role as tour manager, possibly because he had a vested interest in the success of the project and, as an old friend, could be persuaded to do it for less money. Miller, with visions of blown-up amps and tour vans still haunting him years later, says now that the group "won't pay the market value for anything, and it always ends up biting them on the bum."

> MILLER: The tour never came together. They should have been touring in a coach, like other bands. You save money because you don't need hotels, and you get a driver. But Robert won't drive at night. So we're in this tiny little van! They tour in seventies, eighties style.
>
> They were embarrassed, and that made them not want to discuss [how] the tour [was going]. It was way below my expectations of how good they were going to be.

Miller was in any case in a difficult, because ill-defined, position: was he their friend or their employee—and if he was an employee, whose employee was he?[15]

The person who ended up bearing the brunt of the tour's problems—and adding a few extra ones himself—was the drummer they hired for this tour. Miller remembers that a list of potential drummers for the shows was drawn up: Janet Weiss was at the top, followed by Glenn Thompson (who at that time was dedicated to his post-Custard band, the Titanics); others who were mooted included Clare Moore, Jim White (of the Dirty Three), and Nick Allun, who'd played in the Apartments and Fatima Mansions. In the end, however, Forster called in an old friend, Matthias Strzoda, who had played drums in Forster's backing band in Germany some years earlier. It was a decision all involved would soon regret, and it displays again the haphazard approach the Go-Betweens take to important decisions—an approach many find endearing until they find themselves dealing with the fallout. Strzoda's recollections of what was clearly a very unhappy tour for all concerned suggest a band still coalescing and uncertain of how to tour at

The European touring lineup in 2000, with Matthias Strzoda *(Sarah Neal)*

their "level" in the new millennium.

Once preparations got under way, Strzoda recalls that he, Forster, McLennan, and Pickvance had only four days of rehearsal, each about three hours long, "leaving the shaky parts somewhat ... shaky" from his perspective. Not only was he underprepared for the tour, but he found it hard to get on the same wavelength as the others, who shared a background and knew one another much better.

> STRZODA: Early on, when things like "you're here to keep the beat, don't worry about anything else" were coming in my direction, I was laughing. I didn't take it seriously. But when I talked about musical jokes—like turning around the beat (snare/bass drum) for a few bars, for the sake of amusement—the reply was, "don't even think about it!" Well, I wasn't, of course. I was telling a musician's joke among musicians. But this was serious!

Strzoda felt they were hypercritical of his playing:

> After almost every show—right after the show, while the enthusiastic crowd was still yelling for more—there was some talk like:
>
> Grant: "Maybe you shouldn't play that long drum roll in the intro of 'Easy Come, Easy Go.' A short roll, that would be better."
>
> Robert: "Mmm, know what you mean. Or maybe you shouldn't play

it at all. You probably should leave it out. What do you think, Adele?"

Adele: "Well, I don't know . . ."

Grant: "Yes, I agree. Don't play it."

And this and that, tempo, breaks . . . they would always find something. I couldn't believe it! And it's not like there wasn't a forgotten line, a wrong chord, a miscount, or whatever on their part. Robert tried to make a feedback part work during "Apology Accepted" all through the tour and failed. But, man, these are live shows, and little mistakes can even be worth a laugh. But no, no fun. *No fun!* Halfway through the tour, my self-confidence was at a total low. I had become unsure of my ability to even keep a simple, four-to-the-floor beat. It was stupid. What's the use in them putting down someone's abilities, especially when these are offered to make *their* songs shine?

The primary Go-Betweens, for their part, quickly became very unhappy with Strzoda, feeling that his style was often inappropriate and unpredictable. Miller relates that "after the Brussels show, Robert tore strips off Matthias in the band room, which Matthias got very upset about because he did it in front of other people."[16]

Strzoda admits he was "difficult to deal with sometimes," although he adds rather sarcastically that this was because he insisted on "asking questions, even about arrangements and set lists" and "saying what I think sometimes." He thinks that Forster and McLennan basically wanted "a beat box—audible but invisible, dressed up in a suit and tie, and smiling on stage," whereas "I was irritating them—there was no room to care about all that; they were busy keeping their system going."

Photographer Bleddyn Butcher, a longtime friend of the band, picked up on the tension in the touring group when he visited them backstage in London. "There's something unpleasant going on here, and it seems to stem from the one person in the room I don't know. To whom I wasn't introduced. Without saying anything or even talking to anyone, he's exuding attitude." This was, of course, Strzoda.

In Spain, things came to a head.

At BBC Studios in London, 2000 *(Matthias Strzoda)*

MILLER: The thing is, Robert and Grant say one thing to Bob. Robert and Grant say another thing to each other. Bob says one thing to Robert and Grant, another thing to Grant and then another thing to Robert. It's a merry-go-round. My position was trying to *interpret*. I realized, This is no fun, I'm not enjoying the shows. I broke down in Barcelona, I broke down in tears.

In Brussels, Robert asked what I thought of Matthias. And I said, "I think he's terrible." He asked what I thought we should do. I think it was agreed that he should be sacked in Munich. But Munich came, and then there was no mention of it, and we made it to Paris, and then we went off to Madrid . . .

I'd been up most of the night, disputing with hotel reception about the van. We were in Spain to support Teenage Fanclub—it was another of the Go-Betweens' decisions that we had to go to Spain, even though it was six days of traveling, hotels, and fuel, when all we were getting was £2,000 and a support slot. And the deal was that Teenage Fanclub would use our gear, so we had to get to the venues early to do soundcheck.

I get a phone call at about two o'clock in the morning: "You've got to move the van, we've got Japanese tourists coming at five o'clock."

"I'm not moving the van!"

I'm very tired, but we've got to get up at seven to get to Barcelona. Only one more day to go.

Matthias was always the last one on the bus. I'm waiting, waiting. Matthias wanders into the foyer and says, "Steve, I had to pay for my breakfast." Well, I'd paid him his wages, so I said, "So?"

He replied, "You should have told me—it is your job to tell me."

At this point I told him to get fucked. And didn't speak to him again. And that was kind of *it*. I then drove two-thirds of the way to Barcelona; I didn't want to sit in the back of the van.

I'm not a tour manager. I don't want to be a tour manager. I was Robert and Grant's tour manager because we're old friends, I have a credit card, and I work for half-rates—but I'm not going to clean up this mess of a tour because, yet again, it's all their doing. And the price of this is, of course, excommunication.

If the end of the European tour led to the end of the longstanding friendship between Miller and the Go-Betweens, it also resulted, finally, in Strzoda's dismissal.

STRZODA: Robert took the last possible opportunity to sit down in the hotel lobby (with Adele as assistant), trying to enter into something he thought would be a constructive conversation. It was a nice try, honestly, but since he was giving me pretty much the same you-do-this-when-we-kind-of-want-that, and since they were clearly going to ask someone else to play with them in Australia, I left the tour with a very bad feeling. A feeling of not being wanted.

Robert wrote to me later: "It is without doubt the strangest and most unsatisfying tour I've ever done. I'm still trying to work out how it all went so badly." He tried to say it hadn't been working music-wise. Which, if you listen to some of the live tapes, is simply not true. It didn't work on the interpersonal level (and obviously that has an effect on making music)—but it was their fault for not knowing how to change that, while I was the only one trying.[17]

The touring party went on to North America without a drummer, much to the disappointment of their US label, Jetset, which had, says Miller, been promoting a full-band tour as a key selling point, given that Forster and McLennan had not toured there with a band since 1988.

In the same year that Matthias Strzoda tried and failed to become a Go-Between, the group were reminded—once again—of another, more long-term former drummer. The Australian Broadcasting Commission screened an ambitious multipart documentary, *Long Way to the Top*, an anecdotal history of Australian rock.[18] Clinton Walker was heavily involved in scripting the series, and Lindy Morrison played a major part in the episode entitled *INXS: In Exile*, which was only slightly about the group INXS and more about Australian groups of the 1980s and the success some of them enjoyed overseas. Morrison and Nick Cave were the most prominent commentators in this episode, and many viewers were no doubt somewhat surprised to see Morrison begin crying towards the end of the episode, while talking about an apparently rather anodyne topic—the "institutionalization" that the band experienced as a touring unit.

McLennan commented when he saw the episode:

Lindy was quite emotional, but she was looking back at a time when it was a big struggle. People don't realize just how little respect Australian music had in the early 1980s in London, in the bloody home of Empire.

For many viewers, Morrison's outburst was a key moment in the series,[19] though they tend to recall—wrongly—that Morrison's tears came while she was discussing her relationship with Forster. In any case, the choice of Morrison to represent the Go-Betweens on this program indicates that, for many, there is no Go-Betweens without her.[20]

MORRISON: I was disappointed about the reunion, because I'd wanted it to be a body of work that was complete. If they want it to be the Go-Betweens, they can be the Go-Betweens, and if that makes them happy, I'm happy that they go on doing that. [But] they've got such a great sense of art, and I can't understand why they would have wrecked it like that. It really was perfect, the six albums, the way they sat together and the fact that I played on all six of them—I thought it worked as a body of art. It's like having a gorgeous dining-room table and six chairs and someone gives one chair away. It's forever ruined, for me.

Like Lindy Morrison, Glenn Thompson lives in Sydney, and so Thompson, who can lay claim to being both the eighth *and* the eleventh Go-Betweens drummer,[21] encounters his most illustrious predecessor now and again.

THOMPSON: I've met her in studios, and at parties. When David and I had just quit Custard and started the Titanics, she came up and said, "At least you didn't use the name Custard." But we soon found out that we should have!

Despite the touring problems, the revived Go-Betweens project was working so well that Forster and McLennan were soon adamant that the group would stay together this time around—or at least that they, as a duo, would continue to use the name. McLennan insisted in late 2000:

This is an ongoing thing. It's like a soap opera. We're already talking about when we can do the next one. To use another metaphor, it's like a beautiful old car that's been stuck in a garage for years: when you take it out on the road and the engine's purring, you just want to keep driving it.[22]

24
Bright Yellow Bright Orange

Late in 2001 Forster moved back to Brisbane with Karin and their two children (a daughter, Loretta, had been born earlier in the year). Now that Forster was back in Australia again, the Go-Betweens could resume more frequent touring, as they did throughout 2002. These tours were nothing like the extended treks of the 1980s, however.

> FORSTER: We just sort of go out and come back, and work on things again, work on songs, and then go out again—it's earning money but more of a learning experience—and then going back to the Brisbane hole. I'm playing keyboards on stage now, which is good. I really enjoy it. And it gets us out amidst it all.

The revival of the Go-Betweens meant that Forster was able to buy a house for the first time. He and his family settled into suburban Brisbane, living close to his parents, and Forster found himself plunged into domestic activities as never before:

> FORSTER: I'm trying to be handy—painting, choosing floor coverings. We had to rip the kitchen out. I've been going to the hardware store, which is something I've avoided up till now. I've always lived in rented accommodation; I've never had to face this. I'm learning.
> But at the end of the month there's a fair chance we'll be moving in and I'll start writing songs. The last year has been so hectic.

As 2002 went on, plans for the next album started to come together:

> FORSTER: Grant's in full swing. He's written lots of songs and I haven't got many, [so] it's shaping up to be a normal Go-Betweens record. I've written two songs. Actually, I've only written one song in the last two

years, to be totally frank.

I think it's going to be a little bit more lush, a bit more beautiful, a little bit more acoustic. I keep saying "folky," I keep saying "jumpers."[1] I've got this white jumper that I got in Germany. The people who were living downstairs from us were quite wealthy; I don't think we came across as poor victims or anything, but they gave us all these clothes. Wealthy Germans, so it was all designer labels—and there was this fantastic white jumper. It's got this Swedish architect feel about it. To me, that's a big part of the album, but I can't talk too much to Grant about this—he just gets annoyed.

I must say Grant's got a couple of really good songs, he's got one called "Mrs. Morgan" that is an instant classic.

The new album, *Bright Yellow Bright Orange*, was recorded under what seem to have been happy, comfortable, and creative conditions—for the other participants as well as Forster and McLennan:

PICKVANCE: For Glenn and me, playing on this album is like: "At last, we get to do it!" We've played together since Warm Nights, in 1995, and *finally* we get to record. We missed out on the recording of the *Warm Nights* album, which was a bit of a bummer, and [Glenn] wasn't available for *The Friends of Rachel Worth*, but luckily he was up for doing this one. So that was great. I think we play together really well, we have a similar understanding of the songs, so we can just fall back, lean on each other.

I really enjoy Glenn's drumming—it's very relaxed and shuffly, and he texturizes the song so well, he's so in control. He's one of those people who can play anything well—he plays keyboards, he comes up with the riffs that were thrown into this album and tastefully drums up the little parts from the verse, chorus to . . . Yeah, he's great, and we get on well socially, we're good friends. It's nice to have the band as it is—we've known each other for so long, we're friends now.

Recording took place at Sing Sing studios in the inner-city Melbourne suburb of Richmond—a few blocks from the (no longer operating) Richmond Recorders, where *Send Me a Lullaby* had been made twenty-two years earlier. Sing Sing is a top-flight studio in the style of Studio 301 in Sydney, where *16 Lovers Lane* had been recorded. Fans of Australian rock may recall that the Seekers made their comeback album at Sing Sing a few years ago; it is also where the most recent Nick Cave and Dirty Three albums were recorded. Pickvance describes the studio as "big, tall, glassy, wooden, very jouji." McLennan explained to Go-Betweens fans that the different studio meant the new album was "more technicolor—I think *Rachel Worth* is more watercolor."²

Forster and McLennan adhered to their traditional work methods:

> PICKVANCE: They work together really well, actually. It's quite strange—they're like chalk and cheese to me, but I suppose that's how it works. They have between five and ten percent input into each other's songs, although maybe there's more before we are involved. They always oversee the recording of each other's songs, they're in there listening, adding ideas, adding each other's bit, making room for the other bit.

> THOMPSON: Grant and Robert practiced all the songs together for a few months beforehand, so they were very specific about what they wanted. They could hear it in their heads; they didn't leave a hell of a lot to chance. So I was told most of what to play, which I found kind of frustrating. But when we'd finished the album and I listened back, I thought, "I would never have played the drums like that." But I like it, it's really spare.

Thompson seems to exercise a similar presence on these recordings as John Willsteed's on *16 Lovers Lane*; he not only fulfils his basic function in the group, he also fills out the sound with his own pop sensibility. He plays a little guitar and provides keyboards on most tracks (Forster plays keyboards on two songs).

> THOMPSON: Once we were recording, I got the drums on first, of course. Then I sat down at the keyboards with headphones on one ear, listening to the track through the other ear, as they were putting down vocals, and figured out some keyboard lines. I asked if we could add them in. I got a lot of personal pleasure out of that.

The string arrangements on the album were by David Chesworth, a respected Melbourne composer whose music career began with the minimalist new wave group Essendon Airport at around the same time as that of the Go-Betweens. Most recently he has been working in opera.³

While *Bright Yellow Bright Orange* suffers from some of the same problems that bedevil *The Friends of Rachel Worth*—the post-millennial retro-ism of hokey sixties organ sounds, for example—its ten songs are robust and confident. Forster's "Caroline and I" is a light but engaging study of the rather vague parallels between Robert Forster and Princess Caroline of Monaco, with an irresistible melody line rather similar to that of the Buzzcocks' "Paradise." McLennan's "Mrs. Morgan" may not quite be the masterpiece Forster keeps telling us it is, but it certainly has a sumptuous

Relaxing at Sing Sing: the current lineup of Forster, Glenn Thompson, Pickvance, and McLennan *(Sarah Neal)*

chorus. McLennan is once more indebted to a drummer for bringing out the best in one of his compositions: Thompson's playing, together with the backing vocals, heightens all the song's possibilities. "Too Much of One Thing"—an oblique and in some ways surprisingly conservative disquisition on the life of McLennan, with a verse contributed by McLennan himself—is bizarre, needless to say; in this case it is the lyrics and the concept that make the track, not the music (which is simple, repetitive country rock, like an extended intro to an out-take from an early 1970s Neil Young album). "Old Mexico" is affectionately clumsy, and like "Mrs. Morgan," the pop possibilities of its chorus are maximized by Pickvance and Thompson. As for "Make Her Day," if Forster had written it in 1978, rather than 2002, the Go-Betweens would have been on *Countdown* in a heartbeat and had a massive hit single—and it would probably have destroyed them. Its catchy guitar figures, prominent keyboards, and choppy chorus make it one of the best pop songs a Go-Between has written in a long time, if ever.

Fitting in with its vaguely pop-art cover (which recalls the sleeves of early Go-Betweens singles like "People Say"), Forster had come up with *Bright Orange Bright Yellow* as its title—white jumper notwithstanding.

> FORSTER: When our son was born, a very good friend of ours called John Nixon,[4] who's an artist, sent us a small painting. It was one of those boards that artists use . . . It was an L, it was two colors, bright yellow and

bright orange. This was in 1998.

Then we moved to Australia at the end of last year. We bought a house. We were painting our son's bedroom—and I'd honestly forgotten about this painting—and we painted the bedroom bright yellow and bright orange. This was about March this year [2002]. I can remember standing in the room and I looked at it all and I just went ,"oh—bright yellow bright orange." And as soon as I said that I went, "that's an album title." So the actual "bright yellow bright orange" is the color of our son's bedroom.[5]

With the album finished, and scheduled for release in the UK, USA, Australia, Germany, and Japan on various different independent labels, it was time to think about planning tours to support it. Forster told Go-Betweens fans on the band's web site what they could expect this time around, assuring them that this time the touring band would definitely involve both Thompson and Pickvance:

FORSTER: I think the band's great. We played one show last May in Brisbane, an unannounced show during the rehearsals for *Bright Yellow Bright Orange,* and I thought we were just really great. We've come up with a classic lineup. We're going to go out to play and we're going to make a big jump from the way we played on the last tour. I think we're going to knock people flat. So that's why Grant and I are really excited about playing.

I'm going to be playing more keyboards, Glenn's going to be playing guitar. [Sometimes] there's going to be three guitars on stage with bass. I think it can completely break apart and when the four of us come back and do our instruments then it's got power and beauty. I'm really excited. It's going to be fantastic![6]

Thompson and Pickvance are enthusiastic, too, but not surprisingly they have a certain hesitancy that Forster and McLennan don't ever need to have. For one thing, they're effectively employees of the group's founders, however close the ties between them may have become. And the band's history inevitably weighs more heavily on them:

PICKVANCE: Every time I walk on stage I feel like an impostor ... I'm not standing in anyone's shoes, and I hope the people out there don't think I'm trying to, but I tend to think, *Oh god.* When I stand on stage I'm quite happy to stand near Glenn at the back. We're doing our job. But it does feel a bit weird.

Audience members at post-2000 Go-Betweens shows will still call out "Where's Lindy?" though increasingly they are shushed by others in the crowd. Needless to say, "Cattle and Cane" is the song in the live set where Morrison's absence is clearly felt; these days, Forster and McLennan usually play it as a duo. Thompson (who says he stopped trying as a drummer "once I learned how to play drums good enough for pop") has few problems with the bulk of the Go-Betweens' set, but there are elements of the Lindy Morrison legacy that cannot be recreated.

> THOMPSON: It's hard to play Lindy's odd-time-signature drum parts, but I'm rarely required to play drums on "Cattle and Cane." I think those peculiarities come from Robert and Grant writing music around vocal phrases. Although it must be said that Robert has a very "creative" sense of musical time. If the band all start together on a song that Robert has counted in, it's a miracle. Nick Cave is the same . . .

McLennan recently claimed that he's "given up on the commercial success thing—which is very helpful for my state of mind."[7] But this has not stopped him trying to push himself, and the band, into unusual areas, for instance with a new song, as yet unreleased, called "Ashes on the Lawn":

> PICKVANCE: There were two songs we recorded that didn't make it onto this record.[8] One is probably going to be a b-side, and the other was a tricky one because it was quite a surprise as a Go-Betweens song. It *was* a Go-Betweens song because you can hear it's Robert and Grant singing. But music-wise it was a bit of a shock . . . the way it was structured, or recorded, it was really a stadium-rock song. Queen or the Rolling Stones maybe?[9] That one didn't make it on the record, much to Grant's disappointment. I don't know how it was voted out, but, "ten songs on the album"—keep it ten songs. I don't really know how they go about deciding, they decide the order, they decide the songs, what's going to work or not going to work... It's an interesting song. You never know, it might come back.

The Go-Betweens have been dragged into the commercial music industry in a number of other ways, however. "Streets of Your Town," which just failed to reach the top forty in 1988, was sampled by dance artist(s) Milky for a song called "More Than I Can Say"—which itself also stopped just outside the top forty. And in a move that is in some ways even more extraordinary, Australia's largest telecommunications provider, Telstra, recently licensed "Streets of Your Town" for use in their TV ads.[10]

The band have started to become absorbed into the Australian mainstream in other unusual ways, too: Forster and McLennan posed for a portrait by painter Anne Wallace which was submitted for Australia's prestigious Archibald Prize; "Cattle and Cane" was voted one of Australia's best songs in a poll of critics and musicians;[11] and popular politicians—such as Natasha Stott-Despoja, until recently the leader of the Democrats, claimed that the Go-Betweens were one of her favorite bands. And among certain of their peers, most notably Belle and Sebastian, the Go-Betweens seem to have become a popular subject for songs—a bizarre development that is testament to their distinctiveness, though of course it began in the 1970s with the Apartments' "Help."

The narrative of the 1996 incarnation of this book stopped cold in the early days of 1990, with the Go-Betweens' breakup and Forster and McLennan preparing to continue in music. Nevertheless, the subsequent years were reflected in the interviews within the book itself, as the ex-members of the band and their various allies battled each other ideologically among the ruins of the group.

The difference between that ending and this one is very clear. At this point, Forster and McLennan seem determined to carry on with the Go-Betweens after what seems in retrospect to have been not a decisive split, but rather a decade off from the compromises that necessarily go along with being in a band—a decade in which they finished their thirties, entered their forties, and settled down in one way or another before deciding to capitalize financially and artistically on the successes of the original Go-Betweens. Though the differences in their lifestyles are more marked than ever—as suggested in Forster's lyrics in the song about McLennan, "Too Much of One Thing"—and their professional decisions are generally as perverse as ever, their working relationship seems secure. Perhaps more remarkably, with Thompson and Pickvance backing them they seem happy to consider this a new version of the band, rather than a reversion, twenty-five years on, to the original twosome. Some of this confidence no doubt stems from the vibrant new sound they've achieved on *Bright Yellow Bright Orange*, and the strength of its songs. It is the sound of a band no longer in debt to its influences or, more importantly, its past. The Go-Betweens are looking forward.

25
Elemental Things

As I was finishing the revisions to this book, I was unexpectedly offered an additional opportunity to speak to Forster and McLennan when they visited Melbourne for a day to promote *Bright Yellow Bright Orange*. As a kind of bonus track, I offer this transcript of those (separate) interviews, held at a café called Bimbo Deluxe in Fitzroy, Melbourne, on March 7, 2003.

GRANT MCLENNAN

NICHOLS: Why has this new album worked so well?
McLENNAN: It's probably due to the fact that Robert was back living in Brisbane, so we were able to sit down for two to three months together in the summer of last year, go through everything that we had, and get that connection back again. "Too Much of One Thing" is an example of that. I wrote the music and melody and said to Robert, "I think it would be great if you wrote some lyrics for this." Robert liked it so much that he stole the song from me—and sang the whole fucking thing! Well, he gave me one verse.

I think the other thing was being more settled. The magnificent Adele Pickvance being involved. And Glenn coming aboard cemented things. I think we're a really great unit—this is a great lineup of the band. We've had some good ones; this is a really good one. I hope we continue to record and travel with it.
NICHOLS: You've often referred to blindness in your songs. Where does that come from?
McLENNAN: I hadn't really thought about this before, but I did recently notice it myself. I used to wear glasses—until I was fourteen. I had to have operations on my eyes, I had a lazy eye, or whatever it's called. Also,

there's blindness more as a metaphorical thing—to me, many people can't see. Also, I guess, there's a love of obliviousness, of being in your own world—a bit of that.

As far as a theory goes, I'll have to think about that. You've stumped me. That's good. But "blind" can also mean utmost faith, just powering through the world. The song "Going Blind" [on *Rachel Worth*] is all about that.

NICHOLS: You used to write about fires and burning things. A bit less often lately, though.

McLENNAN: A little bit. Part of it is that I'm interested in elemental things. Quite a few poets I like use that imagery. It's been used for centuries. I like that reduction of the world into those essences.

NICHOLS: Mrs. Morgan—where does she come from? She's been in two other songs, as well.

McLENNAN: It's funny, I was in Cairns recently, and I went with my stepfather to an RSL club. Everyone at the table was seventy and above, and I realized one of the men sitting across the table from me was married to the woman who inspired Mrs. Morgan. That's not their real name. I remember when I was a child this woman gave me a piece of sapphire in a rock, it hadn't been polished or cut, and it always stuck with me. She became the first Mrs. Morgan. Then when I did *In Your Bright Ray* she popped up again, because that song "Sea Breeze" takes place at two o'clock on an afternoon in Cairns, as specific as that, and "Mrs. Morgan" came up then.

It's not like I think I have to resuscitate Mrs. Morgan. You would know, as a songwriter, that words just come into your head, and she makes an appearance every now and then. She's getting older, too.

NICHOLS: It sounds like you're saying the person Mrs. Morgan is based on is no longer with us.

McLENNAN: No, she's still alive. I told the man this story and he said he would tell her.

I like those people over seventy. They remember the Fall of Singapore. It's a very North Queensland thing. It's hard to explain to a southerner, that whole generation . . .

NICHOLS: Behind the Brisbane Line.

McLENNAN: Yeah, my mother was sent down to Brisbane during the war because of the fear of invasion.

NICHOLS: I heard you haven't read my book about the Go-Betweens.

McLENNAN: No, my mother has a copy. I'm being honest, I've flicked through it, I've read certain chapters that I was interested in . . . Where are you going with this?

NICHOLS: The question's about you, not the book. If someone had

had a book written about them, even if it was a complete character assassination, most people would find it very hard not to pick the thing up.

McLENNAN: Okay. I'm not interested in memoirs, or autobiographies. With that book, what I—well, I'll be honest, what I've seen doesn't particularly interest me because I've lived it. I cooperated a little bit in the book, and I wish I hadn't. Not that I think you're a bad writer or that you have an axe to grind, it's nothing against you. But Phil Kakulas once asked me, "Why would I want to read something that you've okayed?" And I thought, that's very true. Not that I am seeking a complete character assassination or an analysis of my lifestyle and everyone else's in the band.

I'm flattered, it does appeal to my ego that there's a book on the band. But when I looked at that book, I thought you got the balance wrong. From what you had told me . . . I'm not saying "what you led me to believe," but what I thought you were trying to do was more to look at the early days. And that, to me, was way more fascinating. Then the fact that there was all that record-by-record thing which got smaller and smaller—I thought that was unfair.

Robert wanted it to be *Remembrance of Things Past,* he wanted it to be three thousand fucking pages long. To me there wasn't enough about the music.

NICHOLS: "Ashes on the Lawn" . . .

McLENNAN: What? Who have you been talking to?

NICHOLS: Adele told me there was a really good song called "Ashes on the Lawn" that didn't make it on to the album. It sounds like a really interesting new direction, from what Adele told me.

McLENNAN: Adele, I'm going to have to *talk* to her . . .

We recorded twelve songs for the record, and two of them didn't make it. We wanted ten songs, and we wanted it to come in as close to forty minutes as possible. Now, listening to the record, I don't miss it. But I have a copy of the twelve-song record in a different sequence, and it's a different record. The inclusion of those two songs, and a rearrangement of the songs, makes it a different record; I don't think it would have been *Bright Yellow Bright Orange.*

"Ashes on the Lawn," I'm hoping, is going to be one of those tracks that people are going to talk about, and maybe at some stage we will release it—or we'll do it live. It's a big rock song. And live, it works. We haven't played it live [on stage], but whenever we came to do it in the rehearsal room people looked forward to it. People who have heard the demo and the Sing Sing studio version have asked, "Why isn't this song on the record?" So it might be our "Blind Willie McTell."

NICHOLS: It's kind of stadium rock?

McLENNAN: No, that does it a disservice. It's still very much an intimate Go-Betweens experience. But it's bigger. Robert and I sing it together, the whole song we sing together. It's an actual joint vocal. We've never done that before. And the chorus doesn't have words. The song has a really great Robert Forster lyric as well; it's one of those songs I wrote the music for and had some lyrics, and he wrote more lyrics to it.

NICHOLS: It's interesting that you're actually sitting down and writing together. Had you ever done that before?

McLENNAN: Once. "Don't Let Him Come Back." I hope—as you said, since we're actually in the one town together—it might be cool for us to actually sit down and jam on things.

NICHOLS: Although "Too Much of One Thing" suggests to me that seeing quite a lot of each other has actually emphasized how different your lifestyles are.

McLENNAN: That's true. Put it this way: we don't go to the same clubs.

NICHOLS: You haven't done a solo record for a while. Given your capacity for writing material, you must have an enormous number of songs sitting around.

McLENNAN: I do have a lot of songs. In the past I would have been chafing at the bit, I think. But I'm just so pleased with the triumph of this record. I'm almost trying to contain my enthusiasm for it, because there's nothing more predictable than someone in a band raving about their genius. But I must admit I'm very happy with the way the record looks and the way it sounds, and how the band sounds. I just know that we are going to kick arse.

    I don't say that lightly. I have not looked forward to touring as much for a long time. I can't wait to show people we're a good rock band. We're risk-takers. I'm very bored with lots of new bands—when you see them, you've seen them before.

NICHOLS: Did you have much involvement with last year's reissues? I imagine some of that material could only have come from your private stash.

McLENNAN: Some of it did. Most of that was assembled by our English record label and by Jonathan Turner, a guy that runs a Go-Betweens web site. His knowledge is encyclopedic. He tracked down some things I'd forgotten I had done, like that "Exception of Deception" song. So it was really weird. Our participation was down to them sending us on CD all the extra things they had, and Robert and I listening to it and saying, in most cases, yes. But there were a couple of cases where we said, "not for a million dollars"!

NICHOLS: What were they?

McLENNAN: They were the ones Phil Kakulas is probably interested in.

NICHOLS: About ten years ago I asked you if you were ever going to do any writing outside music. Do you ever do that?
McLENNAN: I do. I'm constantly working on poems. But that's it. I have written some stories over the years but honestly I'm not happy with them. Whereas poems... That was my first romance with literature, as a child, Henry Lawson and Banjo Patterson. Not that I want to write like that, but I was way more into that than other forms of writing. And I continue to experiment.
NICHOLS: There's a nineteenth-century-ballad element to your lyric writing, so is there a major difference in style in your poems?
McLENNAN: I don't think I'd call it lyric poetry. In general it rhymes, occasionally it's blank verse. But I love the discipline of form in poetry. I think it's incredibly hard to do, and that's why there are so many abysmal poets. *Abysmal.* God! People just open their mouths. It's very adolescent. They should be taken into the headmaster's study and caned on the hands. English is a beautiful language, David.
NICHOLS: Do you have any ideas about the next album?
McLENNAN: I haven't, but Robert did say when we had almost finished *Bright Yellow Bright Orange* that what we should do for the next one is rent a beach house down at Byron[1] and make a kind of soft reggae-pop record.
NICHOLS: He didn't say that, surely!
McLENNAN: He did, he did. Soft, like early Bob Marley. Those great tunes, but a little bit of upstroke there. And I said "no way." But at the moment—it all depends on the material that's going to be written in the future—there's definitely an idea that we all get together in the practice room and jam more—actually play together as a band, like you're supposed to, you know. Just for the joy of playing, a new riff or something, you don't even have a finished song, just go in there and play on that riff for two hours and...
NICHOLS: ... let it speak to you.
McLENNAN: Yeah. Definitely. And Robert and I have often said that a Go-Betweens record could have two pop songs and seven pieces of sound collage. We've got a mandate to do what we want to. Obviously, I think that would be commercial suicide. But we've never been...
NICHOLS: You're no strangers to commercial suicide.
McLENNAN: Yeah, we're no strangers, so it'd probably be a good step.

NICHOLS: Let's talk about "Caroline and I." It's a little older than the other material on the record.
FORSTER: Yeah, it was written in '97.
NICHOLS: Is it really about Princess Caroline of Monaco?
FORSTER: Yep.
NICHOLS: What did she mean to you?
FORSTER: She meant a lot to me when I was between the ages of about fifteen and nineteen. She was a glamour figure. Obviously, from the lyrics, she was the same age as me. She was just someone I felt attracted to. If you think of movie stars at around that time, like Faye Dunaway—she seemed a million miles away, and she was what Hollywood was putting forward at that time, as a face. And Karen Black . . . And pop stars from that time, Helen Reddy or Cher . . . There was no one my age. But [Caroline] was my age. I was attracted to her, and it was like we were living these parallel lives. She went to university at the same time as I did. I went to Queensland University, she went to a university in Paris. It seemed that we were moving in the same direction.

I wrote the song in 1997, just after her [fortieth] birthday had been in the papers; I was living in Germany and they'd made a big thing about it. It just clicked at around the same time as I wrote the music.
NICHOLS: You've written more than one song about parallel lives lately . . .
FORSTER: I know, I know. I didn't realize, but there's "He Lives My Life." It just came out. I don't want to look into the psychology of it, David, but yeah, it must interest me.
NICHOLS: It's the sort of thing people say about the Saints, and they say it about the Go-Betweens, too—that if you'd been born somewhere other than Brisbane . . .
FORSTER: . . . It could be.
NICHOLS: Do you feel like you've missed out?
FORSTER: On what?
NICHOLS: On something—because you were born in Brisbane in . . .
FORSTER: No. I'm quite happy with where I've come from and what I've done. Missed out? No.
NICHOLS: When the extended reissues were being put together last year, and you and Grant were going through the material—was there anything particularly painful there, or particularly revelatory?
FORSTER: Yes, there were things. I was surprised how good the stuff from 1980, 1981 sounds . . . [*Laughs*] You thought I'd never say that! *Send Me a Lullaby*—I've got to completely retwist now and say, "avant-garde

masterpiece." I heard one song, recorded live at the Mosman Hotel, what's it called . . . "Distant Hands"? Yeah, "Distant Hands." Stunned. I listened to that and I just thought: great song, the band sounds amazing, Lindy, myself, Grant—we were bloody good! We'd worked up this whole thing that I'd semi-forgotten about. What a dynamic three-piece band we were.

Even something like "One Word," that funky Talking Heads thing that Grant had, sounds great! I can remember working on that. At the time, I thought it was derivative, but now I listen to it I think there's a cheeky power to the whole song. *Send Me a Lullaby*, was the [London] *Times*' album of the week in July last year. And Robert Vickers told me *Send Me a Lullaby* is selling more than the  other two in the USA. My thing about the album hasn't changed a great deal, but what we were doing around it, just how good Lindy, Grant, and I were as a three-piece—my opinion went up quite a lot.

NICHOLS: What's the next Go-Betweens album going to be like?

FORSTER: There's a temptation to go back to the same studio with Tim Whitten again—we liked that. I have this fantasy of the band . . . that at the moment we're Talking Heads, 1979—a bit sort of *Fear of Music*. I wish Adele would come up with an amazing five-minute looped bass line. Do you know what I mean?

I think [the next album]'s got to be more in the practice room. It's going to be the four of us, circumstances, Grant and I bringing in songs. We've talked to Glenn and Adele about bringing in songs, but I realize now that was a mistake, because Grant and I don't need songs. I find it hard to impose on it, impose a lyric on it. I can do it with Grant, but with Adele or Glenn, they write in a certain style, so it's more like, bring in *less*, bring in a bass line or a guitar riff, and let's jam on it. I can bring lyrics, Grant can bring lyrics. Whether it would make the album or not I don't know but I'd like to hear some of that. That'd be a way to go.

NICHOLS: You're talking about breaking your old rules.

FORSTER: Yeah. We talked to both Glenn and Adele about this before we recorded *Bright Yellow Bright Orange*. And I'd have to tell Adele again. She'd make cassettes of stuff, but all her stuff was songs. And I've realized that's not what we need from her. We need her to write bass riffs. I'd like us to break on through to something like that.

NICHOLS: It sounds like you're coming close to formally inducting Glenn and Adele into the group. They might actually make it into band photos . . .

FORSTER: It sounds like a conspiracy, but it's not. We actually wanted them to be on the cover of *Bright Yellow*, but unfortunately Grant and I were doing the European promo tour while the thing was being done. I had this idea of Grant and myself playing guitars—I very much like that photo and what it sends out—and I thought, let's get Glenn to get a photo taken of himself in his front room playing drums, and a photo of Adele with a bass guitar in her St. Kilda art-deco flat. So I phoned up and said, "Get Glenn to have a photo taken of himself playing drums"... But then everyone in Europe started yelling, "we've got to get the artwork done, we're running advertisements on the tenth of January"—and then it was, like, over! It came very close to them being in the booklet. They'll be in the next booklet.

NICHOLS: Last year, as you were leading up to recording this album, you said "white jumpers." Is it a white jumper record?

FORSTER: Yes and no. The white jumper was Melbourne, it was Sing Sing, it was August, but the white jumper got a little bit burnt in the Brisbane heat.

I don't know where we're going. But that's going to come out in the practice room, too.

NICHOLS: Have you and Grant ever argued?

FORSTER: No. We get tetchy. The closest we've come to arguing—and I think this is documented—is when the Go-Betweens *had* to have a hit single. 1987, 1988—that's where we were at cross purposes to an extent. Besides that, no. And I know it's completely unhealthy. But there's not a lot to argue about. If I lose something I want to do, and give in to him, in a subtle way, I know that somewhere around the corner something's going to happen where he's going to have to give in to me. But major arguments? We spend most of our time arguing against the rest of the world. And being in a band can *be* that. And so you've got to be ... There's enough coming in from the outside.

We had a massive fight with the album, they wanted us to be on the cover. Grant and I had been hounded through Europe: (a) get the cover done while you're doing a promo tour, and (b) you've got to be on the cover. So Grant and I ended up in coffee shops around Europe, looking at the rest of the world and going, "fuck you!" That wasn't meant at you. But do you know what I mean?

NICHOLS: You're under siege.

FORSTER: Yeah. *Still.*

Postscript (2011)

When I wrote the first incarnation of this book over 15 years ago, the internet was just beginning to take its hold—indeed, virtually my first use of e-mail was in early 1996, to correspond with various informants as I was completing the manuscript. The original book was a revelation to many readers around the world, presenting as it did an otherwise unavailable narrative of a group who were seen at the time as an esoteric interest; but you couldn't just google them.

By the time the book's second incarnation was published in 2003, a world of information was, at least potentially, at everyone's fingertips. The music press as a whole was reeling from the impact of the internet on its previously secure role as mediator between artist and fan. The web was not only a means of disseminating information (some of it entirely false, but nevertheless replicated over and over), it also allowed fans to communicate directly between themselves about any type of esoterica one could name (or imagine without naming). In short, the world had changed; information was at once more accessible and less reliable. Quotes from this book, for instance—ones generated by me, and others found by me in otherwise obscure print sources—have turned up not only in various articles on the internet, but also subsequently in other books, then again in reworked or reinterpreted form on the internet. I have had a public argument online with a journalist who I thought had hijacked something from this book, which he claimed he had never read. It transpired that there were just more degrees of separation: he had hijacked it from another source who'd hijacked it from this book.

It is not just information which is available online, of course. Music is now easily accessible over the internet, in pirated and legitimate versions. This accessibility also allows—almost demands—detachment from context. In one sense that's nothing new; twenty years ago you could go to a record store (second-hand or otherwise) and come away with a mish-mash of items. But your records would usually have covers, perhaps even sleevenotes. Today you can easily acquire what amounts to a job lot of fragments of (for instance) the Go-Betweens' career from 1978 to 2004 and make of it what you will. Many people presumably do just that.

I do not intend the above paragraphs as expressions of an old man's sentimentality. I like the internet and I use it a lot. The points I wish to make are these: Firstly, that this book is largely a pre-internet work and, it turns out, one of the last of its kind. New material about the Go-Betweens is constantly being uploaded and generated online: I recommend you make use of it.

Secondly, I would argue that the Go-Betweens are essentially a pre-internet group. As this book shows, in their early stages the band members were magpies with a sense of history. They saw a flow of ideas. It was no coincidence that they also understood that at least one major element of being a rock or pop star was the persona they projected to the world. Almost everyone who passed through the Go-Betweens, and everyone who stayed for any length of time, as well as many of the group's followers, grasped how important this was. The band was from an era in which people made records and sold them with packaging, art, printed lyrics, and live shows. Some aspects of iTunes are heavily reminiscent of the old days of pop 45s (the first ten seconds once again sell the song, for instance), but there are many ways in which it robs the rock world of its glamour. Widespread accessibility is one of these, strangely enough. As I've already mentioned, in the pre-internet era information on particular musicians was difficult to find and only sporadically available—perhaps you knew someone with a pile of *NME*s up to the ceiling, and until it toppled over and smothered them you hypothetically had a resource to call on when you wanted to know something about, say, I'm So Hollow. But these things were rarely indexed, let alone "searchable." Now, what isn't?. It's still hard to find out about I'm So Hollow, but they (and Soggy Porridge) are the exceptions that prove the rule.

These observations are not terribly original; they instantly came to my mind when I thought about revising this book. Of course, it's not really revised; I used to joke that I could write an entirely new book about the Go-Betweens, following the same chronology but using entirely different sources (when I said 'I used to joke', I didn't mean it was a *funny* joke). I have agreed to donate all my interview tapes and other research materials to the National Film and Sound Archive (maybe writing this sentence will make me finally knuckle down to the task of fishing the tapes out from under the house). Perhaps then some day someone else can do exactly that and write a third book to complement this one and Robert Forster's promised memoir.

"The Go-Betweens are looking forward"—that was an apt way to close the second version of this book. Well might they have looked forward: the group managed to pack a lot into its remaining years, in which it could be said vindication was theirs.

Three years following the interviews which concluded this revised history, Grant McLennan died in his sleep. He had just bought a house—his first—in Brisbane; while preparing for a party, he complained of feeling ill and went to lie down. He was found dead later that day, having suffered a heart attack. It was May 7, 2006.

It has been said that Forster and McLennan joked about the Go-Betweens being a three-act play. The second act was the reformed—in fact, reimagined—21st-century version of the group; the third would have been Forster and McLennan in their seventies. Adele Pickvance has said that she thought "we'd be pushing each other up on stage in wheelchairs."

It would be ridiculously glib to try and encapsulate McLennan's last few years and death in any kind of dramatic narrative—real lives can't be shoehorned into Hollywood endings—but nevertheless, those final years were ones in which he experienced much of the commercial success he had long been due. To take one widely reported example of an esoteric insertion into pop culture: the songwriting pair became the name of a shadowy defense contractor in the TV series *24* in 2005, surely a sign that the world had come to terms with the Go-Betweens. McLennan surely enjoyed even more the fact that he was writing some of his best songs (at least, that was Forster's opinion, and Forster's opinion was what mattered most of all). He had also entered into a relationship, with Emma Pursey, which by all reports made him very happy. Some say he intended to announce his engagement to Pursey publicly on the night of the day he died.

It was not *Bright Yellow, Bright Orange* that achieved the commercial success; in fact that excellent album seems to have been temporarily forgotten (time for a reappraisal). Most of the triumph came with its successor, *Oceans Apart*, which the Go-Betweens line-up of Forster, McLennan, Pickvance, and Thompson recorded in London in November 2004. "It's a London record," Forster said at the time, "which means artificial plus organic. Sheen and soil." London's Barbican Theatre hosted a Go-Betweens Day that same year, featuring live performances by the contemporary lineup along with screenings of videos and archival footage of the band.

Oceans Apart was released on various different labels around the world; most importantly for Forster and McLennan's fortunes, however, it began a relationship with EMI Australia, which not only promoted the record (Forster was quoted in the press as saying the label's interest "makes Grant and me very happy") but also acquired their publishing in a lucrative deal which was the reason McLennan was able to purchase a house.

"It's proof that a band can reform for reasons other than nostalgia and financial pragmatism," wrote Alexis Petridis towards the end of a long "CD of the Week" review of *Oceans Apart* in the *Guardian*, "with a maturity that can enhance rather than damage an artist's legacy. More importantly, it is also a Go-Betweens album that stands with their 1980s highpoints." Early problems aside—the mastering of the record was so poor that the UK label Lo-Max agreed, after many complaints, to remaster the recordings and replace consumers' copies on request—most critics were similarly effusive. Forster wrote:

> By then, the whole thing was on an upswing. We got five-star reviews and our first music award. With another album approaching, Grant and I could feel the momentum and goodwill. We were writing well: it felt as if, with our most recent three albums, we were on a run, as we had been in the 1980s.

The award in question was from the Australian Performing Rights Association (APRA); it is often described in the international press as an "Australian Grammy," which needs to be accorded no little irony (few Australians would give an "Australian Grammy" very much status).

The two mainstay Go-Betweens essentially took the year off in 2005, writing songs and attending to other activities, such as finalizing the tracklisting of *Intermission*, the double-CD compilation of songs from their solo years. They were also writing songs, and by the time of McLennan's death were well on the way to having enough material for a new album. According to Forster:

> We had the eight songs. Two of them I had written; the other six were Grant's. One of his was "Demon Days." I remember him phoning me up in late January to say I should come over and hear some new songs. There was excitement in his voice. I went over late one night, which was unusual because we always played during the day. He lived in a small two-storey tower at the back of a house, and I climbed the stairs to his bedroom, where he'd set out two chairs. He then played me three songs. Two of

them were amazing, and one in particular, "Demon Days," I immediately thought was one of the best four or five he'd ever written. It was a waltz ballad, and as he strummed and sang it, with a beautiful instrumental section included, I looked at him in wonder. And I'm glad that at that moment, as the room went still, I said: "For the next 18 months, I'm going to be writing just to catch up with you." He laughed, but it was true.

McLennan's funeral was held at St John's Anglican Cathedral in Ann Street, Brisbane. Forster quipped in his eulogy that "his songs will be remembered for 1,000 years. Sorry, Grant's just told me 10,000 years. He's just added 9,000."

The mourners were led by members of McLennan's family: his siblings Sally and Lachlan, his mother Wendy, and his son Nathan Wallace, whose existence was made known to the wider world for the first time. McLennan had told me in no uncertain terms not to involve his family in my research for the book, or to mention them in the text; hence the absence of these people from the history you have in your hands (and yet another reason why I would not describe this book as a biography, quite apart from the fact that you can't write a biography of multiple people).

Other mourners included Bernard Fanning and Ian Haug of Powderfinger (Haug was, of course, also a member of FOC); Paul Kelly; the producer of McLennan's first two solo albums, Dave Dobbyn; Dave McCormack of Custard, The Titanics, and Cow; Steve Kilbey; Ed Kuepper; Lindy Morrison; and Andrew Wilson (of the Frontier Scouts and the Four Gods, who discovered for the first time that McLennan had *another* lifelong friend called Andrew Wilson as well).

The Premier of Queensland at the time, Peter Beattie, was quick to give McLennan the recognition he deserved. Beattie, who was known for making gifts of Go-Betweens music to international visitors (as indeed is Prime Minister Julia Gillard), established a Grant McLennan Memorial Fellowship in late 2006, awarding $20,000 a year to "allow a talented Queensland songwriter to spend up to two months in Berlin, London, or New York—cities which played a big role in Grant McLennan's career." In announcing the award, Beattie noted that McLennan "put our contemporary music on the world map." The fellowship is administered by Arts Queensland; Forster and Pursey are consultants.

The following year the Go-Betweens were commemorated on a Brisbane walk of fame. And recognition has come in rather stranger forms too. In July 2010 a new bridge across the Brisbane River, referred to in the planning stage as the Hale Street Link, was christened the Go Between Bridge. The choice was made after a ballot of local residents, who chose from a shortlist that included the "Reconciliation Bridge" as well as the provisional name. Brisbane Mayor Campbell Newman observed that "it's a name that works on two levels—not only does it honour one of Brisbane's most treasured musical exports, it also connects Milton and South Brisbane." Forster, helped to launch the bridge with a concert which also featured the exceptionally popular Angus and Julia Stone, Josh Pyke, and Bob Evans: he reminisced on his and McLennan's frequent traversal of inner city Brisbane in the late 1970s, claiming that "the story of the band is really two sides of the river."

There must also have been at least some small element of honoring the Go-Betweens, as well as his own versatile and direct prose, when Forster was awarded the 2006 Pascall Prize for criticism. He had been writing, primarily about music, for the arts and politics magazine *The Monthly* since its first issue, a year before McLennan's death. He has continued to contribute record reviews and observation pieces to the magazine since then, and in 2009 a number of these articles were gathered in a book entitled *The Ten Rules of Rock and Roll*. In awarding Forster the Pascall Prize, the judges described him as "a godsend . . . he writes about popular music with an authority and grace which would be rare in any area of criticism and is all the more striking in a field where criticism is often merely modish." Forster has talked about future writing projects, which may include a memoir.

In July 2007, Forster prepared a series of performances in Brisbane under the title "The Four Ages of Robert Forster." He also recorded *The Evangelist* with Pickvance and Thompson, a "solo album" which included not only songs that would have been his contributions to the nearly-written follow up to *Oceans Apart*, but also three by McLennan which Forster had completed. Like *Watershed* and *Danger in the Past*, *The Evangelist* is a hint of a Go-Betweens album that would never be.

Forster recently gave a keynote speech at an APRA song summit., in which he paid tribute to McLennan by diminishing—unfairly—both himself and the suburbs:

> I was a lot more suburban. He was like, "I have a book to read." He taught me, "You're an artist. You're a thinker. That's your job."

With McLennan's death, Forster has shed some of the artifice that the two contrived in their public personas; for instance, in his widely read reminiscence about their relationship, he dispatches the notion of McLennan as scatterbrained in contrast to Forster's directness and organizational focus. Forster was already branching out into other fields before the end of the

Go-Betweens and is now in a position to observe and enjoy the legacy of the group increase. The experience is clearly a bittersweet one, however, as he must do so without the man who worked as hard as he did to make it happen. Yet both Forster and McLennan had always—from "Lee Remick"/"Karen" onwards—aimed to create a lasting body of work which would touch people with its originality and genuineness. In this, their success is unquestionable. In Forster's words:

> I know this phase had another seven, eight years to go. We had momentum. I was 48 and I knew where the next ten years were going. Suddenly, in one second, that's gone. The end of the friendship. The end of the Go-Betweens. I just had to come to terms with that. Grant was gone.
>
> But, at the same time, we made nine albums. We inspired a lot of people. We'd done something. Grant was very proud of that. We've got that side of things covered. It's just that he's not going to spend the next 20 or 30 years on the planet that he should have.

Notes

Chapter 1: The new Velvet Underground
1 Jack Marx, "Two Wongs Make It Light," *Sydney Morning Herald* (April 24, 1993), 28.
2 Andrew Perry, "We're Going To Become the New Velvet Underground!" *Select* (August 1996), 72.
3 Dave Jennings, "Between Times," *Melody Maker* (March 24, 1990), 24.
4 Andrew Male, review of Go-Betweens CD reissues, *Select* (August 1996), 72.
5 Perry, "We're Going To Become the New Velvet Underground!"
6 Marx, "Two Wongs Make It Light."

Chapter 2: The Australian Go-Betweens Show (1995)
1 Probably some kind of clever association between how conservative and sterile rock "fandom" has become and the presumed dullness of straight people. I wish I'd had a copy of Kath Albury's book (*Yes Means Yes: Getting Explicit about Heterosex*) to throw at them, but it hadn't been published yet. And who knows? It might have caused an accident.
2 Eric Weisbard, "The Go-Betweens," in *Spin Alternative Record Guide* (New York, 1995), 168.
3 Australian radio stations' call signs are prefixed by a number specific to each of the nation's six states. New South Wales stations begin with "2," Victoria's with "3," and Queensland's with "4," all the way up to Tasmania's, with "7." The three letters in 4ZZZ indicate it is an FM station; 4BC, on the other hand, is an AM station. "Public radio" is the Australian equivalent to America's "college radio," but although many Australian public-radio stations began in association with universities—and some retain that link—stations such as 3RRR in Melbourne and 4ZZZ are no longer directly associated with any institution and rely on sponsorship and subscription for their funding.
4 The tapes were never edited, and the interview probably never aired.
5 Parsons was known at the time for his music writing in *NME* and as co-author (with Julie Burchill) of the early punk history, *The Boy Looked at Johnny: The Obituary of Rock 'n' Roll* (1978). He later became a TV pundit and popular novelist.
6 *New Musical Express* was the weekly new-wave bible. Issues reached Australia by sea mail—that is, about two months after they appeared in Britain.
7 Melbourne-based rock magazine. Its catchphrase was "you can't rock without it," though many did.
8 Australia's school system consists of government-run "public" schools and "private" schools mostly run by religious groups. Both receive government funding in different measures. "Private" schools are not always wealthy schools, but the wealthiest schools are generally private schools, and Forster and McLennan both attended wealthy private schools, which in Brisbane are confusingly called "Greater Public Schools." You won't be tested on this.
9 In the 1970s, AM radio in Australia, as in the USA, was synonymous with commercial pop radio.

10. Nicolas Roeg's directorial debut *Walkabout* (1970), about two English children lost in the Australian outback.
11. A reference to Elvis Costello's album *This Year's Model* (1978).
12. Forster is paraphrasing a line from a song on the aforementioned *This Year's Model*. The Sharks belonged to that particularly ugly category of new wave groups, a pre-punk band which changed identity to fit the new scene. This would get them on the national weekly pop TV show *Countdown*.
13. Callaghan was the lead singer/songwriter in the Numbers.
14. 2JJ, a Sydney-based, government-run "youth" radio station. It has since become Triple J, a nationwide FM station.
15. Anyone who thought "Lee Remick" was a *National Lampoon* comedy record probably hadn't heard one: "Lee Remick" is much funnier.

Chapter 3: Brisbane

1. John Willsteed, interviewed by Fiona Dempster, 2001. He adds that "Brisbane was a real, really vibrant sort of place in the mid-to-late seventies," because of the political upheavals and because it was a big city somewhat isolated from the rest of the world.
2. Interview by Virginia Moncrieff, "Ready Steady Go-Betweens," 2JJJ (May 23, 1983).
3. "The Brisbane Devotee," *Cane Toad Times* (August 1979).
4. That is, it took a benign symbol of days gone by—the cherubic, cheeky Harpo Marx—and turned his name into a wry, almost childish, subversive idea. This kind of thing was popular back then.
5. Tony Mockeridge, "Rock 'n' Roll—What Future?" *Radio Times* (March 1980).
6. "The Brisbane Devotee."
7. One of the most notorious practices of the Bjelke-Petersen government was to exert heavy control over street marches, and to declare illegal any that did not meet its criteria.
8. "The Brisbane Devotee."

Chapter 4: "Let's camp it up"

1. "Shake Your Booty" wasn't released until mid-1976; the Godots might have lasted just long enough to include it in their set, but it wouldn't have been an old song.
2. Geyer is a well-known Australian blues singer.
3. Forster, interviewed by Ashleigh Merritt and Allan Martin, 4ZZZ (1979).
4. This changed when Men at Work had a big hit in the USA in 1981 with "Down Under."
5. The Velvet Underground song.
6. Shaun Phillips, "Affairs of the Heart," *Sounds* (August 27, 1988), 12-13.
7. Ibid. McLennan told Frank Brunetti, in 1984, "Robert shared my interest in Ry Cooder." Frank Brunetti, "Go-Betweens: Remembrance of Visions and Hope," in Clinton Walker, ed., *The Next Thing* (Sydney, 1984), 45.
8. In Northern Queensland, 1700 kilometers (1055 miles) north of Brisbane.
9. McLennan, quoted in Marie Ryan, "Exiles from the Lost Australian Dream," *RAM* (June 24, 1983), 9.
10. Quoted in Marie Ryan, "Lush, Languid and Loving," *RAM* (December 7, 1984), 16.
11. Known in 1977 as *Gamut*.
12. Grant McLennan, "Robert Altman's Images," *Gamut* (September 25, 1977), 12.

Chapter 5: "Passenger pop for traveling minds"

1. Jane Cadzow, "Nostalgia Rock Is Toadette's Thing," Brisbane *Courier-Mail* (August 26, 1978), 16.
2. An advance from their days as the Grudge, when their standout songs were "Your Kind Make Me Puke" and "Advance Australia Fair," the latter apparently a parody of Australia's national anthem.

3   Clinton Walker, "Go-Betweens," *Roadrunner* (December 1979).
4   McLennan, interviewed by Clinton Walker (1984). Transcript courtesy Clinton Walker.
5   Diana McRobbie, "The Survivors of Brisbane," Brisbane *Courier-Mail* (May 13, 1978).
6   The Survivors' five albums were never recorded. The tragicomic story of the Suicide label is worthy of a book in itself. Formed as an adjunct label to prominent Melbourne "independent" Mushroom, to showcase and/or cash in on Australian punk music, it was rejected by punk fans as too crass and commercial, though this rejection did not spoil the careers of the groups signed to it. These included many people who will later feature in this narrative—not only the Survivors, but Chris Walsh's the Negatives, Mr. Pierre and James Freud's Teenage Radio Stars, and the Boys Next Door, who later became the Birthday Party.
7   Richard Lowenstein's 1987 film *Dogs in Space* explores this curious mix, in a Melbourne setting. His 2001 film *He Died with a Felafel in His Hand* suggests nothing much has changed.
8   There is obviously confusion in everyone's mind regarding the Grudge and the Numbers, and when one started and the other ended. Since it was essentially the same band this probably doesn't matter.
9   Clinton Walker, "Go-Betweens."
10 Rory Gibson, "Go-Betweens Go All Out for Success," Brisbane *Telegraph* (May 22, 1978), 14.

Chapter 6: "Rob likes the word *go!*"
1   Christopher Isherwood, *Christopher and His Kind: 1929-1939* (London, 1977), 63.

Chapter 7: Funk! Punk! Spunk!
1   In 1978, A$800-1,000 would have amounted to US$900-1,100 or £400-500.
2   The present author's first band made the same mistake in 1985.
3   The Sydney-based fortnightly *RAM* (it stood for "Rock Australia Magazine") was published from 1975 to 1989, and for most of that time was Australia's most respected newsprint music magazine (only the shorter-lived Adelaide magazine *Roadrunner* gave it any real competition).
4   Kim Fowley, *RAM* (March 1979).
5   A. A. Phillips, "The Cultural Cringe," reprinted in his book *The Australian Tradition: Studies in a Colonial Culture* (Melbourne, 1966), 117.
6   The Apartments were not the only Able label band the Go-Betweens tried to pillage. McLennan remembers the band also tried out Mark Callaghan of the Numbers for the second-guitarist role.
7   Wilson also documented the tour with his Super 8 camera, but the footage has been lost.
8   According to Geoffrey Titley, this involved late-night singing of Monkees songs.
9   *Rockhampton Morning Bulletin* (January 17, 1979), 18.
10 "Spunk" in Australia does not have the same meaning as in Britain, where it's a slang term for semen. In Australia, a "spunk" is a good-looking young person.
11 "Pop with Diana McRobbie," Brisbane *Courier-Mail* (January 27, 1979).
12 Forster says he feels it will go nicely on the 17th CD of the Go-Betweens box set.
13 Sources differ on this point. If he played with the group during the north Queensland tour—and he was certainly there for some of the tour—then this may have been his second Brisbane show, for a greater total number of shows. In any case, his tenure with the group was so short it must be irritating to him to be referred to so frequently as an "ex–Go-Between."
14 They changed their name to avoid confusion with a Scottish new-wave group also called Flowers.
15 The studio had meanwhile changed its name to Sunshine.
16 This joke was continued when these songs were reissued in 1986 as half of *The Able Label Singles* EP; by the time they were reissued again on *'78 'til '79: The Lost Album*, it had been dropped, though McLennan was credited with playing harmonica on "Don't Let Him Come Back." And McLennan became Candice when he played bass on the Four Gods' single "Enchanted House."
17 Teekman also mixed the group live on occasion.

18 Eight "Teeki tape" songs, alongside five of the six tracks recorded at Window/Sunshine, make up what was issued in 1998 as *'78 'til '79: The Lost Album*. Forster chose very judiciously from the songs at his disposal—few of the really imitative tracks are included. "The Night," Tim Mustafa's favorite, is a Springsteen pastiche that nearly made the cut but was dropped by Forster at the last minute when he concluded it didn't hold up by itself.
19 A hand-colored version of this picture appears on the cover of *'78 'til '79: The Lost Album*.
20 Once again, sources differ. It might have been a long interview with Dylan in *Playboy*. It takes twelve to fourteen hours to drive from Brisbane to Sydney.
21 Actually, QIT—Queensland Institute of Technology. It became QUT in the 1990s (the "U" is for University). Thank you to Anthea Pitt for pointing this out.
22 David Byrne from Talking Heads. The *Torn Curtain* notes are from the Robert Forster archive.
23 It's not that lost. The ad has been located by Fiona Dempster for her documentary.
24 Ian Wadley: "Hungry Jacks, actually, at the corner of Queen and Albert. The Black Cat was a newsagent, not a café!"
25 Half a world away, a band featuring Stephen Duffy and Dave Kusworth adopted the same name at the same time. The Band had used the name before they became associated with Dylan, which was probably the appeal for both the Birmingham and Brisbane outfits.
26 Robin Gold, quoted in Karen Sprey, "Grand Ideas on a Low Budget," *The Planet*, vol. 2 no. 8 (1981).
27 An edited version of *Heather's Gloves* exists, and Gold has been known to give private screenings. The film's sound, however, is reputedly terrible.
28 Robin Gold, quoted in Sprey, "Grand Ideas."
29 Vickers had moved to New York by the time the film was finished.
30 Pitt Street is a main street in Sydney.

Chapter 8: Zero

1 Like many settler societies, Australia has a population of people identifying as descendants of those who lived on the continent before the arrival of colonizers (in this case, the British in 1788). American readers will see many parallels between the history (and present status) of these people and that of Native Americans in North America. In Australia, people who identify as indigenous make up two to four percent of the population. It is worth noting, too, that they are aboriginals, but also Aboriginal people—the capitalized version being the accepted specific term for Australian native people.
2 Marie Ryan, "Of Skins and Hearts," *RAM* (July 29, 1987), 12-13.
3 Ibid.
4 Other members of Shrew were Diana Priest on saxophone; Marion Redmond on clarinet; Mary Kelly on piano; Bronwyn Nicholls on backing vocals; a woman called Elizabeth, whose last name has unfortunately been forgotten, on double bass; and Robyn Stacey on flute. Stacey remained a friend of Morrison's and photographed the Go-Betweens frequently in the late 1980s.
5 Brunetti, "Go-Betweens: Remembrance of Visions and Hope," 42-43.
6 Ibid.
7 Ibid.
8 By just over five years. Morrison was born on November 2, 1951; Willsteed on February 13, 1957, which (irrelevantly) makes him a year and a day older than McLennan.
9 John Willsteed, interviewed by David Nichols (February 6, 1994).
10 Forster and Zero even did some recording together at 4ZZZ in late 1979. Only one song came close to being completed: it is a peculiar, bouncy, keyboard-oriented affair, and highly appealing.
11 McLennan was not there, having decided to skip Talking Heads in favor of taking in a Jacques Prévert film with new friend Robin Gold.
12 Robert Forster, 4ZZZ interview (January 1979).
13 By the time the song was recorded for *Send Me a Lullaby*, "my Kodak" had become "my camera."

14 Forster, interviewed by Ashleigh Merritt, 4ZZZ (January 1979).

Chapter 9: The Sound of Young Scotland
1   Quoted in Bill Black, "Fair Dinkum," *Sounds* (October 20, 1984), 16.
2   Not to be confused with the Robert Wheeler who plays in Pere Ubu.
3   McLennan also went to Yugoslavia and Greece.
4   Not to be confused with the Reasons Why, a Sydney group of the 1980s.
5   It is said that Elvis Costello had tried a similar approach when trying to find a deal in the mid-1970s, and that A&R people found it too confrontational.
6   Graham Aisthorpe, "How I Spent My Holidays: The Forster Report." *Backstage* (July 1980), 11.
7   Before the Velvet Underground became his full-time concern, Reed had tried writing novelty rock songs for the budget Pickwick label. It's a good comparison as far as "Lee Remick" is concerned.
8   This is possible, but probably untrue.
9   Postcard, *Brochure* (1981).
10 An unfair and inaccurate description of Josef K, in my view.
11 This "girl" was in fact from Brisbane—Judy Crighton, the wife of former 4ZZZ associate Ross Crighton.
12 Interview by Fiona Dempster (2000).
13 Aisthorpe, "How I Spent My Holidays."
14 Ibid.
15 Meaning the Sex Pistols' "Anarchy in the UK."
16 Postcard, *Brochure*. Malcolm Fisher was a pianist who lived above Kelly and Hogarth.
17 "Lee Remick," "Hope," "I Need Two Heads" (with different lyrics altogether from the single version—it begins with the line "Don't you raise your voice at me"), "Eight Pictures" (the ascetic Daly ploughing through the song's drum solo with evident reluctance), "People Say," "Stop before You Say It" (with the entrancing lines "You can fuck him up/You can fuck him down"), "Don't Let Him Come Back," and "Karen."
18 Aisthorpe, "How I Spent My Holidays."
19 Quoted in Fiona Dempster interview (2000).
20 Robert Forster, letter to Andrew Wilson, April 28, 1980, Andrew Wilson Archive.
21 Aisthorpe, "How I Spent My Holidays."
22 McLennan told me in 1983 that "the label we had in mind and the label Edwyn and Alan had in mind swiftly bastardized into something we knew nothing about."
23 An Orange Juice song.
24 37° centigrade, i.e., 98° Fahrenheit.
25 Horne apparently does not recall visiting Robert and Lindy at their home at 329 Fulham Palace Road a few years later. "He's still preaching the same gospel of charts and gossip. He was great to see, although I find his ideas a bit stale," Robert wrote to Andrew Wilson in 1981. (Forster, letter to Andrew Wilson, undated, Andrew Wilson Archive).

Chapter 10: From Brisbane to Melbourne
1   McLennan, interviewed by Clinton Walker (1984).
2   Aisthorpe, "How I Spent My Holidays."
3   That is, in a clipped, new-wave manner reminiscent of the British group Magazine.
4   Bloxsom was another member of Zero.
5   Robert Forster, interview in *Distant Violins* no. 18 (1985).
6   For example, in his book *Stranded: The Secret History of Australian Independent Music, 1977-1991* (Sydney, 1996), 85-87.

Chapter 11: *Send Me a Lullaby*

1. Carlton and Richmond are inner-city areas of Melbourne, and at this time were primarily home to a variety of bohemian, non–English-speaking, young and/or poor people.
2. Quoted in Ian Johnston, *Bad Seed: the Biography of Nick Cave* (London, 1995), 56.
3. A viewing of Richard Lowenstein's film *Dogs in Space* will give the reader a superficial idea of some of the assumptions and behavior of these times. Made a few years after the events depicted, the film features many people from the time cast as themselves or each other (for example, Hugo Race plays Mr. Pierre).
4. It reached the national top twenty in February 1980.
5. In 1979 A$12,000 was equivalent to US$13,400, or £6,000.
6. Richard Cluff, "Tony Cohen," *Sunglasses after Dark* no. 2 (1983).
7. Ibid.
8. Some of the songs were given jokey working titles by Cohen, as can be seen on the log sheets of the 24-track masters (see page 109). "Ambeeant A" was ultimately titled "People Know" and "Out on the Hiway (Man)" became "It Could Be Anyone."
9. Lindy Morrison, quoted in Jim Goodwin, "Go-Betweens Interview," *3PBS Waves* (August 1981), 4. The "Numan Freudski" moniker was almost certainly a joke by Morrison, since James Freud is credited on the album under his own name, but Freud recently claimed it as his own. In his autobiography he writes: "The band and I got on really well, so they invited me to bring in my sax and play on the record as Numan Freudski . . . I was such a crappy sax player that avant-garde was the only way I could bluff my way through the experience." James Freud, *I Am the Voice Left from Drinking* (Sydney, 2002), 96.
10. Forster might again have been exceeding his authority here in suggesting axing McLennan's song. McLennan obviously—and justifiably—thought highly of this early creation: he reintroduced it into the band's set, now singing it himself, in the late 1980s and rerecorded it as a "secret" track on his solo single "Surround Me" in 1992. It's a beaut.
11. Forster, letter to Keith Glass (undated). Courtesy Keith Glass.
12. Forster, letter to Andrew Wilson (undated). Andrew Wilson Archive.
13. Ibid.
14. Morrison believes McLennan colluded with Glass to drop the three "art-rock" tracks, though there is some consistency between that decision and Forster's plea for a chance to revise the album.
15. Forster, letter to Andrew Wilson (undated, probably October 1981). Andrew Wilson Archive.
16. Quoted in Graham Aisthorpe, "Go-Betweens Interview: *Planet* Prints the Aisthorpe Tapes." Reprinted in Missing Link's Go-Betweens press kit.
17. Jenny Watson did the cover art for *Send Me a Lullaby*. Pink and Blue also shared a cassette with Peter Walsh's band Out of Nowhere.
18. John Reid, "Brisbane Born Not the Day before Yesterday," *Semper* (October 20, 1981).
19. This single, along with other Andrew Wilson–related recordings, including some "real" Four Gods songs, appears on the 1999 CD *Amateurism* (Chapter Music). Forster wrote the sleeve notes.
20. In 1982 A$1,000 = US$1,150 or £600.
21. By the "first Postcard," McLennan means Postcard as an independent label, rather than its short-lived incarnation as Orange Juice's vanity label through Polydor.
22. Trevor Block, interview with the Go-Betweens, *Fast Forward* no. 11.

Chapter 12: *Before Hollywood*

1. Geoff Travis, interviewed by Steve Connell (1995).
2. Anyone interested in this kind of lifestyle, for whatever crazy reason, will learn a lot from Ian Johnston's biography of Nick Cave.
3. Forster, who says he finds this description by Morrison distasteful, places the events in Fulham Palace Road in late 1982, after the *Before Hollywood* sessions.
4. Dave McCullough, "Beneath, Between and Behind," *Sounds* (June 5, 1982).

5   Dave Hill, "Raw Paradox," *New Musical Express* (June 26, 1982).
6   *Send Me a Lullaby* is actually an excellent album, and time has treated it well. Subsequent Go-Betweens albums were more distinctive, but *Lullaby* is still a classy piece of work in its own right.
7   She died on September 13, 1982 in a car accident.
8   James Stewart (Grace Kelly's co-star in Hitchcock's *Rear Window*, which is presumably what made the connection in Forster's mind) did not die until nearly fifteen years later, in July 1997.
9   This show marked the first time since the 1920s that early silent film was screened in a way that made performers move naturally, rather than in the speeded-up, jerky style that later technology had imparted to earlier films. Forster might have been responding to this more natural vision of early film.
10 Wait for Ian McFarlane's biography of Ed Kuepper.
11 Forster, letter to Andrew Wilson (undated: 1982?), Andrew Wilson Archive.
12 Grant McLennan, interviewed by Virginia Moncrieff, "Ready Steady Go-Betweens," 2JJJ (May 23, 1983).
13 Everett True, e-mail to author (January 11, 2003).
14 Quoted in Marie Ryan, "Exiles from the Lost Australian Dream."
15 McLennan, interviewed by Moncrieff, "Ready Steady Go-Betweens."
16 Quoted in Marie Ryan, "Lush, Languid and Loving."
17 "Singles: Reviewed by Edwyn Collins of Orange Juice," *Melody Maker* (March 12, 1983), 26.
18 Quoted in David Nichols, "The Go-Betweens," *Distant Violins* no. 4 (1981).
19 Marie Ryan, "Exiles from the Lost Australian Dream."
20 McLennan, unpublished interview with Clinton Walker (1984).
21 McLennan, interviewed by Moncrieff, "Ready Steady Go-Betweens." The format would be repeated by Forster in his song about McLennan on the *Bright Orange Bright Yellow* album (2003). McLennan requested the opportunity to pen a verse for the song, responding to Forster's "impressions, of me and what the song's about," yet again!
22 There was talk at the time that Alison Moyet, the singer in Yazoo, might cover "Cattle and Cane" (which boggles the mind, though the result might have been great); in the late 1990s, veteran Australian Aboriginal singer Jimmy Little equaled the quality of the original on his album *Messenger*.
    McLennan later came to toy with the original concept of "Cattle and Cane"—in one of his closest brushes with self-parody, he changed the words when he performed it live in the late 1980s: now the boy wasn't "waiting for a chance" but cutely "learning how to dance."
23 McLennan, interview with Clinton Walker.
24 Ibid. McLennan might have been reading too much of the work of poet Judith Wright.
25 Discussing his own name's McCartney-Lennon blending with interviewer Chris Hollow in 2002, McLennan remarked, "It's something that I occasionally say to Robert and he just rolls his eyes."
26 "Dusty in Here" was originally entitled "Metal and Shells." The latter title subsequently graced a 1983 US album which combined selected tracks from *Before Hollywood* and its successor *Spring Hill Fair*.
27 Only Collins and McClymont remained from the original Orange Juice by this stage. Malcolm Ross from Josef K had joined on guitar and Zeke Manyika was the drummer.
28 Forster, aerogram to Andrew Wilson (postmarked June 4, 1982). Andrew Wilson Archive.

Chapter 13: "He's the last one to take his coat off"

1   Robert Forster, letter to Andrew Wilson (January 29, 1982). Andrew Wilson Archive.
2   McLennan (and Forster?), notes for *Torn Curtain*. Courtesy of Robert Forster.
3   A double live album of the Beatles live at the Star Club in Hamburg in 1961 was released to great interest in the mid-1970s.
4   Frank Brunetti, "Go-Betweens: Remembrance and Visions of Hope," in Clinton Walker (ed.), *The Next Thing*.

5   A traditional Australian flatbread baked in hot coals.
6   Leslie "Biff" Millar was the Laughing Clowns bassist whom Walsh was replacing: perhaps these two were also engaging in a "handover."
7   Robert Forster, letter to Andrew Wilson (January 29, 1982). Andrew Wilson Archive.
8   This is not the video included on the 2002 reissue of *Before Hollywood*.
9   Vickers, interviewed by David Nichols (June 23, 1983).

Chapter 14: "Can you shut your fucking mouth for a minute?"

1   Meldrum had interviewed the group during one of his trips to Britain for *Countdown*, producing the following unusual exchange with Lindy Morrison:
Meldrum: "Well, this is a pleasant surprise, coming to London and finding the Go-Betweens. I find it almost ridiculous that I have to come to London for you to come on *Countdown*." Morrison: "That's exactly what we said before we came." Meldrum: "And I don't blame you." Replayed on *The 7:30 Report*, ABC-TV (April 22, 1999).
   Interviewer and group then went on a drinking spree that ended with Forster leaving Meldrum's hotel room wearing Meldrum's hat; a struggle ensued for its possession.
2   February 4, 1983. Carpenter was actually 32.
3   In fact it was an EP, *The Tenant of the Room*.
4   The Boys Next Door was the precursor to the Birthday Party. The members recorded an album (*Door Door*) and an EP (*Hee Haw*) under that name before changing the name of the band to the Birthday Party.
5   This was arrant bluster. I was scared for my life at that show, mainly because of the audience.
6   Dag is an Australian term for a socially awkward person, or someone who lacks style.
7   McLennan is falling into quoting from "That Way," a song (ostensibly about Peter Walsh) from *Before Hollywood*.
8   It is this video recording of "Cattle and Cane" that is included on the 2002 reissue of *Before Hollywood*.
9   Casual readers who came to this book looking for some information on the Go-Betweens might be wondering why they should give a loose root about Mr. Pierre's rendition of "Lost Highway." I can't tell you that, but I would like to let you know that after some considerable research it appears to me that this concept never got as far as the recording studio. The Moodists were to have been the backing band.

Chapter 15: Out of Step

1   The recording of "Newton Told Me" surfaced in 1984 as the b-side of the "Part Company" 12-inch single on Sire; it is included on the 2002 extended reissue of *Spring Hill Fair*.
2   Forster, letter to David Nichols (September 20, 1983).
3   To date, it has also been his only such foray.
4   The Go-Betweens' records have been issued on many different labels throughout the world, and only the most compulsive historian/fan would wish to make a full list of the many different releases of the same records via different distribution deals. Throughout this book—with rare exceptions where it seemed relevant to the story—I have focused on the record labels the group had direct dealings with. Usually this means whoever released their records in the country they were living in at the time, although by the end of the 1980s, when Mushroom in Australia, Beggar's Banquet in England, and Capitol in the US released *16 Lovers Lane*, the whole issue had become too confusing for anyone to care about.
5   According to Marie Ryan, "Off the Cliff—and Up!", *RAM* (April 27 1984), 17.
6   At least £2 of the £40 promotional budget was used to send my fanzine a copy of the single—hardly the best way to get your record known, though I certainly treasured my copy.
7   They are included on the 2002 extended version of *Spring Hill Fair*.
8   Quoted in Elisabeth Vincentelli, "The Go-Betweens, Now, Then, and Again: Interview with Robert Forster," *Puncture* no. 37 (1996), 24.
9   At the time £12,000 was equivalent to A$19,000 or US$16,000.

10 Morrison, quoted in Marie Ryan, "Off the Cliff—and Up!"
11 Quoted in Lynden Barber, "Kissing Cousins," *Melody Maker* (November 3, 1984), 30.
12 Don Watson, "Up from Down Under," *NME* (November 26, 1983).
13 A concept dating back to the days of the British Empire. It gave Australians with British parents or grandparents the unlimited right to live and work in the UK.
14 Forster denies doing this.
15 Forster, letter to Andrew Wilson (March 8, 1984). Andrew Wilson Archive.

Chapter 16: *Spring Hill Fair*

1 Marie Ryan, "Lush, Languid and Loving."
2 "The Portable Chat Show" (October 1984).
3 Marie Ryan, "Lush, Languid and Loving."
4 Lynden Barber, "Kissing Cousins."
5 The sentiments of "You've Never Lived" would later also be directed at others; during at least one show on their 1985 US tour, Forster introduced it as being "about the Smiths."
6 McLennan interviewed by Clinton Walker (1984).
7 Clinton Walker, "Stars of the Underground," *RAM* (March 26, 1986), 16.
8 Clinton Walker, "The Band Most Likely to Get a Shot at the Title," *Age EG* (March 14, 1986), 5.
9 Clinton Walker, "Stars of the Underground."
10 Morrison quoted in Chris Heath, "Go-Betweens," *Jamming* (1984), 36-37.
11 Ibid.
12 Mat Snow, "Money Can't Buy You Love," *NME* (October 13, 1984), 16.
13 Biba Kopf, "The Band That Holds You Also Harms You," *NME* (1984).
14 Marie Ryan, "Lush, Languid and Loving."
15 Ana da Silva, aka Anna Silva, was Judy Crighton's next door neighbor. Crighton had already done the Go-Betweens a favor by introducing them to Postcard; she performed another by hooking them up with da Silva.
16 Marie Ryan, "Lush, Languid and Loving."
17 It is included on the 2002 extended reissue of *Spring Hill Fair*.
18 Forster interviewed by David Nichols, *Distant Violins* no. 15 (1985).
19 The songs were "Secondhand Furniture," later recorded as a b-side; "The Power That I Now Have," which, reworked, became "To Reach Me" on the next album; "Five Words," with new lyrics making reference to a warlock married to a voodoo doll, a parson sent up for arson, and so on; and "Rare Breed."
20 Grant McLennan, "Images," *Gamut* (September 25, 1977), 12.
21 Grant McLennan, "Annie Hall," *Gamut* (August 5, 1977), 16.
22 Quoted in John Mullen, "They Shoot Horse (Breakers) Don't They?" *Rave* (November 23, 1994), 17.

Chapter 17: *Liberty Belle and the Black Diamond Express*

1 Mike Ticher, "Go-Betweens," *Snipe* (September 2, 1985), 14.
2 Quoted in Marie Ryan, "Lush, Languid and Loving."
3 Quoted in David Nichols, "The Go-Betweens," *Smash Hits* (February 11, 1985).
4 As Forster and McLennan would have been very much aware, Elektra was Television's label for their first two albums.
5 Presumably this was never a serious possibility.
6 Forster, letter to Andrew Wilson (September 1985). Andrew Wilson Archive.
7 Robert Vickers, interviewed by Fiona Dempster (2001).
8 Quoted in Clinton Walker, "The Band Most Likely To Get a Shot at the Title."
9 Quoted in Danny Kelly, "Liberteens," *NME* (February 8, 1986), 31.
10 Quoted in David Nichols, "Robert Forster Part 1," *Distant Violins* (1985).

11 David Nichols, "The Go-Betweens," *Smash Hits* (February 11, 1985).
12 *Puncture* no. 12 (Fall 1986), 4.

Chapter 18: *Very Quick on the Eye*
1 For some reason, the Boys Next Door contribution to this release was credited to the anagram "Torn Ox Bodeys."
2 Quoted in Peter Docherty, "Go-Betweens," *M62* no. 3 (October/November 1988).
3 Quoted in David Nichols, "Robert Forster Part 2," *Distant Violins* no. 18 (1986), 5.
4 For an attempt to dress a thing up as something more, just look at the umpteen reissues of early Bee Gees material that Festival Records in Australia have been involved with since the mid-1960s. The Bee Gees have had an extensive career and every time they had a new hit or a new look, Festival would release an album of their very early Australian recordings with a current picture of them on the front.
5 Keith Glass, letter to the Go-Betweens (June 1, 1985). Courtesy Keith Glass.

Chapter 19: *Tallulah*
1 Slang term for "derelict" (street person).
2 Quoted in Simon Reynolds, "Exiles in Love," *Melody Maker* (March 7, 1987), 14.
3 Morrison, interview by Fiona Dempster (2001).
4 I was a Go-Betweens fan for more than five years before I realized Robert and Lindy had been in a relationship. I only found out when I overheard two friends of the band in London laughing about the *NME*'s Mat Snow belatedly discovering the fact.
5 Danny Kelly, "Liberteens." Forster, incidentally, denies any such fucks, glamorous or otherwise.
6 With all due respect, the Servants' album *Disinterest* is a Piltdown Man–like missing link between *Send Me a Lullaby* and *Before Hollywood*.
7 Quoted in Simon Reynolds, "Exiles in Love."
8 Quoted in Ralph Traitor, "In Between Days," *Sounds* (February 28, 1987), 26.
9 Doctor and the Medics.
10 Quoted in Bernard Zuel, "The Go-Betweens: Keeping the Faith," *On the Street* (June 17, 1987), 21.
11 I don't think Forster would ever say "dunno."
12 Quoted in Donald McRae, "A Different Kind of Pension" *NME* (February 28, 1987), 47.
13 Forster, "Hair Care with Robert Forster," *Debris* (December 16, 1987). Quoted in Mal Peachey, "Go Boldly," *FSM* (June 1987), 41.
14 Ibid.

Chapter 20: *16 Lovers Lane*
1 Quoted in Andrew Collins, "Inbetween days," *NME* (June 10, 1989), 13.
2 Quoted in John O'Donnell, "You Can Go Home Again," *Rolling Stone* [Australian edition] (May 1988), 77-79.
3 Ibid.
4 Michael Gudinski, founder and proprietor of Mushroom until 1999.
5 Bob Johnson, interviewed by Fiona Dempster (2001).
6 Quoted in David Nichols, "The Go-Betweens: Grant and Robert Ride Again," *Puncture* no. 44 (1999), 12.
7 She means he consumed all the band's complimentary booze each night.

Chapter 21: Parting Company
1 Newtown is an inner-city suburb of Sydney where people in bands (including the present author) used to live in the 1980s, before the yuppies moved in.

2   Forster, interviewed by Fiona Dempster.
3   At the time A$200,000 was the equivalent of US$120,000, or £72,500.
4   I don't wish to insult the reader's intelligence, but just to clarify things, this is a metaphor.
5   Willner was a hot producer at the time, having recently conceived and masterminded several highly regarded various-artists tribute records, including *Amarcord* and *Stay Awake*.

Chapter 22: Danger in the Past

1   In fact this was not just the first album release of this track but its first official release altogether. It was included on the vinyl and cassette versions of the album but not the CD, because of sound quality concerns. It had to be mastered from a cassette dub, the original tape having been lost when it was sent to Beserkley. Improved digital sound technology has since come to the rescue of recordings like "The Sound of Rain."
2   Clinton Walker, original MS of review of *The Go-Betweens 1978-1990* for *Rolling Stone* [Australian edition] (February 1990). Courtesy Clinton Walker.
3   Forster wrote his reply in the margin of the original manuscript of this book, while he was fact-checking it.
4   *Cleopatra's Lament* received a very limited release. I had a cassette promo copy of it when it was released, but have never seen a CD of it.
5   Interviewed in 2001 by Fiona Dempster, Morrison claimed: "Beggars Banquet did the foulest things. [They] refused to admit that Amanda was actually entitled to an artist's royalty, that she'd ever signed a royalty agreement. And that is just so outrageous! It was only because I'd been so good at keeping all the paperwork together that I had the contract that she'd signed." When she went to Beggars Banquet in 1992 to inspect their books, she says she was "treated like a pariah. I was taken into a room—they were very nervous, extremely nervous, and all I wanted was to sort out the accounting—but no one would really talk about what was happening. For instance . . . Robert and Grant were touring Europe and they were still using the Go Betweens account to do that touring so that the money they were touring on, the tour support, was coming out of my future artist royalties. You know, that's up to 1995. I mean it's just outrageous. Stuff was going on and I had no money, I had no power. I became political then about following up on copyright issues . . . See, it's the noncomposers who end up in the gutter in the end."
6   Marci Cohen, "Jack Frost: The Perfect Marriage," *B-Side* (Aug./Sep. 1991).
7   Ibid.
8   Terry Ericsson, *Sound Affects* no. 14 (December 1991/January 1992).
9   A rumor at the time of *Snow Job*'s release was that it was actually just songs recorded during the 1990 sessions that had not made the first album.
10 Some additional recording was done at Preussen Ton Studios, also in Berlin.
11 Often referred to affectionately as "the Smackery" in Melbourne. I couldn't resist bringing this up because I still think it's amusing, but I am not implying anyone was taking drugs at the Berlin sessions.
12 Quoted in Peter Holmes, "The Good Seed," *Sydney Morning Herald* (April 23, 1993), 20.
13 A live version of the song, recorded in Brisbane and included on Forster's CD single "2541," shows the kind of treatment, and response, it can get.
14 Strzoda is a drummer and songwriter who has worked with power-pop trio Die Antwort, electronic disco performer Andreas Dorau, and Nick-Drake-meets-Stereolab six-piece Ja König Ja, among others.
15 This lineup ("with all our names misspelled" in the CD booklet, Strzoda says) backs Forster on "Tower of Song," his contribution to the Leonard Cohen tribute album *I'm Your Fan*.
16 The two-guys-and-a-female-drummer group Smudge were an interesting proposition themselves. Readers outside Australia might know the work of their main songwriter Tom Morgan from the many songs he cowrote with Evan Dando for the Lemonheads in the 1990s, particularly on *It's a Shame about Ray* (1992).
17 I am reminded of a show I saw McLennan play at this time in Sydney when Penny Flanagan and Julia Richardson sang backing vocals on some songs: Richardson playfully grabbed

his 49ers cap. Flushed and embarrassed, he stooped for her to replace it, which she did immediately, turning to the audience and acknowledging the faux pas—while all three were singing a song. Incidentally, the cap was a present to McLennan from Peter Blakely, a young and accomplished soul singer who had major chart success in the late 1980s, and who also wore a lot of hats. McLennan's friends over the last decade have often expressed surprise over his "gangsta" clothes.

18. Of course, McLennan's friends did not take this seriously. During interviews for the first incarnation of this book I noticed a mailing tube from photographer Bleddyn Butcher on McLennan's kitchen table addressed to "G. Dub McLennan" (a play on "V. Dub," an affectionate term for the Volkswagen).
19. In 1991, I asked McLennan who Sweetpea was, but he declined to say.
20. Those who like to read liner notes will have noticed that Quarry also designed the cover of McLennan's third album, *Horsebreaker Star*.
21. According to John O'Donnell's press release for *Watershed*, Paul Kelly played harmonica on "Black Mule."
22. It also confirmed McLennan on a peculiar path of continued lyrical references to starting fires; his other abiding lyrical obsessions include blindness and "Mrs. Morgan."
23. Quoted in Holmes, "The Good Seed."
24. Ibid.
25. Quoted in Larry Crane, "The Go-Betweens," *Tape Op* no. 14 (1999), 38.
26. Quoted in Elisabeth Vincentelli, "The Go-Betweens, Now, Then, and Again," *Puncture* no. 37 (1996), 24. The "dark star" idea comes up again in Crane's article.
27. People who read sleeve notes attentively will have noticed that Forster refers to this error in the acknowledgments to *Warm Nights*.
28. An Australian supermarket chain. The name is no longer used and so for many it remains associated with Australian suburbia in the 1960s and 1970s.
29. A medium-sized inner-city hotel on Parramatta Road, Sydney.
30. Her father was a jazz pianist, one brother is a composer, and another brother and a sister have their own band.
31. Quoted in Elisabeth Vincentelli, "The Go-Betweens, Now, Then, and Again."
32. Larry Crane, who engineered *The Friends of Rachel Worth* in 2000, recalls going out for karaoke "a couple of times" with the band: "Grant did the best version of 'Daydream Believer' without even looking up at the words."
33. She has, however, made a point of recording one track playing acoustic bass on each of the two post-2000 Go-Betweens albums.
34. Robert Christgau, "No Sex, No Funk, No Yellow Brick Road," *Village Voice*, July 25, 1995.
35. Ibid. Christgau reports the show as taking place on July 5.
36. Thompson remembers there being three "Go-Betweens" shows in Brisbane at this time. Forster and McLennan did not, however, officially bill themselves as such: the Zoo show described in chapter two was billed under their own names.
37. *Les Inrockuptibles* is often referred to in Go-Betweens promo material as "a French newspaper." It is a newspaper in the sense that *NME* is a newspaper.
38. Quoted in "Interview with Robert Forster and Grant McLennan of the Go-Betweens, 25th November 2002," www.jturner.dircon.co.uk/webinterview20021125.html.
39. Allen & Unwin (Australia) is an independent company, with no remaining ties to its original parent company in the UK.
40. Though the album is definitely titled *In Your Bright Ray*, creative owners have the option of turning the cover booklet around to pretend they own a Grant McLennan album called *The Magic Club*.
41. Larry Crane, recording *The Friends of Rachel Worth*, was also surprised by McLennan's willingness to allow others to make artistic decisions about his work. He recalls: "At one point, he did several vocal takes of a song and left me to comp his best takes. I was very honored that he would let me make that call."
42. Which was, of course, played by McLennan.
43. Successful in Australia, at least, where they consistently make the top ten with their strongly

melodic guitar-based pop.
44 I have to admit this is what instantly occurred to me when I first heard the band's name. Probably I listen to too much Oz rock.
45 There was also a post-Buzzcocks outfit featuring Steve Diggle and (briefly) John Maher called Flag of Convenience who often abbreviated their name to FOC and sometimes, strangely, to Buzzcocks FOC.
46 The first, self-titled (on Festival), and *Kiss Tomorrow Goodbye* and *Heroic Blues* (on the Cockayne label). All are highly recommended, *Heroic Blues* most of all.
47 Pickvance was replaced as bassist in the Speckled Band by Mia Schoen, when it became clear that Go-Betweens commitments would be too pressing.
48 The drummer for the sessions is Temucin Mustafa, with the exception of "Karen" and "Lee Remick."
49 Except "Man O' Sand to Girl O' Sea," which is the Rough Trade single version (i.e., the second of the three studio recordings) rather than the version recorded for *Spring Hill Fair*.
50 Robert Forster, sleeve notes to *Bellavista Terrace*.
51 It's interesting to note that even this close to the fully fledged Go-Betweens reunion/re-activation, Forster is referring to the group in the past tense.
52 This was of course *Les Inrockuptibles*, for whom Forster and McLennan had performed a Go-Betweens show.
53 "The Go-Betweens Go Again," ABC-TV's *The 7:30 Report* (April 22, 1999).
54 Quoted in Franklin Bruno, "Second Firsts: The Go-Betweens Return," *Portland Phoenix* (September 28, 2000).

Chapter 23: Unfinished Business

1 McLennan, interviewed by Chris Hollow in *Inpress* (January 2002).
2 "New Go-Betweens Record.. *Puncture* no. 46 (2000), 4.
3 Forster, interviewed by Fiona Dempster. One song of Forster's that did not make the final album was "Sleeping Giant," which he wrote about his son, Louis. Forster now intends the track to become a b-side: "I've now retitled it 'An Old Song That I Wrote about My Son.' Because it's [from] 1998. He's four now. It was just after he was born . . . I like the song . . . I'm scared of turning into Graham Nash, you know, the sort of person who writes about their children. It's a scary area. But I think it is done quite well."
4 Forster, interviewed by Fiona Dempster.
5 Crane adds: "The acoustic version of 'Surfing' does not [now] exist . . . We erased the reel of extra takes and leftover bits—on purpose."
6 Miller says McLennan told him, "the only people I talk to about my songs are Robert and Bob"—the irony being, of course, that Miller was only doing this under instruction from those two people.
7 Crane adds: "There was a list of thank-yous for the Portland session that never ran. Jeff Saltzman assisted on initial engineering, Janel Jarosz loaned a twelve-string acoustic guitar, Brian Dickel loaned an upright bass, Joanna Bolme picked them up at the Seattle airport, etc. Somebody must have lost this list along the way. Sam Coombs loaned a lot of guitar, amp and bass stuff."
8 Kevin Sampsell, "One Comeback That Doesn't Suck: The Go-Betweens' Robert Forster Talks about Their New CD," *Portland Mercury* (November 9, 2000).
9 Joshua Klein, *The Onion*, www.theonionavclub.com/review.php?review_id=3710.
10 For instance, Mr. Cold Meiser in "A CD Consumer Weather Report," www.cdconsumer.com/featgobe.htm.
11 They debuted as a band in Australia; their first album was recorded in Australia; and their first permanent drummer, Laura McFarlane, was Australian.
12 Quoted in Franklin Bruno, "Second Firsts: The Go-Betweens Return."
13 Quoted in Paul Malone, "Welcome to Part 2." *The Voice* no. 8 (November 2000).
14 There is a Rachel Worth who teaches at the Bournemouth Art Institute in England and recently published *Dress and Textiles* (Dovecote Press), a book in the "Discover Dorset" series.

I tracked her down, and she wrote to me: "Of course I have heard of the Go-Betweens. I have no idea where the title of the record came from, but this may interest you. In my last position as senior lecturer at Staffordshire University, I sometimes used to play for my students the video of the film *The Go-Between*, starring Julie Christie and Alan Bates and based on the novel of that name by L. P. Hartley. As a historian by training, I often used to quote to my students the first line of the novel: 'The past is a foreign country: they do things differently there.' So when I first heard of the album by the Go-Betweens, you can imagine that I was intrigued/amused at the title. Pure coincidence?? I don't know."

15 It's a classic mistake in indie circles, one that allows the unscrupulous to mix up music networks, friends, and employment arrangements in one big mess, so that friendship is often sacrificed for satisfactory working conditions, and vice versa.
16 Miller adds that he was not there when this occurred. He also says that whenever he asked McLennan about Strzoda the response was, "I think he's fantastic. He's doing a great job."
17 Strzoda concludes: "Truth is: Despite the fact I'm the guy who left the Go-Betweens after only eighteen shows because he thought they were behaving like fools, I still feel love for those ragged two and their music." Miller is less conciliatory.
18 *Long Way to the Top* was the brainchild of Greg Appel, who, as chief songwriter and guitarist in the Lighthouse Keepers, had played shows with the Go-Betweens in the 1980s in both Sydney and London.
19 I base this contention only on my own experience of talking to friends at the time the show was being screened.
20 Or perhaps that the program's producers knew she would be outspoken and interesting whereas Forster and McLennan would be guarded—and difficult to fit into a broad sweep of interviews.
21 Although some lasted for a night, and one for a decade: Gerard Lee, Lissa Ross, Bruce Anthon, Dennis Cantwell, Temucin Mustafa, Clare McKenna, Lindy Morrison, Glenn Thompson, Janet Weiss, Matthias Strzoda, Glenn Thompson.
22 Quoted in Malone, "Welcome to Part 2." McLennan, incidentally, can't drive.

Chapter 24: *Bright Yellow Bright Orange*

1 The Australian jumper is akin to the American sweater.
2 Interview with Forster and McLennan, November 25, 2002, www.jturner.dircon.co.uk/webinterview20021125.html.
3 An Essendon Airport retrospective CD was recently issued on Chapter Music.
4 Readers with scarily brilliant memories will recall that Nixon was a member of Pink and Blue, who shared a cassette release with the Go-Betweens in 1980.
5 Interview with Forster and McLennan, November 25, 2002, www.jturner.dircon.co.uk/webinterview20021125.html.
6 Ibid.
7 Quoted in Malone, "Welcome to Part 2."
8 In fact, there must have been three, as two were included on the bonus disc for the album, and neither of these were "Ashes on the Lawn."
9 Bear in mind that Pickvance is an avowed Queen fan.
10 The music used on TV ads is a parallel universe to the pop charts. I am told that selections from the early 1980s Flying Nun back catalog were used in television advertising in New Zealand in the 1990s. This is perhaps more understandable, since it can be seen as a part of the New Zealand sound, and part of its culture. "Streets of Your Town" is not a very familiar song, though, to mainstream Australia, and it's difficult even to see it as easy to edit for mass consumption.
11 It was not, however, in the top ten, as often claimed. APRA media release (May 2, 2001).

Chapter 25: Elemental Things

1 Byron Bay is a notorious idyllic hippie paradise in northern New South Wales.

ABOUT THE AUTHOR

David Nichols was born in Melbourne in 1965. He started publishing his own fanzine, *Distant Violins*, in 1980, before working as a freelance writer and subsequently as features editor of the Australian edition of pop magazine *Smash Hits* from 1983 to 1991. His music writing has appeared in a wide range of periodicals in the USA, Great Britain, and Australia. His drawings and comic strips have also graced the pages of many unusual and obscure publications, as well as record sleeves, t-shirts, and Converse shoes.

Parallel to his journalistic work, Nichols has pursued what someone once kindly described as a "unique musical vision" as the drummer for numerous bands, beginning with the Cannanes, of which he was a founder member in 1984 and left in 1996, through Crabstick, Blairmailer, Huon, Driving Past, and the Grey Tapes. The most recent release on which he features is an EP by the Mia Schoen Group.

In 2001 he was awarded his PhD in history and now lectures in urban planning at the University of Melbourne. His recent books include the collections *Deeper Leads* (co-edited with Keir Reeves) and *Community: Building Modern Australia* (co-edited with Hannah Lewi), and the social critique *The Bogan Delusion*. In 2012 he will publish *Trendyville*, co-authored with Renate Howe and Graeme Davison.

David Nichols lives in Broadmeadows, a suburb of Melbourne, with his wife, the painter and musician Mia Schoen, and their beagles.

www.ingramcontent.com/pod-product-compliance
Lightning Source LLC
Chambersburg PA
CBHW021054080526
44587CB00010B/253